S0-BHG-784

Quality Management for Educational Technology Services

LB
1028.3
R544
1994

Quality Management for Educational Technology Services

A Guide to Application of the Deming Management
Method for District, University and Regional Media
& Technology Centers

Mark L. Richie

Published by the
Association for Educational
Communications and Technology
1025 Vermont Ave., N.W., Suite 820
Washington, DC 20005

Alliant International University
Los Angeles Campus Library
1000 South Fremont Ave., Unit 5
Alhambra, CA 91803

© 1994 Association for Educational Communications and Technology

Library of Congress Catalog Card Number 94-70545

ISBN 0-89240-073-0

AECT President: Kent Gustafson
AECT Executive Director: Stanley D. Zenor

Edited, designed and typeset by AAH Graphics (703) 933-6210

No part of this work may be reproduced or transmitted in any form or by any means, electronic or mechanical, including photocopying, microfilming, and recording, or by any information storage and retrieval system, without written permission from the publisher.

Additional copies of this book may be purchased by writing to the Publications Department, Association for Educational Communications and Technology, 1025 Vermont Ave., N.W., Suite 820, Washington, DC 20005.

Dedication

For my Folks, who gave me experiences that shaped my life.

For my Family, who gave me the time, space and encouragement that allowed this to be written.

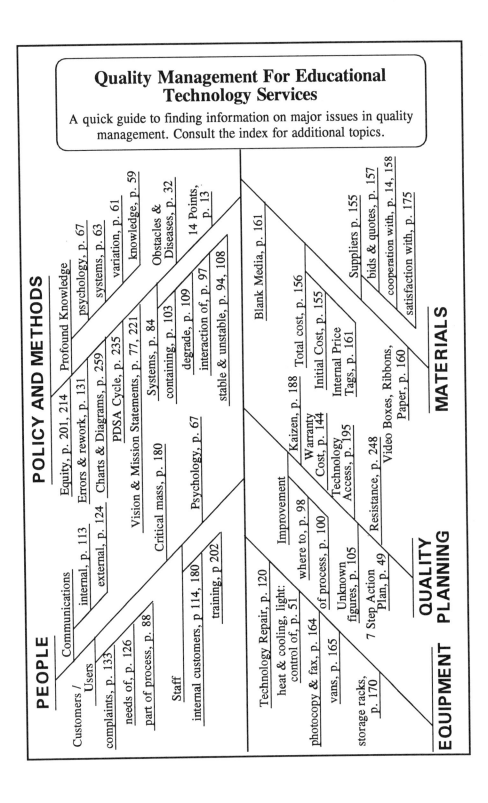

Quality Management For Educational Technology Services

A quick guide to finding information on major issues in quality management. Consult the index for additional topics.

POLICY AND METHODS

PEOPLE

MATERIALS

QUALITY PLANNING

EQUIPMENT

Profound Knowledge
psychology, p. 67
systems, p. 63
variation, p. 61
knowledge, p. 59
Obstacles &
Diseases, p. 32
14 Points, p. 13

Equity, p. 201, 214
Errors & rework, p. 131
Charts & Diagrams, p. 259
PDSA Cycle, p. 235
Vision & Mission Statements, p. 77, 221
Systems, p. 84
containing, p. 103
degrade, p. 109
interaction of, p. 97
stable & unstable, p. 94, 108

Communications
internal, p. 113
external, p. 124

Critical mass, p. 180

Psychology, p. 67

Customers / Users
complaints, p. 133
needs of, p. 126
part of process, p. 88

Staff
internal customers, p 114, 180
training, p 202

Blank Media, p. 161

Total cost, p. 156
Initial Cost, p. 155
Internal Price Tags, p. 161

Kaizen, p. 188
Warranty Cost, p. 144
Technology Access, p.195
Resistance, p. 248
Video Boxes, Ribbons, Paper, p. 160

Improvement
where to, p. 98
of process, p. 100
Unknown figures, p. 105
7 Step Action Plan, p. 49

Suppliers p. 155
bids & quotes, p. 157
cooperation with, p. 14, 158
satisfaction with, p. 175

Technology Repair, p. 120
heat & cooling, light: control of, p. 51
photocopy & fax, p. 164
vans, p. 165
storage racks, p. 170

Contents

Foreword

FROM ITS VERY BEGINNINGS, THIS BOOK HAS BEEN A CHALLENGE. In the fall of 1992, I challenged the author to put into writing his experiences in implementing the total quality management (TQM) philosophy in an educational setting. Mark accepted the challenge, and agreed to have the book ready for publication in 1994. The ultimate challenge, however, is presented to you the reader. Through this book, Mark is challenging each of you to no longer do "business as usual," but to apply the principles of total quality management to the operation of your center and the way you manage people and services.

This book is pragmatic in its approach, based upon ten years of research, study, and practical application by the author. It is based in the real world education setting of a regional media center. Mark shares anecdotes, side comments and examples from his experiences with TQM. Unlike other authors who write books on management philosophy and style, but never manage anything or anybody, Mark has transformed the way his center does business by applying the principles of total quality management.

Quality Management for Educational Technology Services shows how the quality management approach pioneered by Dr. W. Edwards Deming in Japan allows educational service centers to expand services and be more flexible by reducing waste and rework. The author explains why offering "service with distinction" may be the best defense against arbitrary budget cuts. He illustrates how higher user satisfaction, better utilization of resources and better service reliability are major benefits that can be achieved by using the quality management principles outlined in this book. This book is your guide to changing the way you do business and manage people.

In closing, I want to acknowledge and thank the author. Mark Richie is a good friend and a professional colleague. He has been an active member of AECT for many years, giving unselfishly of his time, energy and talents to the association and profession. He is a Past President of

NARMC, an AECT national affiliate organization. As an author, he willingly sacrificed the many long hours of preparation and writing needed to produce this book. With publication of this book, Mark has made a significant contribution to everyone who wants to apply the principles of TQM in an educational service center setting. Thanks, Mark.

Stanley D. Zenor
AECT Executive Director

August 1994

Acknowledgements

THERE ARE MANY PEOPLE WHO HELPED MAKE THIS BOOK POSSIBLE. They provided encouragement, support, ideas, anecdotes and occasional abuse. Without their collective concern for the success of this book, I would not have been able to complete my work or enjoy the level of satisfaction I have in the finished product.

First, let me thank AECT Executive Director, Stan Zenor, who asked me to write this book in October 1992. Without his initial ideas and encouragement this book would never have happened.

Throughout the entire process of writing and editing I relied on Brian Blecke, Manager of Total Quality Marketing at Films Incorporated, to read the manuscript for content and conformance to the philosophy of Dr. Deming. Brian invested a tremendous amount of time and energy reading and commenting on the contents as the work progressed. I am indebted to him for the clarity of thought he provided and the insights he brought to our discussions over the last 15 months. I am also grateful to Brian and Films Incorporated for arranging my participation in a second four day seminar with Dr. Deming.

Four other colleagues provided me with valuable assistance as manuscript readers. They are Shirley Crehan of Bucks County Instructional Materials Service, Pennsylvania; Chuck Forsythe of Montgomery County Instructional Materials Service, Pennsylvania; Janet Williams of the Special Projects Center, Punta Gorda, Florida; and Susan Tucker of the University of South Alabama. They reviewed the manuscript for readability and kept the content focused so that the book would meet the "Monday morning needs" of media and technology managers in the field. I thank them for their comments, ideas and encouragement.

I would also like to thank Dr. Joyce Gerdau who allowed me to participate in an experimental "collaborative inquiry group" as part of her doctoral research at New York University. My participation in the process over a five-month period influenced many of the comments in this book on organizational planning and the value of team-building.

I owe a world of thanks to my family and especially my closest friend, Arlene Albert. Her encouragement helped me when writing became a chore. She gave me the space and the time to write, and listened when I needed to talk and when I was stalled. Her patience with me was a valuable asset. To Arlene, Jessica and Andrea, thanks.

Much of the background for this book came from 11 years with the Burlington County Audio-Visual Aids Center in New Jersey. The center provides instructional materials, technical assistance and staff development programs in support of the educational needs of 63,000 students and 5,000 teachers. And although the center is stuck with a name imposed by the 1949 legislation it operates under, it supports the emerging technologies that will be the tools for education far into the next century.

Over the years the AVA Center board of directors gave me the freedom to experiment, risk and fail on occasion. They have always provided philosophical and fiscal support for new ideas and services. No media and technology director could ask for a better board of directors. I thank them for their support.

The staff of the AVA Center deserves a tremendous round of thanks as well. They are dedicated to the mission of the center. They are committed to making our users proud to use our resources and seeing that they get what they need exactly when they need it. I am very proud of their accomplishments and the level of service they give to the educators of Burlington County.

I have had the privilege of being a member of the National Association of Regional Media Centers for over 11 years. It has been a rewarding and professionally stimulating experience. The professional relationships developed with fellow members over the years have been a source of great personal pleasure. The opportunity to exchange ideas and listen to the experiences of other media and technology professionals from across the country has been invaluable.

I would also like to thank Dan De Santis, George Brown, George Ferris, Don Bagin and Donald Gallagher. Their collective influence over the years materially prepared me for the success I have enjoyed in my work and helped give me the confidence required to write this book.

A special thanks to Herb Brassleman who, many years ago, let me know that I wasn't alone in my effort to make some sense of regional media center performance data.

Many thanks to my old friend Bruce Leonard for designing the cover and making me look good.

Finally, my sincerest thanks to Dr. W. Edwards Deming for creating the philosophy of quality management upon which this book is based. Studying his work changed my life and profoundly influenced the way I carry out my responsibilities as a manager. Dr. Deming died December 20, 1993, shortly after this book was finished. He leaves a legacy of global proportions and he will be greatly missed.

Mark L. Richie
January 1994

Read This First

THERE WAS A MAN WHO LIVED MOST OF HIS ADULT LIFE WITHIN A FEW miles of the White House in Washington, D.C. He developed and taught a management method that brought Japan from the ashes of war to pre-eminence as a world economic power. Prior to 1980 he was virtually unknown in the United States. In Japan he is so revered that the most prestigious award for quality in that country is named for him: an American statistician and physicist. His name is W. Edwards Deming.

In 1980, he was featured briefly in an NBC documentary, "If Japan Can, Why Can't We?" In the beginning of the 1980s all manner of United States corporations and government agencies adopted the Deming method of managing for quality. One of them, Florida Power and Light, a public utility, became the first U.S. company to capture the Japanese Deming Prize for quality.

Ford, Xerox, Nashua Paper, Harley Davidson and thousands of others had, by 1990, made the Deming quality method a corporate way of life. Government agencies like the Internal Revenue Service, Health and Human Services, the Department of Defense and the United States Navy all began to adopt the Deming method. City governments like Madison, Wisconsin and Austin, Texas also made the Deming quality method work for them.

There may even be hope that in the '90s the quality efforts in Washington will bear fruit. During a speech to a gathering of American labor and industry leaders in July, 1993, President Bill Clinton credited Dr. Deming's work as the inspiration behind his "Reinventing Government" initiative. He even recommended to the audience that they read, *Dr. Deming: The American Who Taught the Japanese About Quality,* by Rafael Aguayo.[1]

During the 1980s as well, a number of isolated attempts were made to use Deming's management principals to improve the quality of education. In 1990, Dr. William Glasser published *The Quality School,* as an approach for transforming American education by applying a quality philosophy. In 1989 the American Association of School Administrators formed the Total Quality Network. The Network provides a support system and sponsors training sessions that bring the principles of Dr. Deming to bear on improving the system of education.

The purpose of this book is to help educational media/technology managers and staff improve the quality of their services through the study and application of Dr. Deming's management principles. Managers of campus educational technology centers, audio-visual centers, regional and district media centers, intermediate units, instructional material services, corporate audio-visual units, computer centers and government technology training centers can all benefit from this book.

In the early 1990s an explosion of articles were published and books written on the subject of quality improvement for business and education. The danger that accompanies such an explosion is a parallel emergence of overnight experts, pre-packaged training kits and traveling consultants. They are eagerly met by frustrated educational managers hoping for a quick fix, cookbook approach or a "model" to adapt to their own circumstances. If the reader knows little or nothing of Dr. Deming, let your education begin here. Dr. Deming cites Seven Deadly Diseases of American management. One of them is the "hope for instant pudding." The desire for fast, visible results is born of the short-sighted style of management that typifies American corporations and American education. Companies look only to the next quarter. Schools look only to the next report card, or at best, next year's standardized test results. Quality management requires willingness to take a long term view.

This book is not a cookbook. It does not provide a model that can be imported and adopted to any educational, government or university technology service center. It is also not an academic treatise on the subject of quality service. You may find some sections are repetitive or explain similar concepts in slightly different ways at various places in the text. This has been deliberately done to accommodate the tendency to skip around a book like this searching for parts that have a direct bearing on a specific management problem. Repeating connections to theory and examples offered elsewhere in the book is an attempt to accommodate this kind of reader without losing important information. The Topic Finder Cause and Effect Chart at the beginning of the book was created to help readers find key concepts quickly, especially when using the text as a reference after reading it all the way through.

Above all, this book is a guide book for self-education. It provides a discussion of the Deming method as it applies to the environment of an educational technology service center. As you read this book and others on the Deming method, some of the concepts will appear incredibly simple. Quality management has been described by more than one author as a "blinding flash of the obvious." The difficult part comes when it is time to integrate all of the simple little things into a cohesive whole.

"Quality improvement is a do-it-yourself effort," says quality consultant and author Stephen George. Applying the Deming philosophy effectively can only come from personal study and application to the unique features of your organization. It is your system to improve, your problems and your services. The Deming philosophy provides an approach and a method for improvement, but it cannot specify what improvements are to be made.

You can watch videotapes, read books and articles, consult with experts and train everyone in your agency, but only the personal commitment, followed with action by top management of the organization, can make it happen. Only management has the power to improve the system of production and service that employees must work in. And only management has the power to combat the destructive forces in the work place that rob an employee of pride and accomplishment.

The Deming method is centered on a philosophy of continuous quality improvement. It is a long and never ending journey.

Continuous quality improvement is not a goal; it is a state of being. Visible and measurable benefits from using the Deming method take years to realize. Yet results that are more difficult to measure, but just as important, like a happier staff and greater user satisfaction, may surface far sooner. Developing a quality service agency takes a long time. It is hard, frustrating work that at the same time is paradoxically enriching and rejuvenating.

As the 20th century ends, the United States may finally begin to understand the meaning of quality. That you are reading this book is indicative of how far the idea of quality has spread.

While reading this book and studying the work of Dr. Deming, it

While reading this book and studying the work of Dr. Deming, it may be useful to keep the following two items in mind. Each, in its own way, is a humbling indicator of the challenge that quality presents.

"The Deming Prize is like your learner's permit for driving. It means you have read the manual and you can pass the test. It doesn't mean you are an expert."

Richard Dobbins,
Quality Improvement Development,
Florida Power and Light.

"In the race for quality, there is no finish line."

Found scrawled on a chalk board
behind the service counter of an
equipment rental center near the
author's home.

[1]"Moneyline." *USA Today,* July 29, 1993. Section C, pg. 1.

A Note on the Deming Method and "TQM"

THIS BOOK IS BASED ON THE TEACHINGS OF DR. W. EDWARDS DEMING. IT is the result of research, reading, study and ten years of struggle and practical application in a regional educational media/technology center.

Elements of quality improvement methods developed by other quality leaders such as Walter Shewhart, Joseph Juran, Armand Feigenbaum and Kaoru Ishikawa are also applied within this book and are noted where appropriate.

The term TQM or Total Quality Management has been intentionally avoided in this book. The term Total Quality Control was originated by Dr. Armand V. Feigenbaum in 1957.[1] It has since evolved into Total Quality Management and has become a catch-all term for a variety of quality improvement techniques and practices. Ardent students of quality management tend to view TQM as the practice of quality improvement based on the application of statistical process control and the use of quality tools such as control charts, cause and effect diagrams and Pareto charts.

The difference between TQM and the teachings of Dr. Deming are perhaps best described by one of his students and a highly regarded quality consultant, Dr. Kosaku Yoshida. "TQM is an analytical concept," he explains. "the Deming philosophy is a holistic concept."[2] TQM provides the tools for analysis of processes within a system. The Deming philosophy guides our actions.

Dr. Deming does not use the term TQM in his work or in his seminars.[3] At best, the phrase "Deming Quality Method" could be applied, if necessary, as a label to his philosophy. In deference to Dr. Deming and in order to stress the origin of the management theory this book is based on, the term TQM is avoided.

[1] Ishikawa, Kaoru. *What Is Total Quality Control? The Japanese Way.* Englewood Cliffs: Prentice Hall, 1985. Pg. 90.

[2] *Made In Japan "Whole"-istically.* Videotape. Los Angeles: Quality and Productivity, Inc., 1989.

[3] Walton, Mary. *Deming Management At Work.* New York: Perigee Books, 1990. Pg. 148.

Quality Management for Educational Technology Services

Chapter 1

THE DEMING PHILOSOPHY: BEGINNING THE JOURNEY WITH NO END

SOMETIME IN THE LAST FORTY YEARS THE UNITED STATES BEGAN losing ground. From the end of World War II, through the 1950s, the world market would buy almost anything we produced. Untouched by the destruction of war and superbly organized for mass production, we out-produced, and out-sold any three other nations combined. But somewhere along the line we slowly lost our status as the major supplier of industrial goods to the rest of the world.

Innovations born in the United States, and for a variety of reasons never developed here, were bought up by corporations in other countries, chiefly Japan. The VCR, invented in the United States, became identified almost exclusively with Japan. The microwave ovens developed by Raytheon are now built mostly in Japan and Korea. The first industrial robot was installed in a GM assembly plant in the 1960s. By the end of the 1980s, Japan had four times as many industrial robots as the United States and today no industrial robots are manufactured in the United States at all.[1]

Something was happening, and America didn't notice. As new industrial nations emerged, they approached business in a different way. They began to see that volume production no longer mattered. What mattered now was how well the product was made.[2] The growth of better international communications, air cargo and overnight delivery service made the world smaller. Political boundaries mean very little in a global market place.

America continued to manage business based on financial plans, quarterly reports and return on investment. Japan's growing industries made management decisions based on what satisfied the customer.

The difference began to hurt America. In 1959 Japan built a total of 1,600 fork lift trucks while the United States built 30,000. By 1980 U.S. production was three times greater. In the same period Japanese production grew 60 times and three of the five top-selling fork lift trucks in the world were made in Japan.[3]

In 1970, 98 percent of all color televisions sold in the United States were manufactured by U.S companies. By 1988 it was 10 percent. Is it any wonder? In the late '60s Motorola advertised a color television with the "Works In a Drawer." It actually advertised the "advantage" it had when the set *had to go in for repairs!* The buying public didn't know much, but it knew that it didn't want a TV that had to go in for repairs.[4]

In 1970 nearly all machine tools sold in the United States were also made here. In 1989 the figure was 35 percent. Only 25 percent of the telephones sold in the United States today are made in the United States. Only one percent of the tape recorders sold here are made here.[5]

In the mid 1960s the United States held 15 percent of the world market in financial, insurance and banking services. It was less then seven percent by the end of the 80s. The rules changed. The first Nissan product arrived in the United States in 1969. From 1980 to 1990 Japanese imports rose from 20 to 30 percent of the U.S. market. And it is not a matter of culture or something unique to the Japanese work force. Japan now has eleven automobile assembly plants and several television factories in the United States with quality output as high as their counterparts in Japan. The Honda plant in Marysville, Ohio makes cars and motorcycles for the U.S. market and export, including back to Japan![6]

We Can Do It, Too

In 1986 General Motors and Toyota began a joint venture to build the Toyota Corolla and Chevy Geo Prizm in the United States. Called New United Motor Manufacturing, Inc., or NUMMI, they selected a GM plant in Fremont, California that had been shut down because it was no longer productive and had, according to GM, the worst work force in the country.[7] The joint venture brought in five Japanese managers from Toyota, removed much of the automated equipment that GM had installed and hired back 85 percent of the original work force. Within 18 months after start up, the plant was 50 percent more productive than the average GM plant, had defect rates as low as a plant in Japan and had cut the absentee rate from 25 percent under GM to four percent[8]—American workers producing quality at a level expected by Toyota. Obviously these must be very special workers, highly skilled, the best of the best. Not really.

The difference is the way they are managed. In fact, written English skills are not a requirement for employment and some employees cannot read, write or do the most basic math. Management is responsible for employee training, and the average worker in a Japanese owned auto plant in the United States gets about 300 hours training versus about 50 hours U.S. companies provide.[9]

Contrary to popular belief, little of the training is in "basic skills." In addition to skill training for the job, workers receive training in problem-solving, interpersonal relationships, conflict-resolution, teamwork and cooperation. Managers at NUMMI have found that "teamwork easily compensates for educational deficits" among workers. The general press would have us believe that tomorrow's basic workers will need increasingly higher levels of education in order to meet global competition. But Japanese auto and electronic manufacturers have repeatedly proven in the United States that quality management and training for better cooperation and teamwork make the difference; not better math or writing skills. In fact, a study done by Stanford University of several high-tech Silicon Valley companies did not find any skill requirement for the basic work force that required more than an eighth grade education.[10]

Examples, frequently ignored, demonstrating the success of

Deming's work in America abound. In 1974 Motorola sold its Chicago television assembly plant to Matsushita. American workers were turning out television sets with an average of 150 defects per hundred built. By 1979, using the same work force, the defect rate had been reduced to an average of four defects per 100 built.[11]

In 1975 Sony Corporation built a television assembly plant in San Diego. Its culturally diverse work force created a plant that, within three years, was named by Sony as one of their ten best plants world wide.[12]

In 1978 Firestone had to recall ten million steel-belted radial tires that the National Highway Traffic Safety Administration had linked to 41 deaths and 70 injuries when the tires came apart in use. Between that, the oil crisis and internal quality problems, Firestone was in big trouble. In 1983 Bridgestone Tire purchased a Firestone plant in Tennessee. Within two years, operating with quality management and with unionized American workers, its scrap and defect rates were as low as any of Bridgestone's 16 plants around the world. The plant went from producing three grades of tires to two: grade A and scrap.[13] Another example: With the same work force, Sanyo reduced defect and warranty rates by 90 percent in an Arkansas television plant it purchased from a U.S. company.[14]

While Japan was overtaking United States productivity in the '70s and '80s, in typical American style there was a continuing hunt for some factor that could be blamed. Wage differences were blamed, until Japanese wages came to parity with the U.S. Tariffs; soft exchange rates, and automation were all to blame according to some.[15] We overlooked the crucial factor: management. We looked at what had been produced, the erosion of US markets, the result. But we failed to learn how it had been done, the method. We overlooked quality. We can't blame the Japanese, we did it to ourselves.[16]

This book is not about Japan, it is about method. It is about the why and the how of personal and organizational transformation specifically applied to educational technology services in a variety of settings. American industry has only just begun the work of applying quality management principles to service and production. Early adopters like Ford, Xerox, and Motorola provide valuable history lessons and visible evidence that managing for quality reduces cost, raises quality and improves productivity. They now have roughly 13 years of experience and improvement to their credit. Other companies, large and small across the country, have begun serious adoption of the quality principles used by Japanese companies—the principles largely associated with Dr. W. Edwards Deming.

To compete in a global economy, American business has had to completely rework the way it does business and how it thinks of quality. Evidence of progress after ten years is beginning to be felt in the United States. Once the defect rate of U.S. cars was 300 times greater than that of a car made in Japan. Now it is 25 times greater. Improvement, but nothing to write home about. Toyota has a number of North American parts suppliers. In 1990 it brought the best suppliers together for a meeting. The best suppliers had an impressively low defect rate of one-tenth of one percent, or 1,000 errors per million. Toyota explained that if they wanted to remain suppliers of Toyota parts they would have to meet the defect rate of their suppliers in Japan whose quality was 100 times better; just ten defects per million parts.[17]

Don't you think it is time for us to catch up? Such a misguided thought. "Do you think the Japanese will stand still while somebody catches up?" asks Dr. Deming.[18]

It Starts with Education

The capacity for American management and employees to think in terms of defects per million, cooperation, teamwork, process improvement and quality has to start with education; in American schools. The American Association of School Administrators began the Total Quality Network in 1989 as a means to bring quality management to education. The Association for Supervision, Curriculum and Development has devoted entire issues of *Educational Leadership,* its professional journal, to quality management. And *Kappan,* the publication of Phi Delta Kappa, has carried numerous articles on quality schools over the past several years.

Just where quality management will take American education and whether it will have a lasting impact as a method for educational reform depends on variables too numerous to list. The experience in the educational community will mirror the experience in U.S. business. Visible results may take years to show up. There will be numerous false starts, misapplication of theory and examples of bad practice. Overnight experts and packaged "quality education" kits will enter the picture and divert energy from the transformation that is required. The downward pressure of detractors will take a toll as well.

What is required is personal study and personal transformation. As managers of technology services that directly support education, we have an obligation to help improve instruction by providing the best educational materials, support and services possible. As education becomes more dependent on computers, satellites, videodisc, CD-I and long distance data networks our role becomes all the more important. Managing technology with the rules used twenty years ago will no longer work.

The first break with the past requires educating our colleagues that educational technology in not the "answer" to educational reform. Installing a computer lab, a satellite dish and a fiber optic network can no more improve education than the installation of a blackboard 300 years ago. How technology and information are *managed* is what is important. What will the technology be used for? What need does it fill? What kind of instruction will it deliver? These are all useful questions. Ultimately the educational community must recognize that the quality of interaction between teacher and student and between technology and the user must be managed with the aim of improving the quality of learning.

As a media manager the value of studying the quality philosophy of Dr. Deming is therefore two fold. First, we can better manage our service center for continual improvement of products and services. To deliver superior service that meets and exceeds the demands of education creates greater user satisfaction.

Our second reason for studying the Deming method and becoming personally transformed is so that we may act as a resource for the educational institutions we serve. As a source of information and training materials, with the experience of practical application within our agency, we can be in a better position to assist others to learn.

The transformation is not easy and does not come quickly. The philosophy of Dr. Deming is totally unorthodox compared to the current system of management in the United States. To break with old, comfortable ways is difficult enough. Harder still is to accept that you will become, as Dr. Deming put it, "an exile among your peers."

Management in Education

Since the end of World War II education has borrowed a series of management techniques from business and industry and attempted to force-fit them into the practice of educational administration. Over the years this has yielded a series of acronyms such as PERT—Program Evaluation and Review Technique; MBO—Management By Objectives; SBM—Site Based Management and PIP—Personal Improvement Plan. It has also generated a series of discipline and instructional methods, in most cases named for their progenitors.

In that half-century, many of the same problems as before still exist in education, some more acute than ever. Thousands of other problems have emerged to plague the educational system and complicate administrative functions. None of the management techniques tried so far truly addresses the flaws within the system that allow the problems to exist. Like the American management methods they were spawned from, they are short-sighted, number-crunching, near-term, results-oriented methods that fail to create long-term improvement of the system. The system remains the same while frustration levels build among teachers, parents and administrators. To paraphrase Dr. Deming, the methods are "all practice and no theory." In short, the practice produces no new knowledge because there is no theory on which the actions are based. Dr. Deming explains, "Without theory, one has no questions to ask. Hence without theory there can be no knowledge." Knowledge cannot exist without theory.[19]

Dr. Deming's point is that no matter how well-intentioned the practice is, it cannot possibly create long-lasting, effective improvement because there is no underlying theory as a foundation.

Educational technology centers, audio-visual centers, regional and university media centers, intermediate units, instructional materials services, corporate audio-visual units and government technology training centers have existed in one form or another since just after World War

II when audio-visual instruction was adapted from war-time training to the classroom. The management evolution of educational technology has mirrored the management techniques tried by educational administration in general, with similar results.

Under the rationale of "accountability" management frequently delegates the responsibility for creating a quality service to a level that has no control over the flaws in the system that cause problems and block quality. The middle or lower lever supervisor, and ultimately the worker, is blamed by upper management when things go wrong. The call for "accountability" is simply a way to find someone to blame.[20]

Frustration and resentment is created when people are blamed for the errors that occur as a result of doing what the system demands of them. Dr. Deming's often repeated axiom is, "The worker is not to blame." Ninety-four percent of the quality problems in this country are directly related to the system, and the design of the system is management's responsibility. The problem is M A N A G E M E N T. "Quality is made at the top; in the board room."[21]

Without a commitment followed by action from the top management of any organization, efforts to create quality will fail. Ultimately, quality becomes the job of everyone, but it has to start at the top.

Deming Fundamentals

To use the Deming quality method in educational technology management, or in any management area, requires an understanding of several fundamental elements. Note the phrase, "requires an understanding." This is the theory, the foundation upon which all activities of a quality organization are based. Build a poor foundation and the house will not stand. The fundamentals are these:

- The 14 Points
- 7 Deadly Diseases
- Profound Knowledge
- The Obstacles to Adopting A Quality Philosophy
- The Deming Flow Diagram
- The Deming/Shewhart PDSA Cycle

In the context of educational technology services, this chapter will review the 14 Points and their linkage to profound knowledge. Chapter 2 will review the diseases and obstacles described by Dr. Deming. The remaining elements and their implications are covered at various points throughout the book. Chapter 4 contains a fuller discussion of profound knowledge. Study of the 14 Points in greater depth is available by reading *The Deming Management Method* by Mary Walton, Perigee Press, 1986. A deeper appreciation of profound knowledge can be gained by studying *New Economics For Industry, Government and Education,* by W. Edwards Deming, MIT Press, 1993.

Introduction of Profound Knowledge

Before we begin examining Dr. Deming's 14 Points, a brief introduction to his theory of profound knowledge is useful. Students of Dr. Deming may find it difficult to find references to profound knowledge in earlier works by and about the Deming method. Dr. Deming first wrote his thoughts on profound knowledge in 1989 in a paper delivered to the Institute Of Management Science at Osaka, Japan.[22]

There are four parts to the system of profound knowledge that work together to provide the philosophical foundation of Dr. Deming's work. The four parts are interrelated and must be seen as a whole, not as separate pieces.

Understanding of Some Psychology allows us to understand people, the most important part of any system. Psychology allows us to learn how

---

THE SYSTEM OF PROFOUND KNOWLEDGE

Understanding of Some Psychology

Understanding of Knowledge

Understanding Variation

Appreciation of a System

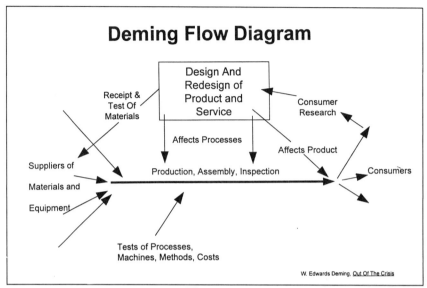

Figure 1-1

people interact with each other and how they affect the operation of a system. Since adopting a quality philosophy requires a fundamental change in the attitude and behavior of people in an organization, psychology allows us to understand how people change. It lets us see what motivates change, what causes resistance to change and how new ideas are adopted.

Understanding of Knowledge gives us the power to take data and raw information and turn it into knowledge with the aid of theory. Monthly activity reports to upper management generally consist of raw data: numbers. They tell what was done, but not why. Numbers do not offer us insight as to how a process can be improved. Knowing the difference between information and knowledge is key to understanding this part of profound knowledge.

Understanding Variation is the basis for understanding the behavior of a process. Any system that produces a product or provides a service is subject to variation. Some variation is created by the system itself. Call them errors if you like, but most errors, or variation, are part of the system and are called "common cause" errors. Errors, or variation, that are unusual and not caused by the system are called "special cause" errors.

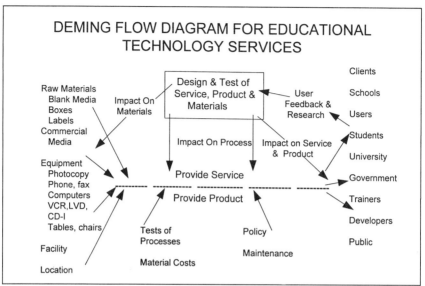

Figure 1-2

Profound knowledge of variation allows us to know the difference between the two kinds of variation and what can be done to correct them. Common cause errors can only be reduced or eliminated if the entire system is improved to eliminate the cause of the variation. Special cause errors, if they are likely to occur repeatedly, must be traced and individually corrected to keep the system stable.

Appreciation of a System requires us to view our educational technology center as a "system of service," not just a collection of departments and functional areas. Knowing that we manage a system of service means that we recognize the internal customer/supplier relationship that exists between each component in the system. The Deming Flow Diagram in Figure 1 illustrates the flow of information and material through a process to accomplish aim of the system. Figure 2 shows the Deming Flow Diagram adapted to the system of educational technology services. Instead of looking at our centers as an organization chart, profound knowledge shows us the system that we have for delivering services. It teaches us that the interactions between processes within the system should be the focus of our attention.

DR. DEMING'S FOURTEEN POINTS

POINT 1   Create constancy of purpose toward improvement of product and service.

POINT 2   Adopt the new philosophy.

POINT 3   Cease reliance on mass inspection to achieve quality.

POINT 4   End the practice of purchasing on price tag alone.

POINT 5   Improve constantly and forever the system of production and service to improve quality and productivity, and thus constantly decrease costs.

POINT 6   Institute training for the job.

POINT 7   Institute leadership.

POINT 8   Drive out fear.

POINT 9   Break down barriers between departments.

POINT 10 Eliminate slogans, exhortations and targets for the work force asking for zero defects and new levels of productivity.

POINT 11 Eliminate work standards, quotas, management by objectives, management by the numbers and numerical goals. Substitute leadership.

POINT 12 Remove barriers to pride of work.

POINT 13 Institute a vigorous program of education and self-improvement.

POINT 14 Put everybody to work to accomplish the transformation. The transformation is everybody's job.

This is an abbreviated form of the 14 points. For a complete text of each see *Out of the Crisis*, by W. Edwards Deming and *Dr. Deming: The American Who Taught the Japanese About Quality*, by Rafael Aguayo, Simon and Schuster, 1990.

The Fourteen Points

The 14 Points consist of seven *dos* and seven *don'ts* for management to follow. Like the system of profound knowledge, they are not a list of options or choices. The road to being a quality organization begins with study and adoption of *all* 14 Points. The author failed to grasp this at the beginning of his quality journey and probably delayed reaping the benefits of the Deming method by three or four years. You cannot pick and choose the points you like and reject the others as unworkable or not applicable to your center. They are not menu items that can be selected at random. They work together and mutually support each other. They are, as Lloyd Dobbins puts it, "of a whole."[23]

The following discussion of the 14 Points covers each point in an abbreviated form and relates its importance to the management of educational technology. The 14 Points will be referred to continuously throughout the book.

Point 1: Create constancy of purpose toward improvement of product and service

Constancy of purpose means that the organization must know what its aim is. It must have a clearly defined reason for existing and know what business it is in. Each process in the larger system of the agency must also know what its aim is in relationship to the aim of the organization as a whole.

Every employee in your center must be able to identify the internal customer of the process they work in and must recognize the ultimate aim of the center as well. If we all know what the aim of the organization is, then we have a basic, common principle to guide our actions and set the agenda for long-range planning.

The quest for quality improvement must permeate an organization inside and out, at all levels. Quality is not a sometime thing that only applies to one department or one function. A quality system is deployed across all functional areas and includes everything from how the phone is answered to the selection of software. Every staff member must know that continuous improvement is the only way the agency will sustain a quality service and thrive.

Management must be the force that leads the drive for continuous improvement.

Point 2: Adopt the new philosophy

Nothing will change in a system until there is a profound personal transformation in someone who has the power to change things. That means a manager or administrator. Only management can change the system. How to change it and what to change it into flows largely from the attitudes, philosophy and past experience of the individual. If their past experience has been with the American style of management, then their approach will be the same. The agency may function, but the attitude will impede improvement of the system.

The Deming method will work only if leadership fully adopts and understands the philosophy of management embodied in the 14 Points and profound knowledge. Adopting them, as we will see, requires action.

Point 3: Cease reliance on mass inspection to achieve quality

End of the line inspection, whether you are checking purchase orders or shipping lists, only finds the defects. Even if you find an error just before it goes to a user, it is too late. It costs the same to deliver services with errors as it does to deliver services correctly. Correcting errors is called rework, and rework is a cost. What if the defect gets to the user site, as in the case of delivering an incorrect videotape? Driving the correct item out to the client's location is a warranty cost, and, if out of control, can lead to heavy losses. According to a formula developed by Federal Express it costs 100 times the initial cost to correct an error once it gets into the hands of the customer. Chapter 8 details the waste associated with rework and how to calculate the cost of warranty. Dr. Deming asks, "When does it cost less to do something right the second time?"[24]

Quality cannot be inspected into a process or service. Instead, create a process that reduces the opportunity for errors to occur in the first place. Note the use of the word "reduces" rather than "eliminates."

Can all errors be eliminated from a process? According to Dr. Deming, no. A system that runs with no defects all the time would defy logic and violate laws of statistical probability.[25] All systems create random variation in performance. The aim of improving the system is to narrow the variation and come closer and closer to the ideal or target value for the process.

In America we try to "meet specifications." In Deming management the intent is to create the most desirable outcome for the system. The difference is best described through the observations of Genichi Taguchi, originator of what is known as the Taguchi loss function. A specification for the arrival time of a delivery van on a regular delivery route might be expressed as "anytime between 9:00 and 9:15." Specifications assume that any value between the specification limits is acceptable to the process and everything just outside specification is unacceptable. However, there may be an optimum time for arrival of the van, a specific target value such as 9:10. The Taguchi loss function says that the farther the actual arrival time is from either side of the target value, the greater the loss to the system.[26]

A frequently cited example of the loss function at work is the optimum temperature for an office environment. If most people in an office function at their best when the temperature is 68 degrees, then any movement of the temperature to either side of 68 will begin to degrade worker performance. The farther away from the optimum value, the greater the loss will be. At 72 degrees or at 66 degrees, the performance change may not be noticeable. But at 80 or 50 degrees it will become apparent.[27]

Point 4: End the practice of purchasing on price tag alone

Under most state bid and quote rules, the purchasing agency has an option to make final decisions in the best interest of the organization. Requirements detailed in bid and quote requests can also include life cycle maintenance costs and potential resale value as factors in determining the total cost of a purchase. What is "total cost"? It is the sum of all the expenses that will be incurred by the purchasing agency over the lifetime that the product will be used. That includes the initial cost, plus repair, routine preventive maintenance, supplies, employee training and possible resale.

While a low initial cost may appear to be in the best interest of an agency, Dr. Deming asks, "What are you getting for your money?" What is the total cost of ownership? Dr. Deming was once asked how much a pair of shoes he was wearing cost. He replied, "I don't know, I'm not done wearing them yet."[28]

If the low bidder on an order of 1,000 video boxes imprinted with your agency name ships 1,000 and ten arrive broken or defective, the contract requirements have not been met. When their response to your complaint is, "You have to expect some defects," there are two alternatives. Deduct the cost of ten boxes, pay the bill and do business elsewhere, or work with the supplier to help it meet the requirement for 1,000 defect-free boxes in the next order. Working with suppliers is a form of cooperation that Deming encourages as part of the pathway to quality.

Chapter 9 deals with the concept of "total cost" and expands on the need to work with suppliers.

Point 5: Improve constantly and forever the system of production and service to improve quality and productivity, and thus constantly decrease costs

Although the Deming way of quality requires adoption of and adherence to all 14 Points, Point 5 contains a significant message for students of quality improvement. Taking the sentence apart is instructive.

"Improve constantly and forever" is a notion most Americans do not understand. American management and American education are goal driven. We like to see a "light at the end of the tunnel," or bring a project to closure. We are masters at being close enough. Point 1 stresses "constancy of purpose." Point 5 says that the effort to improve our agency, school, regional, government or university media service never ends and has no finish line. It has the aim of continuous improvement.

"The system" can be glossed over when reading Point 5, yet is a pivotal concept for understanding how the quality of an organization is improved. We frequently blame the system or say we work in a school system but fail to grasp what a system is. According to Deming:

A system is a network of interdependent components that work together to try to accomplish the aim of the system.[29]

The output of an organization is the result of how well the components of the system work together and is directly dependent on the management of the interactions between the component parts. Dr. Deming uses an engineering term, explaining that a system functioning at its best has been "optimized." Optimization only occurs when all of the processes that go into the system are working together effectively toward a common aim.

It is always management's job to ensure that all components work in cooperation with preceding and following stages toward optimization of the system and that the system supports the aim of the organization.[30] Chapter 6 discusses the system of service in greater detail.

The Deming method tells us that 94 percent of the errors and defects produced by an organization, factory or service are a direct result of flaws in the system, not the worker. It is a statistic most managers do not want to hear.[31] Why? Because it clearly shifts the burden of responsibility from the employee to management.

"Production and service" are mutually dependent elements in Point 5. It does no good for a university computer lab to have the finest, cutting edge computer technology on hand if the hours of operation are inconvenient, or the lab assistants are ill-trained and surly. The educational resources available through a technology center can be the best on the market, but if the system that makes them accessible to the users is defective, it really doesn't matter.

Note the order of the wording of Point 5: "Improving the system" comes before "to improve quality and productivity." We cannot tell people to be more productive or simply ask them to improve the quality of their work. Posting banners that say, "Do Your Best," "Others Are Depending On You," and "Quality Depends On You" won't do it.

Urging employees on will not make them work any harder or reduce the number of errors. If we paid every teacher in America twice what they are making now, the level of student performance would not improve. Until fundamental improvements are made to the system of production and service, or the system of education, nothing will improve.

Quality and productivity improvements are natural outcomes of working to improve the system. Yet such a simple concept is so completely misunderstood.

Improvements to the system thus "constantly decrease costs." Frequent references to decreasing the cost of production and service in books on the Deming method and Total Quality Management are troubling to managers of educational and government agencies. "We are not a corporation. We have no bottom line or profit margin," they protest.

There is a "cost" to doing anything: providing a service, delivering videotapes, originating distance learning programs, or manufacturing an automobile. And the cost of doing something correctly is the same as doing it incorrectly. The burden of additional cost comes from finding and fixing defects. Any improvement to a system of service or production that reduces the possibility of creating errors, scrap or defects will lower the cost of producing the product or rendering the service. To the system of education, loss due to creation of defective service might be lost bond issues, declining public confidence, and reduction of tax support.

In an educational service agency, the reduction of errors produces a valuable commodity: time. Time previously spent on rework, correcting errors, following up on snags, and handling complaints can be used to expand and improve the service.

Point 6: Institute training for the job

Dr. Deming views the lack of employee training as a major cause of errors and defects. Major corporations spend large sums of money to train workers and keep them current with changes in procedure and technology.

Two kinds of training are important in Point 6. The first is proper training for the job itself. Driving a delivery van, answering phones, using a scheduling computer, labeling videotapes—any function in a technology service center requires training. Training for the job should also include teamwork, cooperation, systems thinking and problem-solving skills. Using one worker to train another to do the same job is not acceptable unless it is supervised by a competent manager.

The second kind of training is about the mission and aim of the organization. Most employees don't see beyond their own job function because they have not been shown the rest of the system. Most departments don't see beyond their own work to the larger system either. If Point 1 is followed, all staff and all departments will know their individual aim and the aim of the organization as a whole. They will know what the aim of the organization is because they have been taught as a result of the training received through Point 6. Training for the job involves skill training and training in how a specific job fits into the overall flow of the system. Teaching a person what they will be doing is important, but teaching them why they are doing it gives meaning to the work and builds self-esteem in the worker.

Checking out materials, answering the phone, helping a user, aiming an up-link, using a scheduling computer, labeling a videotape; any function in an agency that supports the use of educational technology requires training. And since most such agencies or departments are small, multiple responsibilities make formal cross-training important as well.

Turning a new employee over to another employee doing the same work for on the job training doesn't count. Deming and other quality leaders point to this practice as an example of management ducking its responsibility for the performance of the system. Managers and supervisors are directly responsible for how well a system performs. It is therefore imperative that new personnel be trained according to the standards and practices of the system by someone whose job it is to train people. A large organization may have an entire training department with a formal curriculum and performance requirements. But in the more typical smaller organization, management must take an active role in training people for their jobs.

The practice of allowing workers to train other workers is similar to playing "whisper down the lane" with the quality of the organization. It is a dangerous source of variation in the process that may be impossible to trace when things go wrong later. As the "training" is passed on, it becomes altered, diluted and creates deviation from the original performance requirement. Eventually the hapless employee will be called on the carpet for failing to perform adequately, when he was only doing his best.

Worker training worker is especially dangerous in an organization where annual reviews or meeting performance goals plays a part in determining promotions or raises. There is no benefit to training new co-workers well if someday their performance will make the worker with seniority (the old hand) look bad.

Of course new workers can be helped to learn their job by other employees. Old hands have much to offer the rookie that will help performance improve quickly. Cooperation between workers is essential for continuous improvement to work and the skill of working cooperatively needs to be taught as well. But first the employee must be formally trained in what the job is and given the skills to carry out the work.

The second kind of training, about the mission and aim of the organization, is essential to bring new people into the system as quickly as possible. Most new workers have not experienced the philosophy of continuous improvement in a work place. Most have come from traditional environments where phrases like, "close enough for government work," and "leave it for the night shift," are the norm. All employees need to understand the larger mission and aim of their organization. This includes part time and student-workers as well. They need to know where their work comes from and who gets their work next. "Who depends on me?" They need to know who is the ultimate customer. Armed with this information, workers can make vital contributions to improving the system of production and service.

Point 7: Institute leadership

First there were administrators. The job of the administrator was to maintain the status quo. They kept the bureaucracy running and didn't make waves. Then the idea of management arose, defined as "getting things done through other people." In the new economic age that is no longer enough. Leadership provides vision, shows people the way, coaches better performance and provides the resources so that they may do a better job. Leadership in a work unit, department or division drives the organization forward, but only so far as the top management can see. If leadership's vision is only into the next quarter, it can't possibly lead beyond that point. "America looks at the next quarter. The Japanese look at the next century."[32]

Dr. William Glasser, in his work on quality schools refers to traditional management as "boss-management." Managers who have learned the Deming way of quality will become "lead-managers," according to Glasser.[33]

Dr. Deming was fond of saying that "quality is made in the board room." That also applies to a regional media center, a school media center, a university television studio or a multi-state satellite consortium. Can you apply quality management within your work unit or department alone? Of course. In any system of production or service that you can control, you can put Deming's philosophy to work. Many who have started to use the Deming philosophy in education began in a single classroom. The fortunate ones saw their methods adopted upward through the system.[34] But real transformation of an organization can only happen with serious commitment from the top. If top management fails to be involved, or attempts to improve the quality of the system without fully understanding the theory that guides their actions, there will be no lasting, systematic, change for the better.

Ford Motor Company is one of the largest and most successful American companies to embrace the Deming method. Dr. Deming would not work with Ford until the president of the company attended his four-day seminar on quality and statistical process control.[35] Deming would not invest his time unless he could see commitment from the top. That was in 1981. By 1992, Ford's U.S. market share had gone from 18 percent to almost 25 percent and the cost of the warranty was cut by 45 percent.[36] Within four years of using Deming's methods new owner complaints dropped by 59 percent.[37] By 1992, five of the top ten automobiles sold in the United States, domestic or imported, were Fords. FORD no longer stands for Fix Or Repair Daily.

The success of Ford or Xerox or Nashua Paper did not come from a piecemeal approach to quality. As you continue study of the 14 Points, remember that you cannot pick only the ones you like and leave the rest. They all work together if you let them.

Point 8: Drive out fear

If Dr. Deming's philosophy is to have an even chance of working, management must make this point work every day. Fear comes from impending change, the unknown, anticipation of annual reviews, fear of making a mistake, the desire to please the boss, worry over job security and many other sources. Fear creates a kind of paralysis that prevents people from contributing to the improvement of the work place. Workers have seen new management ideas before. They have experienced the anxiety of getting a new supervisor and have endured departmental reorganizations. Launching a "quality program" with a kick-off day, banners and meetings only adds fuel to the fires that create fear. To drive out fear, workers must see a visible change in the attitude and behavior of management. Even the most benign boss creates a certain amount of fear in employees simply because they are not certain what he or she will do next. As you learn to use the Deming philosophy, some of the fear creating behaviors you may have will disappear. As employees begin to learn about the new philosophy they will know something about the principles that guide your actions and your actions will become more predictable. If you can live the philosophy every day, trust can be built. Without mutual trust much of the real work of improving performance cannot take place.

If you want a visible place to start, get rid of the time clock and eliminate annual performance reviews.

Point 9: Break down barriers between departments

Point 9 can be taken both figuratively and literally. Some corporations no longer have offices for upper management, preferring to place their desks on the shop floor or in general work areas. The new arrangement removes the physical barrier between managers and workers. It promotes higher visibility, better communications and fosters an atmosphere of cooperation. For private conversations and planning sessions numerous conference rooms are made available. Some of them were formerly executives' offices.

While the removal of physical barriers between departments or functional areas may be less practical, the removal of procedural and organizational barriers is possible and essential.

The Deming method of management promotes the cooperation of individuals in a system to work toward the common aim of the organization. Under traditional American management practice each functional area within an organization is largely isolated from the next. The business office doesn't know much about production, production doesn't know much about product design, product design doesn't know much about customer service and so forth. Organizations that are so organized are, by definition, suboptimized. Chapters 6 and 10 provide greater insight into the negative effect of organization charts. Among other things, they create a silo or chimney effect in which information flows up and down but not across functional areas. In some cases the organization chart promotes internal competition for scarce budget resources or better equipment. It distracts attention from the client and diverts work activities into self preservation.

One of the most visible results of breaking down barriers between departments in U.S. industry is the creation of the Ford Taurus. It was the first car built in the United States using the Deming approach to design and quality. Instead of starting in the design department and being handed to engineering and so on down the line, Taurus was put together with a team of people from each of the departments that would have anything to do with the car. Sub-groups within the team went so far as to meet with auto body professionals to find out how to build a car that would be easier to fix if it was in an accident. Taurus was introduced in 1984. By 1992 it was the most popular passenger car sold in America, domestic or imported.

General Motors started an entire new division, Saturn, based on the cross functional approach advocated by Dr. Deming. Within its first two years of operation, Saturns were ranked in the top three automobiles with the highest customer satisfaction. In 1993 new Saturns had the highest score ever in a J. D. Powers owner-satisfaction survey, out-ranking Mercedes-Benz and Toyota.[38]

Continual improvement in the system of producing goods and services can only happen if individuals understand their place in the larger picture of the organization. Since the ultimate product or service is the result of interactions between all the processes in the system, people have to communicate effectively between departments. The barriers to communication have to go.

Point 10: Eliminate slogans, exhortations and targets for the work force asking for zero defects and new levels of productivity

There is a minor industry in America selling motivational posters to corporations. The posters carry a cartoon or photograph, and some slogan or phrase that is supposed to remind workers to do their best, work harder and pull together. Managers buy these actually thinking it will improve their work force. Instead it creates resentment and perpetuates the adversarial relationship between worker and management.

Dr. Deming tells us that workers are already doing their best. Prodding them to do better without changing the flaws in the system that allow errors to occur raises frustration and lowers morale. The intrinsic desire to do a good job is eventually crushed.

Zero defects? In the Deming method there is no such thing. Random variation in a system will produce errors no matter how hard the employee works. Can we limit the number of errors? Certainly. The system can be redesigned to reduce variation. The process of production or providing a service can be redesigned to remove the need for most rework and inspection. Where the process design has been optimized, there can be no other way to do a job but the right way. But exhorting workers to "do a better job" or "cut down the number of errors" can't fix the system that allows the errors to happen.

Posters, slogans and banners do not create quality, raise customer satisfaction or reduce waste. Improving the system does.

Point 11: Eliminate work standards, quotas, management by objectives, management by the numbers and numerical goals. Substitute leadership.

This is one of the hardest concepts for new students of quality to grasp, perhaps because it goes against traditional Western management in such a tangible way. Dr. Deming frequently quotes Ardel Nelson, personnel director at McClellan Air Force Base in California, who describes such practices as driving a car while looking in the rear view mirror.[39] Numbers and performance appraisals only tell you where you have been. Numerical goals and performance objectives can always be met by juggling the figures. The system is never touched because you are now producing a number instead of a product or service. Better numbers never increased customer satisfaction or improved productivity.

When the Department of Transportation demanded that airlines meet new on-time performance standards, the airlines simply changed their schedules to allow more flight time. More flights arrived "on time" and even more arrived early.[40] When a school board set a new target for reducing the number of students listed as late each day, the administration changed the criteria that defined lateness. The goal was met, the problem remained the same.

Leadership that promotes continuous improvement in the system will improve performance. Between 1980 and 1985 the number of new car complaints at Ford dropped 59 percent. Ford did not set a goal to reduce customer complaints by 59 percent in 5 years. Ford focused on what pleases the customer and worked to change the system of production that allowed defects of workmanship to exist. By putting all their energy into improving the system, the drop in the complaint rate took care of itself.

Point 12: Remove barriers to pride of work

To use the Deming method one must believe the following: nobody takes a job with the intent of doing it badly. The demoralized, beaten worker generally gets that way because the intrinsic motivation to do a good job has been destroyed. Flaws in the system destroy it. Poor working conditions, misguided management, merit ratings, poor training, bad lighting, inadequate tools, defective raw material, poor process design, faulty product design, and numerical goals all conspire to prevent workers from taking pride in their work.

The worker knows he is powerless to change any of the flaws in the system, yet he will be blamed when things go wrong. The frustration of being powerless breeds resentment and creates a roadblock to productivity, quality and pride. A Japanese visitor to the United States once remarked, "In Japan we expect employees will perform the work at hand. In America, you expect the employee will not." It is management's responsibility to change the system.

Unfortunately, past management practice builds barriers by creating regulations and detailed procedural requirements that add little to the value of a service. Management consultant and author Peter Drucker once observed, "Most of what we call management consists of making it difficult for people to get their work done."

Point 13: Institute a vigorous program of education and self-improvement

Point 13 looks similar to Point 6 yet is not. Point 6 seeks the institution of regular and systematic training for the job to be done. Point 13 goes beyond the work place and focuses on improving the education of the individual. Investing in the education of the work force returns the organization more widely read employees—who are more likely to see beyond individual tasks and understand better their role in the system as a whole. Employee self-esteem is raised through their own work at self-improvement and this produces workers more likely to make constructive contributions to improving the work process.

In many educational agencies the professional staff is reimbursed for taking additional courses. Raises are frequently connected to completion of additional college courses. This is an example of Point 13 at work. However, the benefit should extend to all employees: support staff, drivers, custodians and technicians. The scope of the courses eligible for reimbursement could be extended to include G.E.D. preparation and high school adult classes. There may even be employees within the organization willing to conduct classes on beneficial topics such as financial planning, child care, plumbing or word processing.

Point 14: Put everybody to work to accomplish the transformation. The transformation is everybody's job

Tomorrow? Not necessarily. But eventually everyone in your organization, or at least within the scope of your authority as a manager, must be involved in the transformation and the process of continuous improvement.

Managers new to the Deming method can find themselves creating more problems than progress if they conduct mass orientations and training sessions too early in the transformation. Brian Joiner, a student of

Dr. Deming's and a noted quality consultant, actually discourages much front-end training, pointing out that conducting a lot of training sessions only "gives the illusion you've done something."[41] Without tangible action on the shop floor or in the office, the employee can see no connection between the training and the realities faced each day in the work area.

The experience of the United States Department of Health and Human Services is typical of the results that come of an overeager desire to adopt Point 14. Health and Human Services embarked on a comprehensive program to make every employee aware of the move toward a quality, customer-oriented organization. And, that continuous improvement would always be expected.

Unfortunately there was no method or structure in place to accomplish the transformation. Employees left sessions with their hopes up. But after a few weeks, when nothing appeared to have changed and the agency was still running the way it always had, the hope turned to cynicism. Quality management had become just another government buzz word, another management fad. For Health and Human Services it was a long road back to get people to adopt the new philosophy and believe in the power of quality management.[42]

A key lesson everyone in an organization must remember is that quality doesn't happen overnight. Once real improvement to the system has begun it will take time for the improvements to show up in measurable or visible ways. It may take years. Ironically, more subtle, less tangible evidence may appear first. Improved worker attitudes, fewer fires to fight and a new interest in making the organization a better place to work in may appear.

Later in this book the idea of creating a "critical mass" of people who will begin the transformation will be covered. The philosophy of quality cannot be spray painted over an organization. It must spread from one point to another, from one functional area to another. And, like strands on a spider web, it must extend in all directions within an organization.

Eventually, everybody in the system will be part of the process that makes a quality organization.

[1] Dobyns, Lloyd. *Quality . . . Or Else: The Revolution in World Business.* Boston, MA: Houghton Miflin, 1991. Pg. 24.

[2] Ibid., pg. 27.

[3] Imai, Masaaki. *KAIZEN:The Key To Japan's Competitive Edge.* New York: McGraw-Hill, 1986. Pg. 179.

[4] *In Search Of Quality: Quality Through Systems.* Videotape. Northbrook, IL: Coronet/MTI Film & Video, 1991.

[5] George, Stephen. *The Baldridge Quality System: The Do It Yourself Way To Transform Your Business.* New York: Wiley & Sons, 1992. Pg. 22.

[6] Dobyns, pg. 240.

[7] Weisman, Jonathan. "Some Economists Challenge View That Schools Hurt Competitiveness," *Education Week,* November 13, 1991. Pg. 1. And, *Quality . . . Or Else: Vol. 2.* Videotape. Chicago: Films Inc., 1991.

[8] Agayo, Rafael. *Dr. Deming: The American Who Taught the Japanese About Quality.* New York: Simon & Schuster, 1986. Pg. 48. And, Dobyns, pg. 113.

[9] Bracey, Gerald. "The Second Bracy Report On The Condition Of Public Education." *Kappan,* October 1992. Pg. 115.

[10] Weisman, Jonathan. "Skills in The Schools: Now It's Business' Turn." *Kappan,* January 1993. Pg. 367.

[11] Dobyns, pg. 127.

[12] Barker, Joel. *Discovering The Future: The Business Of Paradigms.* St. Paul, MN: ILI Press, 1985. Pg. 65.

[13] Walton, Mary. *Deming Management At Work.* New York: Perigee Press, 1991. Pgs. 187–189.

[14] George, pg. 23.

[15] Gabor, Andrea. *The Man Who Discovered Quality.* New York: Penguin, 1990. Pg. 4.

[16] Aguayo, pg. 7 & 240. And, Dobyns, pg. 39.

[17] Ibid, Dobyns. Pg. 37.

[18] Walton, Mary. *The Deming Management Method.* New York: Perigee Books, 1986. Pg. 67.

[19] Deming, W. Edwards. *The New Economics For Industry, Government and Education.* Cambridge, MA: MIT, 1993. Pg. 106.

[20] Langford, David. "Why Are We Here?" *Focus In Change,* The National Center For Effective Schools Research & Development, Fall 1992, Number 8. Pg. 10. Quoting David Langford who began the application of quality management at Mt. Edgecumbe High School School in Sitka, Alaska in 1988.

[21] Deming, pg. 35 and in Four-Day Seminar, February 16–19, 1993. And, Gabor, pg. 127.

[22] Deming, W. Edwards. "Foundation For Management of Quality in the

Western World," a paper delivered at a meeting of the Institute of Management Science, July 24, 1989, Osaka, Japan. Reprinted in *An Introduction To Total Quality For Schools,* American Association of School Administrators, 1991.

[23] *The Fourteen Points, Volume 1, The Deming Library.* Videotape. Chicago: Films Incorporated, 1988.

[24] A quote also attributed to Philip Crosby in, *Quality . . . Or Else.* Pg. 91.

[25] Deming, W. Edwards. *Out of The Crisis.* Cambridge, MA: MIT Press, 1986. Pg. 141 & 479.

[26] Ibid., pg. 141.

[27] Deming, *The New Economics,* pg. 221. And, Dobyns, pg. 84.

[28] Contributed by Brian Blecke, Director of TQM Marketing, Films Inc., Chicago, quoted from a Deming Four-Day Seminar, St. Louis, October 1992.

[29] Deming, *The New Economics,* pg. 50.

[30] Aguayo, pg. 177.

[31] Deming, *The New Economics,* pg. 35.

[32] Line delivered by the villain in the Clint Eastwood film, *Line of Fire* while posing as a big wheeling American investor.

[33] Glasser, William. *The Quality School.* New York: Harper Collins, 1990. Pg. 26.

[34] *Focus On Change.* Madison, WI: National Center For Effective Schools Research. Fall 1992, Number 8. See articles on David Langford and Theresa Hicks.

[35] Gabor, pg. 126.

[36] Fellows, Gary. *The Deming Vision: SPC/TQM For Administrators.* Milwaukee, WI: ASQC Quality Press, 1992. Pg. 4.

[37] Walton, Mary. "Making America Work Again." *Philadelphia Inquirer Magazine.* March 11, 1984. Pg. 22.

[38] "The Heartbeat Of America." Frontline. TV program. Public Broadcasting Service, October 13, 1993.

[39] Walton, Mary. *Deming Management At Work,* pg. 225.

[40] Dobyns, pg. 168.

[41] Walton, Mary. *The Deming Management Method,* pg. 204.

[42] The Role Of Total Quality Management in Improving the Vision of Government Employees, Session 409, AECT INFOCOMM Convention, Washington, DC., 1991.

Chapter 2

DISEASES OF MANAGEMENT AND OBSTACLES TO THE TRANSFORMATION

THE FOURTEEN POINTS DESCRIBE ACTIVITIES REQUIRED TO IMPLEMENT organizational transformation. They are essentially a prescription of seven things that must be done and seven things that must not be done. This chapter describes some of the barriers and pitfalls that will be found along the way.

Dr. Deming cites a series of diseases and obstacles that must be cured or overcome before quality performance can become a reality. The list has changed over the years, but it is essential to understand what you are up against when pursuing quality in America. A few of the more pervasive diseases are covered here. Their numbers correspond to Dr. Deming's list in *Out Of The Crisis,* page 97.

Seven Deadly Diseases

Disease One—Lack of constancy of purpose

Very simply, lack of constancy of purpose is the opposite of Point 1 of the 14 Points.

A successful organization has a defined purpose, mission and vision of its future. The organization as a whole understands that it has the power and the methods at hand to create the future as well. Living that purpose and mission everyday is a difficult task. It is too easy to fall back on old ways when the going gets tough. A lead-manager can easily revert to being a "boss" when confronted with circumstances which she finds threatening. It takes personal study and a deep philosophical transformation to overcome Disease One and create an environment where there is no other choice but to maintain constancy of purpose.

Disease Two—Emphasis on short-term profits

For the purposes of a non-profit educational or government agency, substitute "results" for profits. Emphasis on short term results is one of many elements that trouble critics of the Deming method when applied to education and government. Because Americans tend to look only for the obvious, they see the word "profit" and use it as evidence that quality management only works for corporations.

To see beyond that takes an ability to see how short term thinking limits opportunities for continuous improvement. Sports teams look to the next game, or at best, to the play offs. Sales people look only for a "good quarter." Government agencies, schools and universities launch a variety of multi-year projects, the benefits of which are lost when the funding expires. A technology center spends $200,000 on a down-link video center and schedules every possible teleconference event it can find in the first six months to prove how valuable it is.

Strategic plans may contain elaborate milestone and Gantt charts to plot movement toward a specific goal. As the goal becomes closer, creative energies wane. There is a tendency to drift because "we are so close, we're bound to get there." And once the goal is met, another "project" is hatched and another goal set. Projects become the focus of attention instead of improving the process.

A quality organization knows what its aim is and what its purpose is. It also knows that the continuous improvement of the process that creates products and service is a never-ending challenge. Quality is an endless journey, not a place of arrival.

Disease Three—Evaluation of performance, merit rating or annual review

Of the 14 Points, Point 11 seeks to cure this disease. It must be cured simply because it does not work. If 94 percent of the poor performance in an organization is the fault of the system, how can the worker be made responsible for it? It is impossible to encourage teamwork and cooperation while ranking people against each other at the same time. Dr. Deming points out that under such a system the poor performer is an asset to the good performer; it makes him look good.[1]

Evaluation systems pit one employee against another, build fear, reward short term results and do nothing to improve the system of production or service. The merit review and annual evaluation are also major causes of low productivity, poor morale and high absenteeism. According to Deming, reviews "leave people bitter, crushed, bruised, battered, desolate, despondent, dejected, feeling inferior, some even depressed, unfit for work for weeks after receipt of rating, unable to comprehend why they are inferior."[2]

A 1965 study of performance appraisals at General Electric concluded that employee reviews were of "questionable value." The defensiveness created by appraisals that pointed out areas for improvement actually produced "inferior performance."[3] Yet they continue to be standard procedure for most corporations, schools and government agencies.[2]

Technology service agencies and other media centers dealt with in this book tend to be part of larger bureaucracies over which media managers have little or no control. Sometimes there are union rules on raises and evaluations. Sometimes there are civil service regulations or local administrative policies or some combination of all three to contend with. It may be impossible to do away with annual reviews altogether under these conditions. But at the very least, they can be made a constructive part of the process that leads to continuous improvement of the system. If handled the right way, an evaluation system that helps employees understand and improve their work over a long period of time is useful.

If raises are already separate from the evaluation process, so much the better. Raises may be based on years of service or job title but not on performance within the title. In most civil service regulated agencies and universities, the raises come every year and are totally unrelated to performance. But the annual review must still take place.

It may be possible to evaluate workers in sub-units within a technology service center on a group basis. Using the aim of the organization, the purpose of the unit, and the improvement of quality indicators within the larger system as reference points, the group could construct a reasonably good assessment of their performance during the past year.

Unfortunately this is only reporting what has happened and is similar to driving a car by looking in the rear view mirror. It is a report on past actions with no connection to the future. The evaluation exercise with the work team will have value only if it is used as the basis for improving the system. If all of the people in the work team have some experience with the Deming method they understand that their performance is only as good as their interaction with the system they work in. It is the result of many factors, many of which they have no control over.

If implemented constructively, the bureaucrats higher up will have an "employee evaluation" to file away and the work group will have a useful tool for developing teamwork and improvement.

The only evaluation that really matters is based on progress toward improvement of the system.

Disease Four—Mobility of management

Mobility of management in technology service agencies takes on several forms, all of which are destructive to teamwork and the improvement of the system. In some cases, where the technology unit is part of a larger organization, managers are rotated or promoted through various departments on a regular two- or three-year cycle. The manager never has enough time to fully learn his job or understand the function of the unit he is to manage.

Frequent reorganizations of universities or educational intermediate units have the same net effect. Overnight the manager of the technology unit becomes part of another department with a new administrator who may be totally disinterested in supporting technology and media services. Funding can be decreased and personnel transfers occur based on personal choices, old allegiances and a lack of knowledge. The opposite can occur and be equally destructive. An administrator, finding that technology services are now part of his responsibilities, may proceed to micro-manage the unit into the ground based on false assumptions, guess-work and absence of knowledge. Administrators find themselves assigned to this position because someone else thought, "Hey, give it to so and so. He understands this technology stuff."

If this cycle repeats itself a number of times, the technology manager also leaves—out of frustration—breaking continuity and creating more decline within the unit as employees brace themselves for the changes a new manager will bring. Ultimately workers do just enough to get by, absenteeism rises, productivity drops, the quality of service declines and the whole technology unit may be lost in the next agency reorganization.

Disease Five—Running a company on visible figures alone

Like Disease Two, emphasis on short term profits, Disease Five gives government and educational managers some trouble. Somehow they can't get past business terms like "profit" and "company."

Substitute the word "agency" for company and continue. Deming uses this disease as an example of management by result, or focusing on what has already happened. In other words, looking at a system after it is too late to do anything. Driving by looking in the rear view mirror.

In a government, university or educational technology center visible figures can take many forms. Cash flow from a video rental service or from a technology repair service is important. Revenue from sponsoring a satellite teleconference may allow purchase of additional equipment or provide seed money for the next conference. Group purchasing activities may generate a positive cash flow. And cutting corners in May or June to end the year with a surplus is also using visible figures to manage.

Counts of anything related to the service are also very visible numbers. A regional media center may count the number of items shipped, the number of teachers served and the number of requests turned down. A down link site may enumerate the conferences held or the number of people attending. A repair unit may track items repaired, turnaround time or returns for rework. And in many cases these numbers may be important as a gauge of productivity. But to try and manage a technology center on these figures alone will not lead to improvement of service or expansion of the user base.

Dr. Lloyd Nelson is Director of Statistical Methods for Nashua Corporation; a man who understands numbers. Yet one of his most important contributions to quality management, frequently quoted by Dr. Deming, is that "the most important figures one needs for management are unknowable."[4]

The constant loss due to rework, waste and errors is never factored into the management of most organizations. There is unknowable loss to the organization from angry and dissatisfied users as well. The productivity within the organization is affected by poor training, cheap materials and poor process design to an extent that may never be known. The effect of these losses can never be calculated and the cause never corrected by the workers within the organization. Workers are totally powerless to correct the faults in the system that prevent pride in work and allow losses and errors to occur. The system of production and service is the responsibility of management. Management must account for the impact of these losses.

Disease Six—Excessive medical costs

As this book goes to press the United States Congress is wrestling with a national solution to Disease Six that may or may not render a cure. The scope of the national debate on the issue validates the concern Dr. Deming raised about its effect on quality and productivity. Early public discussions about the national health care plan already focus on the wasted time and money spent on unnecessary paperwork and loss due to correcting billing errors. Improvement of paper processing alone could save millions.

Disease Seven—Excessive costs of liability

Corporate, government, university and school budgets are being slowly eroded by legal fees and out-of-court settlements. There is no movement or interest in the government to regulate the conditions under which individuals may bring suit against a corporation, school or service agency. An agency may act in good faith, adhere to government regulations, conform to safety codes, even offer compensation for any kind of real or imagined damages and still end up paying to protect itself in a law suit.

Obstacles to the Transformation

Over the years some diseases have been reduced to obstacle status. Deming looks at the obstacles as being easier to cure than the diseases.[5] In all cases they must be recognized and dealt with if they impede change and improvement.

Until 1992 Dr. Deming had no enumerated list of obstacles. Then, as part of his work for the Deming Video Library, he created a list of "Six Western Ideas That Are Obstacles to the Adoption of the Deming Philosophy."[6]

The list is a collection of myths that are taken as truth in Western society and, when put into practice, fail to create an environment where improvement is possible. They are still accepted as true by many workers and managers because they do not know that there is an alternative. Once the alternative is presented as part of the Deming philosophy, it is amazing how quickly they become recognized as myths. The following is a review of the obstacles most frequently mentioned by Deming and his disciples.

Our problems are different

As quality management principles began to flow into education during the late 1980s and early '90s, this became the rallying cry of jaded administrators unwilling to consider the new philosophy. The failure of administrators to recognize that the Deming method transcends all products and services is without boundaries. Our problem is quality and quality is made in the board room.[7]

"The problem is always the same; *management*."

W. Edwards Deming.

New technology is the answer: The supposition that solving problems, automation and new machinery will transform industry

A favorite solution to decline of productivity and lack of excellence in America is the notion that new machinery, computers and technology will help. This appeals to both industry and education. Since this book is aimed at educational technology managers in a variety of work settings, a little time on this obstacle in particular is appropriate.

Technological innovations such as computers, fax machines and robots are no more likely to produce either quality or productivity improvement than purchasing a new fleet of cars for the local police force. New cars do not make the officers more effective. The ratio of arrests to convictions will not rise and the rate of crimes per year will not drop. When making a comparison at this kind of level, the reader may be inclined to agree. Even to the point of saying, "Well, that's obvious!" Yet many otherwise intelligent and educated people, in spite of evidence to the contrary, will imbue technology with special powers that it simply does not have. They agree with the police car analogy but protest that since computers and other technologies are so powerful, they can't help but make people more productive.

Take the analogy closer to the world many technology managers understand, into the computer itself. If a computer is up-graded from a 85 MB hard drive to a 350 MB drive, does it make the spread sheet program easier to use? Will the number of errors in data entry drop? No; it has just made the storage space bigger—like buying more filing cabinets.

The same applies if we install all new computers that run at four times the speed of the old systems. Has accuracy improved? Will the worker thus become four times less likely to make a mistake? Will productivity rise by a factor of four? No. It would defy logic if it did.

Yet this myth that technology, all by itself, has the power to improve productivity and transform America, from the factory to the classroom, continues to be promoted in both the popular press and academic literature. Numerous articles have appeared in the academic and educational technology literature since 1980 proporting to explain how technology will be the driving engine behind school reform. The myth is perpetuated because of a failure to view the work place or the classroom as a system.

That this myth exists among people who are otherwise technologically literate is one of the great paradoxes of the post-industrial age. We work with and teach others about computer systems all the time. If someone suggested that buying a laser printer would allow a secretary to make fewer errors and type faster, it would be dismissed with a scoffing laugh and a puzzled look.

Computers are so powerful, they just have to make us more productive, right? A study undertaken by the Massachussetts Institute of Technology Sloan School of Management examined the productivity benefits corporations realized through the investment in computer technology over a ten-year period. The study concluded that there was no positive effect and that there might be evidence of a negative effect on productivity. The study reviewed the drop in computer technology costs against their vastly increasing power. It looked at the rising corporate investment in technology over ten years: a 400 percent increase. Yet productivity during the same period remained flat.[8]

An article in a well known computer magazine reviewed the report and attempted to postulate explanations for this apparent violation of logic. It suggested several explanations, two of which have a direct bearing on our study of the Deming method.[9] First is that, "while computers help individuals get work done, the structure of corporations is based on old methods of doing work—hierarchy-bound dinosaurs unable to take advantage of new ways of working." Exactly. The computer has been tacked on to an existing system. The system has been made bigger, but the processes within the system remain the same. Therefore the output remains the same.

The other explanation provides a direct link to at least one disease and three of Deming's obstacles:

- Hope for instant pudding
- The unmanned computer
- The supposition that solving problems, automation and new machinery will transform industry
- Running a business on visible figures alone

The article aptly points out that computers allow us to do more useless things. Given access to an incredible amount of information, we tend to try and find some way to use it. The rationale being that, if it's in there, it must hold the answer to becoming more productive. The MIT report explains that the computer has given management a tool for reporting sales and production figures much faster and in much greater detail. Business reports on sales that previously were done monthly are now tracked weekly or even daily, "causing more frequent evaluations—more work." Production figures can now be reported on an hourly basis. And because it can be done, it is done. But does it add any value to the company? Does the increased data about the company help improve the process of production and service? Does it tell us *how* to improve? Of course not. It only furthers the disease of running an organization on visible figures alone.

Information, no matter how fast we can get to it, is not knowledge. Information is a point in time, a snap shot. Knowledge includes a dimension of time and derives from theory. Information accessible in an instant is worthless unless there is a theory to guide its use. Dr. Deming makes the theory of knowledge part of the system of profound knowledge, discussed more in Chapter 4.

Computers allow us to produce reams of reports. Statistics and figures do nothing to alter the way the information is used. Bad decisions based on more data, produced more quickly, are still bad decisions. We have been working on improving the rear view mirror; we made it bigger.

Focusing so intently on the perceived solution, technology, we fail to see the problem. The problem is management of the system as a whole.

Yet this is exactly what is being done on a much larger and potentially dangerous scale, every time some well-meaning corporate president, politician or educational leader calls for more technology to be purchased for our schools and universities.

The story of General Motors and New United Motor Manufacturing Inc. found in Chapter 1 is another illustration of the misguided hope that installing new technology alone will improve productivity and quality.

In the early '80s General Motors decided that the reason for Japan's highly competitive position in the world auto market was its application of high-technology computers and robots. GM embarked on a massive retooling of assembly lines to include robots wherever possible. It reasoned that if workers were making mistakes, they could be replaced with machines that didn't get bored and never made mistakes.[10]

Over $70 billion was invested in this approach including the purchase of a computer company, Electronic Data Systems, owned by H. Ross Perot. They even gave him a seat on the General Motors board. The result was that by 1987 General Motors still had the highest production costs per car in the industry. It took 41 man-hours to build a mid-size car and GM's market share had fallen ten points from 1980 to 35 percent of the U.S. market. Ford, which embraced the Deming philosophy more fully and earlier than GM, was building the Taurus in about 25 hours and had gained three points of market share.[11]

The NUMMI venture brought in five Japanese managers from Toyota, hired back 85 percent of the original work force, and within 18 months after start up, the plant was 50 percent more productive than the average GM plant. When the upper management of GM visited the plant, it was dismayed to find much of the recently installed robotic technology had been removed by the Japanese managers to help make the plant *more productive!*[11]

Same plant, same people, producing higher quality at a lower cost with more productivity. What was different? Knowledge. The Japanese brought with them their most valuable commodity: knowledge as taught by Dr. Deming.

The Japanese managers understood the obstacle to productivity that technology for its own sake can present. They knew that only when the whole system is improved will quality go up and cost go down.

The same applies to an educational technology service center, where ever it is located. Buying the latest media tracking computer won't halt the decay of service quality. Only continuous work to improve the system that produces the service will. And only the manager or director has the power to do it.

Failure to see technology as just one piece of the total system of production and service can be destructive to any organization. Individual productivity might improve but the output of the organization is not the sum of the efforts of individuals. It is the product of the multiplier effect caused by the interaction between processes and activities, a concept that is discussed in Chapter 6. Who is responsible for improving the interactions between activities in a system?

Hope for instant pudding

A phrase Dr. Deming credits to James Baken of Ford describes the need for a fast course of action to create visible, short-term results. An organization in crisis may turn to the Deming method or enlist the aid of one of thousands of overnight experts in quality for help, only to be disillusioned at the lack of immediate results. A patchwork of fixes may get the organization through the crisis but it will not create the transformation required to grow and flourish. A series of articles in the early '90s examined the disappointment many companies felt with their quality efforts. These articles in the general press are seized upon by detractors of quality management as evidence of its failure to change United States companies. The deeper story is that 69 percent of companies who, with constancy of purpose, stuck with their efforts beyond the first three years saw measurable improvement in quality and customer satisfaction.[12]

The Deming method is not a quick fix. It is not a cookbook, a formula or a management style. Nor is it a program that is kicked off with a special event and concluded with a party six months later. It takes time; a lot of time. And it takes work. The work of quality improvement cannot be delegated to someone else because you are too busy. Others may be involved, but the responsibility is management's alone. Collect the tools, study the methods, adopt the new philosophy and go to work because quality improvement is truly a do-it-yourself effort.

Search for examples

This follows the "hope for instant pudding" as an obstacle to the transformation. In a desperate hope for a quick fix, department heads, managers and presidents of companies will look for a successful model to copy.

This obstacle may be more difficult to overcome in education. Much of the way we train educators is by observation of successful teachers. Curriculum design relies on finding examples of good courses at one school and adopting them at another. Numerous federal grants to fund innovative educational programs include a requirement that the program be "exportable" to another school.

The United States government's approach to promoting quality as embodied in the Malcolm Baldrige award, advocates "benchmarking" as a tool to achieve quality management. Benchmarking is a process in which one organization (company, government agency, technology service center, etc.) observes and gathers performance data from another organization that is perceived as being a quality leader. The data and observations are then used as a performance standard against which the performance of the organization can be judged. The intent is that the organization will begin improving its quality performance to approach and beat the benchmarked organization.

The Baldrige Criteria seeks information on how a company selected sources of information to benchmark for competitive comparison and where it was applied to improve the company. But there is no guidance on selecting a method by which the information gleaned from one organization can be translated into quality improvement in another. Benchmarking can lead to useless comparisons and setting impossible goals if there is no understanding of the theory and methods used to achieve the quality level that is being benchmarked.

It is important to understand the *process* used by the benchmarked organization to implement changes that produced high quality performance. For this reason Dr. Deming sees the practice of benchmarking as a "search for examples" and, therefore, dangerous and misguided.[13]

This is not to say that benchmarking is totally useless. Only that it can lead to false hope by creating performance goals to aim at in a vacuum of method. The "world class" organization being measured may have gotten that way by sheer coincidence or through unrelated events such as the failure of a competitor.

On the other hand Dr. Joseph Juran, another highly respected authority on quality management, sees benchmarking in a different light. He sees it as one of the most important and useful trends in modern management. [14] A more detailed discussion of benchmarking as it relates to quality planning appears in Chapter 12.

Regional media centers and all educational technology centers can benchmark as well. Turnaround time on equipment repairs, time to generate invoices, rate of errors in filling video orders, return complaints on poor repairs, training time in a computer lab, equipment scheduling errors, system of handling orders, cycle time to buy replacement videotapes, purchase order errors, delivery delays, user satisfaction and a thousand other points can all be benchmarked.

The comparison need not be within the same industry. Xerox benchmarked L.L. Bean when it wanted to improve its warehousing and distribution system. Xerox estimates that of the ten percent gain in productivity it achieved, three to five percent of it came directly from benchmarking L.L. Bean's warehousing methods. Xerox also has a comprehensive ten-step process for evaluating benchmarked information and finding the methods behind the data. [15]

Regional, university and large district media centers might do well to study the methods of United Parcel Service, Federal Express and United Airlines.

Dr. Deming tells us that "it is hazard to copy." He warns that there is no number of examples of success or failure that will help another organization improve quality. Only by knowing the guiding principles by which the organization operates can you begin to know how quality is improved. Observing another operation to learn how to improve your own produces nothing unless there is an understanding of the theory by which the improvement is made. [16]

This is the primary reason why quality control circles failed in the United States during the 1980s. They were widely copied from Japan with no understanding of the theory behind their structure or function. It created a false start (another obstacle) for quality improvement in the United States and probably delayed wider acceptance in industry by six or eight years. More about QC circles can be found in Chapter 12.

Quality improvement "depends totally on knowledge of the 14 Points and of the diseases and obstacles and the efforts" put forth by management.[17]

Our troubles lie entirely with the work force

This obstacle may now be elevated to the level of myth. It is a common and widespread belief among Western managers and executives that the work force is to blame for the poor performance of a corporation. Even if no other obstacle existed, this one alone would prevent management from taking steps to begin improvement of the system.

To make the Deming method work in any organization, management must recognize that up to 94 percent of the problems, errors, waste and rework are caused by the system, not the workers.[18]

Anywhere from 15 to 40 percent of the cost of producing the product or service goes to pay for the wasted time, effort and material it took to produce it.[19] Think about that in an educational technology service center in terms of time wasted correcting errors, looking for things, reloading software, and answering complaints.

Workers can only produce to a level the system will allow. Replacing them with robots, urging them to do better, making them feel good, doubling their pay, threats, quotas and motivation seminars do nothing to improve the system. It is the responsibility of management to improve the system and help workers improve their performance.

We install quality

Quality cannot be inspected into a product or service. End-of-the-line inspection is too late. The defect is already there. However the process can be redesigned and improved to a point where there can be no other outcome but a quality product and service. At that point, continual improvement can begin.

The fallacy of zero defects

Demanding that a department produce zero defect work does not change the system that produces the defects. It also ignores the mathematical logic that there is natural variation in everything. Much of Dr. Deming's work is based on statistical theory which he spent a lifetime developing and putting into practice. Systems of production and service, like an educational service center, are not exempt from the laws of variation.

To explain the formulas used to determine the limits of variation that a system creates, known as statistical process control, or SPC, is far beyond the scope of this book. Dr. Deming recommends finding a person with at least a master's degree in mathematics to help you learn the basics of SPC when it becomes necessary. Formulas for calculating control limits in a variety of situations that would apply to any organization can be found in *Out of the Crisis,* by W. Edwards Deming; *SPC/TQM for Administrators,* by Gary Fellers; *Understanding Statistical Process Control,* by Wheeler and Chambers; *The Deming Management Method,* by Mary Walton; and *Improvement Tools For Education (K-12),* published by PQ Systems.

The Deming Library, a video series available through Films Incorporated, Chicago, contains valuable information on the nature of variation. It is of paramount importance to understand that the limits of variation are created by the system itself. They cannot be arbitrarily assigned because "that's what we think can be achieved."

For example, in a regional media center a major task is to deliver video/film materials ordered by teachers to local schools. An average regional or large city video/film center may delivery 30,000 items per year. The normal variation of delivery errors per month or week can be determined with statistical process control methods.

The determination is made by plotting the number of packing errors discovered over the course of 15 to 30 delivery cycles. Through the application of mathematical models developed by Walter Shewhart of Bell Labs, the limits of variation created by the system can be determined. Only from this base of information can efforts be made to improve the system and drive the number of errors down. Continued observation of the system will determine if the improvement has had a positive effect.

A common error on the part of managers new to using statistical methods to analyze system performance is to set a goal of × number of errors or × percent of defects. The goal is arbitrary and fails to allow for an analysis of exactly how the system is *presently* performing. Many other books on the Deming method are laced with stories of good intentions gone bad because of a failure to understand this basic aspect of SPC.

There are many more obstacles to transformation, but those discussed above the most common. The following six obstacles are Deming's view of the great inhibitors to lasting transformation.[20]

Six western ideas that are obstacles to adoption of the new philosophy

1. Competition is more effective than cooperation.

2. There is no way everybody can win.

3. It is more important to please the boss than the customer.

4. Someone is to blame for every problem.

5. Concentrate on fixing the parts, and the system will take care of itself.

6. Once you get a college diploma, you are educated.

Think of this as a true/false quiz. Give it to yourself and give it to your boss. If you answer "false" to all six statements, congratulations. You are ready for the transformation to a new management method. If your boss answers "true" to any two or more of the statements, you have a lot of work to do.

Chapter 3 details seven distinct stages of transformation that will be experienced during your study of the Deming method. You may already recognize some of their characteristics as you read. Don't worry too much about where you are on the road to quality, but recognize that all seven stages need to be experienced. Skipping from stage one to stage six, for example, will prevent your organization from making the sometimes difficult transition that is required.

1 *A Theory of a System: The Deming Library.* Videotape, Films Inc. Chicago, 1993.

2 Deming, W. Edwards. *Out of the Crisis.* Cambridge, MA: MIT Press, 1986. Pg. 102.

3 Gabor, Andrea. *The Man Who Discovered Quality.* New York: Penguin Books, 1990. Pg. 253.

4 Deming, pg. 121.

5 Ibid., pg. 126.

6 *The Prophet Of Quality: Introduction to the Deming Library.* Videotape. Chicago: Films Incorporated, 1992.

7 Guayo, Rafael. *Dr. Deming: The American Who Taught The Japanese About Quality.* New York: Simon & Schuster, 1990. Pg. 49.

8 Loveman, Gary. *An Assessment of Productivity Impact of Information Technologies.* Cambridge, MA: MIT, 1986.

9 Levy, Steven. "The Case Of The Purloined Productivity." *MacWorld,* March, 1993. Pg. 57.

10 *Quality . . . or Else: Vol. 2.* Videotape, Films Inc., Chicago 1991.

11 Gabor, pg. 216.

12 Aguayo, pg. 48.

13 "Study: Perseverance Necessary To See Payoff." *Total Quality Newsletter,* June 1993. Pg. 4.

14 Dobyns, Lloyd. *Quality . . . Or Else: The Revolution in World Business.* Boston, MA: Houghton Miflin, 1991. Pg. 181.

15 Godfrey, A. Blanton. "At The Cutting Edge Of Quality: Ten Clear Trends for Quality Over The Next Decade." Wilton, CT: Juran Institute. Paper presented at the US Chamber of Commerce's Quality Learning Series, February 26, 1993.

16 George, Stephen. *The Baldrige Quality System.* Wiley and Sons: New York. Pg. 79.

17 Deming, pg. 128.

18 Ibid.

19 Deming, W. Edwards. *New Economics For Industry, Government and Education.* Cambridge, MA: MIT Press, 1993. Pg. 35.

20 Deming, *Out Of the Crisis,* pg.12.

21 Op. Cit. *The Prophet Of Quality.*

Chapter 3

DEMING'S SEVEN STAGES OF TRANSFORMATION

DEMING'S POINT 1 SAYS; "ADOPT THE NEW PHILOSOPHY." POINT 14 says, "Take action to accomplish the transformation." The first is the mental change that must take place to accept the wisdom and the workability of the other thirteen points. The last is the call for the action required to make it work. This is easier said than done. Changing how people behave is always more difficult than changing what people *say* they will do.

In response to people asking "how" to take action, Dr. Deming adopted a seven step plan, paraphrased below, that he credits to Dr. Phyllis Sobo of the Philadelphia Area Council on Excellence.[1]

1. *Struggle*. Management will struggle with all 14 Points, the deadly diseases and the obstacles. Management will reach agreement on their meaning and on the direction to take in order to accomplish the transformation.

2. *Take pride in adopting the new philosophy*. Management will take pride in adopting the new philosophy and the new responsibilities it brings. They will have the courage to break with tradition, even to the point of exile among their peers.

3. *Create critical mass*. Management will explain by seminars and other means why change is necessary. It will create a critical mass of people within the organization who must understand the 14 Points, deadly

diseases and obstacles. Without this critical mass and understanding, management is helpless.

4. *Understand the customer/supplier relationship in every system.* Every activity in an organization is part of a process. Any process can be divided into stages. A flow chart is a means by which to see the relationship of one stage to another and the total process they represent. Work flows from one stage to another. At each point where the work changes hands—worker to worker, department to department—a customer/supplier relationship exists. The final stage may deliver the product or service to the ultimate customer.

5. *Construct an organization to guide the continual improvement of quality.* Put in place a method and structure in which suggested improvements may be tested and studied. The Deming/Shewhart Cycle of Plan, Do, Study, Act, expanded-on in Chapter 12, provides a method for studying improvements and predicting the results of change.

6. *Create teams to improve the input and output of every stage in the process.* Everyone can belong to a team and many teams may be composed of people from different functional areas. The team must have an aim and recognize the customer it will serve.

7. *Implement statistical process controls as part of the organizational structure.* Apply statistics to the appropriate areas for the purpose of understanding variation of the process and better understanding the results of change to the process.

For an agency beginning the journey to becoming a quality organization these seven steps can be invaluable tools for plotting the course of action. Their sequence is important. Organizations that skip around in their implementation may create more chaos than improvement. To add another dimension to the plan, add a time line. To quote Jack Hillerich, President of Hillerich and Bradsby, the company that makes Louisville Slugger baseball bats, "It takes years . . ."[2]

Aside from that accurate but somewhat vague assessment of the time involved, consider this. If you are just starting to become interested in quality and the study of the Deming method, the time spent in the first two stages will be much shorter than for your colleagues who began ten years ago. In the early '80s there were few support groups and almost nothing published in general business publications, let alone education literature, on the Deming method.

Now and in the future, you are less likely to be subjected to the exile noted in stage two. The diffusion of information about Dr. Deming's work has spread exponentially since 1986. Far more people at least recognize his name even if they misunderstand his message.

You and Your System

Management works ON the system,
workers work IN the system.

> *Myron Tribus, Director, MIT*
> *Center For Advanced Engineering*
> *Study, and frequently quoted by*
> *Dr. Deming.*[3]

The success or failure of management's effort toward the transformation may hinge on whether it has a clear understanding of systems thinking.

Understand your personal relationship to the system. If you are the director or manager of an autonomous technology service agency, not part of a bigger organization like an intermediate unit or university, then congratulations: you are the manager responsible for working ON the system and improving it. If your center or department is part of a larger organization then you must begin to practice recognizing what parts of the system you can control, that is, things you can work *ON*. And, which things you can't control. As soon as you realize the problem is something you can't control, you are IN a system. You have crossed over to your "containing system."

Something as simple as controlling the temperature to create an optimum working environment in summer and winter can force you into the containing system. If you, as the manager, can't control the temperature, then you are IN the system and just as powerless as the lowest paid part-time worker to do anything about it. Your responsibility as a manager may include making every effort to correct the temperature, but at the point where further efforts are counter-productive, recognize that it is out of your control and belongs to a system someone else controls.

In a large, multi-department organization like a university, parts of the system over which you have no control can adversely effect the performance of your department. The actual delivery of audio-visual equipment across campus may be the responsibility of a courier in the transportation department. The university media center may have the finest equipment and the most accurate scheduling system, but if the equipment is misdelivered or delivered late by the courier, it doesn't matter. The complaints will come to the media center. The reputation of the media center will suffer. Can you control the delivery people in this case?

Probably not directly. But armed with the 14 Points and the profound knowledge of Dr. Deming, you will find a way to break down the barriers between departments and overcome the obstacles to providing quality, accurate service.

At some point the struggle and reading about quality management must translate into action. Understanding the customer/supplier relationship and systems thinking is crucial for top management and the critical mass of employees. It is a useful place to begin breaking down internal barriers, promoting better communications, gaining cooperation and developing teamwork toward continuous improvement. To understand the internal customer/supplier relationship requires looking at the systems within your organization.

Systems of Production and Service

Whatever your educational service agency does, it is the result of a system. Arranging satellite teleconferences, providing distance learning courses through fiber optic networks, teacher training, software previewing, video/film library circulation, technology repair, printing, cooperative purchasing, video production, reference research: these are samples of the diverse range of products and services managed through a technology service center.

A system receives input and produces output. The input comes from suppliers and the output goes to the ultimate customer or user. Within the system there may be many processes, each of which can be broken down into many stages. As the work flows through the system, at each point where the work changes hands, a customer/supplier relationship exists. Each change point also provides the opportunity for errors and waste to creep into the service or product.

It is important to provide training in systems thinking to all employees involved with process improvement. Traditionally, most employees and even department heads operate in isolation within the system. They must be allowed to see the system as a whole. Flow charting can help do this, but they must also learn how to think along system lines. The performance of a system is the result of various interactions within the system. By the same token, problems and errors are caused by complex and dynamic interactions as well. Unfortunately we tend to see the world in a linear fashion, full of cause and effect relationships that we assume are valid. Over the years management has developed a "find and fix" mentality. Find the apparently obvious cause to a problem, and fix it. The find and fix mentality creates only short term solutions, puts out fires and perpetuates the isolation of processes from the bigger system.

Quality organizations depend on team work and cooperation. This is acheived by teaching employees to see beyond the limits of their own tasks and learn their relationship to other components of the system. Teaching everyone to think this way is very important. Peter Senge points out in *The Fifth Discipline* that if only one or two people see a problem from a systems perspective, their observations will be easily discounted by fellow workers. As the skill of systems thinking becomes second nature within an organization, discussions about emerging problems will shift away from find and fix fire fighting toward understanding the underlying causes embedded in the system.[4]

To help everyone begin to see the system as a whole, a flow chart is used to graphically represent the flow of information and materials through the system. In a quality organization using the teachings of Dr. Deming, the flow chart replaces the traditional organization chart. Each process is represented by a box along the way indicating that some work is being performed at that point. A separate flow chart may exist for the various stages within each process in the system as well. Using a flow chart in an organization begins to let people see their place in the total system. They can see where their work came from and where it is going— not only to the next person in line but to the ultimate user.

Chapter 6 explains the process of flow charting in greater detail.

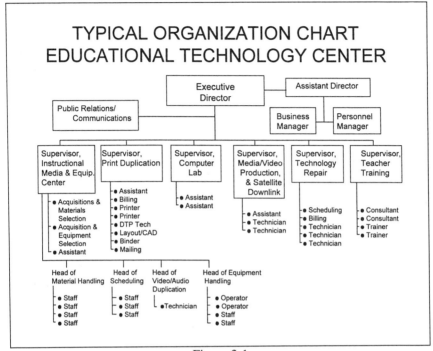

Figure 3-1

The act of flow charting can be a great team-building exercise. The flow chart also helps develop a much more realistic organization chart. Traditional organization charts only show who reports to whom. They tell nothing of the services, products or activities required to accomplish the mission of the organization. The flowchart conveys meaning to the worker and manager alike. Involving everyone connected to a process in the flow charting exercise can reveal wasted motions, redundant activities and opportunities for improvement. The action toward the transformation has commenced.

Statistical Process Control

One of the most unsettling and most misunderstood aspects of quality management for a novice is statistical process control or SPC. Note that of the seven stages of transformation, SPC is the final phase of action.

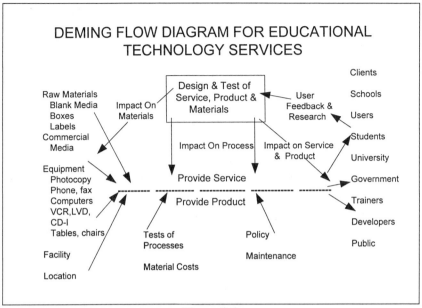

Figure 3-2

It also represents a relatively small part of all the activities that go into quality management. In 1988 David Langford began the use of Deming's philosophy in an Alaskan high school. He explains, "When I first started this process, I thought statistical analysis was 99 percent of the process and human relations was one percent. Since we've been in it for two years, I'm now realizing it's just the opposite." Take Langford's word for it and you have just saved two years.

This book is an introduction to quality management as it specifically relates to educational technology service agencies. Because a technology center will have advanced far beyond the scope of this book by the time it is ready to look seriously into using SPC as a quality improvement tool, the mathematics of SPC will not be dealt with here. Dr. Deming's book, *Out Of the Crisis*, and Mary Walton's, *The Deming Management Method*, both provide a general introduction to the formulas used for SPC. One of the best text books on the subject is *Understanding Statistical Process Control*, by Wheeler and Chambers, published by SPC Press, Knoxville, TN.

Statistical process control is not as difficult as it sounds and many educational institutions are in a position to have access to qualified math educators who might assist with training in SPC applications. In addition to the titles mentioned above, many of the sources on quality management mentioned at the end of this book contain valuable information on using SPC. The appropriate application of various data collection methods and formulas can yield useful information to guide the improvement of technology services. A discussion of system stability as it relates to SPC is located in Chapter 6.

It was pointed out earlier that the order in which an organization goes through the seven phases is important. Some corporations and educational institutions have seized upon SPC to the exclusion of other elements of the Deming method. Quality improvement can not be accomplished with statistics alone. Without a theory of management upon which action is based, statistics are maeningless numbers.

Dr. Deming provides a theory of management that puts numbers in context and guides the decisions that are the result of observing the system. The theory is referred to as a System of Profound Knowledge. It is the foundation upon which implementation of the 14 Points is grounded.

[1] Deming, W. Edwards. *Out Of The Crisis*. Cambridge, MA: MIT Press, 1986. Pg. 86; and, Walton, Mary. *The Deming Management Method*. New York: Perigee Books, 1986. Pg 87.

[2] Quoted in *Quality . . . Or Else, Vol. II*. Videotape. Chicago: Films Incorporated, 1991.

[3] Tribus, Myron, and Yoshikazu Tsuda. "Creating the Quality Company." *Quality First: Selected Papers on Quality and Productivity*. American Quality and Productivity Institute, 1987. Reprinted in *An Introduction to Total Quality for Schools*, 1991.

[4] Senge, Peter. *The Fifth Discipline*. New York: Doubleday, 1990. Pg. 267–269.

[5] Dobyns, Lloyd, and Clare Crawford-Mason, *Quality . . . Or Else: The Revolution in World Business*. Boston, MA: Houghton Mifflin, 1991. Pg. 259.

Chapter 4

A SYSTEM OF PROFOUND KNOWLEDGE

IN ALL OF DR. DEMING'S WORK THE IDEA OF *PROFOUND KNOWLEDGE* may be the most difficult to get top management to think about. First, it sounds like some gimmick from a high priced, get-in-touch-with-your-inner-potential, self-help video purchased late at night from a cable channel. It also sounds terribly complex. "Profound" sounds so deep. Avoid the temptation to skip this chapter. The answer to the question, "How do I begin?" starts here.

It is not all that complex, nor is it that simple. There are many people who are practitioners of the Deming method who do not understand profound knowledge and are doing quite well. The system of production and service they are responsible for can show very gratifying gains in quality and productivity without their understanding profound knowledge. The gains could be so much deeper and enduring if they did.

To implement and live the Deming method requires using the 14 Points, curing the deadly diseases and overcoming the obstacles to transformation. The 14 Points are used best within the context of profound knowledge.

Accepting new ideas about managing people may be difficult, but it is more difficult to actually change day to day management behavior. The potential user must be willing to reject certain long-held beliefs about themselves, others and management. This requires mental transformation.

57

Brian Joiner, a quality consultant and long-time associate of Dr. Deming calls it a "change of state, as from ice into water."

Changing your management style, attitude and outlook on things will be very hard. It will be very easy to backslide into old management ways when things get tough. Posting the 14 Points next to your desk might help. Sometimes Point 1, will jump out at you in times of trouble: "create constancy of purpose."

If it only took money to adopt the Deming method, the United States would have captured the world automobile market long ago. But better quality and better productivity cannot be bought. The transformation must begin in the mind, with the understanding of theory. Conversely, if one begins to change behavior and take action toward quality goals without a full mental commitment, aided by study, the efforts will fail. The organization's advances will be lost when it runs on hard times and management finds it easier to slip back into the old way of doing things. Implementing the 14 Points with an understanding of profound knowledge gives strength to the commitment to quality.

The System of Profound Knowledge consists of four parts, each of which supports and interacts with the others. Some aspects of profound knowledge may appear to be obvious to the reader; other parts may take some thought. The unique contribution of Dr. Deming is linking the four parts into a system that allows us to see management in a different way and to apply the 14 Points with meaning and deeper understanding of their implications.

The four parts of the System of Profound Knowledge are:

- Theory of knowledge
- Appreciation for a system
- Knowledge about variation
- Understanding some psychology

As Dr. Deming explains, it is unnecessary for top management, a department head, director or unit manager to be expert in one part or any combination of parts of profound knowledge. A general understanding of each part and how it relates to each of the others is a good start. The 14 Points logically flow out of profound knowledge and as one begins to work with the Deming method on a daily basis, situations arise that will trigger connections between the two. As this happens learning will take place and a better understanding of your system will emerge. It is important for now to know that the four parts exist and that they are, as Lloyd Dobbins puts it, "of a whole."[1]

Profound knowledge may best be understood by arranging the parts to show how one flows into the other. Let's start with a theory of knowledge.

Theory of knowledge

Knowledge and information are two different things. In the post-industrial information age politicians and other speech givers are fond of pointing out that information is now doubling every eighteen months. Although the amount of usable information may be doubling at a much slower rate. Information is data. Raw facts, numbers, plots, lines and words in a row. Only when information is placed in a context and applied to a specific situation based on certain assumptions, can it become knowledge. In 1993 the federal government proposed legislation providing incentives for private ventures to build a so-called "information super highway" throughout the United States. And although politicians and well-meaning educators are quoted in the general press saying that this highway will improve learning, it will not. No amount of "greater access to information" will improve learning, health care or the trade deficit without theory to guide action or without improvement of the systems that use the information.

To understand what knowledge is, one must understand that knowledge cannot exist without theory. Theory poses the question "why?" Without theory, there is no way to use information.

Most regional media centers and other technology centers accumulate loads of circulation and utilization data in their media management computers. Corporations do the same with sales and production figures. A calculator and a filing cabinet could do as much. That is not knowledge. Even when it is printed out in a report to show sales, invoices, circulation, lost material, requests turned down, or errors made it is still just information. It does not predict nor does it use technology to improve management. The speed at which computers process information and prepare reports does not help anyone to understand the future or the obligations of management. Only knowledge of the system can allow us to predict the possible outcomes of a proposed change.

Information is historic. What we require for management is "a statement that predicts future outcome, with the risk of being wrong," as Dr. Deming explains. He emphasizes the importance of management being able to predict future performance based on theory and observation of past performance. Just having a weekly report of numbers does not do that. "Any statement that does not predict is information. Knowledge has temporal spread." he concludes.[2]

The pervasive use of computers to manage information may have inadvertently furthered the use of management by objective and management by results to the continued detriment of organizations that rely on such methods. It is historical management; the rear-view-mirror analogy again. The results from the computer only tell us where we have been. They offer no knowledge about the future or how to improve the system.

American industry continues to install new computers and expect them to help boost their competitive position and be more productive. In spite of a 400 percent increase in capital outlay for computers in one eight year period, white collar productivity in the United States registered no gains, much to the surprise of many technology advocates.[3] How could it? How could the installation of computers improve the system of production and service? It can't and it never will. Unless the technology is part of a planned, systematic improvement effort aimed at changing the system to reduce waste, lower rework and improve quality, it is nothing more than something new added to the old system. The hole just gets bigger.

Knowledge comes from questions based on theory. Without theory, Deming teaches, there can be no questions.[4] The theory may be based on a guess or a hunch or a gut feeling, or a skip digit random sample, or five years of research. "How can we improve the circulation of video-discs to our schools?" "How can we reduce the loss of computer disks?" "How can we improve reception on the down-link?" "What will be required to prevent power failures in the computer lab?" These questions are all based on theory and will require information to answer. The answers will yield knowledge. Experimenting, or trying a new approach, may produce better results in all four of these cases. If it does, knowledge has been produced; the system has been improved. Even if better results are not achieved, Dr. Deming has pointed out that we have still learned something: we have learned what will not work. New knowledge has been created and we will have to go back and find another theory, make a new prediction.

One of the deadly diseases is the statement, "We rely on our experience." Experience in the absence of theory produces nothing. Deming sees it as one of the chief dangers of using benchmarking, as it is typically practiced, to improve quality. Visiting another educational technology center to learn how they have achieved a certain level of proficiency and attempting to replicate their methods back home can do more harm than good. Without understanding the theory that guides their actions you are depending only on their results for guidance. And results of any kind are only information. The fact that a specific university media center has a national reputation for outstanding service does not mean their performance is the result of a specific plan or method. Only by deep inquiry and study, much more than can be done in a one- or two-day site visit, can you reveal the theory behind the practices that have resulted in superior performance, or if the performance is even connected to a specific method.

Dr. Deming delivers a simple warning about studying the achievements of others, "Never mistake coincidence for cause and effect."[5]

This brings us to knowledge of variation. Once we know that the data we gather can be processed into knowledge, we will need to recognize there will be variations in the data—and in just about everything else.

Knowledge about variation

Managers and workers need to know about variation. Information on utilization of resources offered by an educational technology center can be instructive for understanding variation. How many videotapes are circulated, how many hours of teleconferencing are offered, how many computer keyboards are repaired, are all counts that might show up in an annual report or a monthly report to management. There is no absolute to these numbers and they will vary from month to month and from year to year.

On its face, that sounds obvious. But the reports typically wind up in the hands of the uninformed but well-intentioned who may ask why the circulation is off this year, why there were fewer teleconferences or why the repair shop did fewer keyboards. The search for the answer to these questions creates untold hours of wasted time each year both in education and industry. It leads to a phenomenon described by Brian Joiner as "management by the last dot," or "two dot management."

In an effort to track the performance of an organization, management typically looks at the last weekly or monthly report. If management doesn't like the last dot on the chart, it looks back another month. With two dots, management draws conclusions and makes decisions.[6] It might as well start using a set of dice as a management tool. Dots on a chart do not tell us how to improve.

The truth is that everything varies. Things go up or down, they get better or worse.

The question is, what can we learn from variation in a system? Variation is one way the system talks to us. We can ask, is the variation stable or unstable? If it is stable, then it is predictable. Anything that is predictable is manageable. Dr. Deming tells us that management is prediction. Prediction is based on information applied to a theory; the first part of profound knowledge. What do we mean by stable?

A stable system will produce the same results, within a certain range, over and over again. The stability may have a very wide range and be undesirable and still be considered stable. Take the example of a regional media center that delivers videotapes and laser discs to many schools each day. It may own several trucks and have set routes for delivery to a certain number of schools each day. The time the trucks return to the center may vary from day to day because of the length of the route, number of school stops and the number of items to pick up or deliver. Weather and traffic may contribute to the variation as well. Yet over a period of many weeks a predictable pattern may emerge for the return time of each truck on each day.

The time will not be exact. It will vary. On Monday the trucks may return between 1:00 and 1:22 p.m. On Tuesday it may be between 2:10 and 2:38. On Wednesday it may be between 12:55 and 1:10, and so forth.

If the arrival time varies within a certain range on a consistent basis, we may assume the system is stable. What can be learned from this variation? We can decide if the arrival range is acceptable. We can study the range of variation to determine if it can be reduced. Is the arrival time creating staffing problems in the center? Are people waiting around for an hour on some days for a truck to arrive? If we have several trucks, is there a conflict for unloading space or is too much material arriving at once? If you can predict when each truck will arrive on each day, you can plan the use of staff time much more productively. The system is talking to you. It is telling you what it is capable of doing.

Will it do any good to tell the drivers to "do better" and "get in on time from now on?" No, not a whit. The drivers are only performing as well as the system they work in.

How these issues are addressed and how to identify an unstable system will be discussed in Chapter 8. Here they serve only to give a relatively simple example of variation within a larger system. This brings us to the third part of profound knowledge.

Appreciation of a system

A system is defined by Dr. Deming as "a network of interdependent components that work together to try to accomplish the aim of the system."[7] It is the interactions between all parts of the system that create the total output of the system. It is why the *sum* of the processes never results in the end product. Just adding together all the contributions of the parts does not take into account the multiplying effect of the interactions between the parts.

If management owns the responsibility for improving the system of production and service, then it must learn something about systems thinking, mentioned earlier and something about operations analysis. Modern operations analysis, or operations research, grew out of the experience of using scientific investigation techniques to improve the performance of allied forces during World War II. Unlike previous approaches that only looked at individual components of the system, operations research took a "whole-system" approach. The collection of performance data was applied against statistical models and also took into consideration outside factors that affected the results of the system. Analysts not only took into consideration the strategies, people, training and equipment involved, but the "interactive features of the system" as well. Analysis considered alternate approaches to a specific problem and through system modeling provided a higher degree of prediction that a specific improvement would work than the trial and error methods previously used.

The efforts of various operations research groups during the war sought to optimize the performance of systems by learning how the best units performed and training others in the same techniques with the aim of creating greater uniformity of results. Operations research was largely responsible for the allied success after 1943 in defending convoys against German U-Boats.[8]

The methodology described above should sound vaguely familiar to the student of the Deming method. It represents the same kind of system thinking and scientific analysis advocated by Dr. Deming. The military establishment has had the benefit of this method since 1939. The Deming method now allows it to work for any organization.

All of us live and work in some form of system. In education some speak of a "school system" but do not give the words a second thought. For an organization to successfully adopt and implement the Deming method, top management—the director, manager or department head— must begin thinking about what a system is and how their organization functions as a system. If they continue to see each function, process or department as a disrelated piece of the system, the organization will never improve.

For a system to function productively, that is, toward the aim of the system, there must be communication and cooperation between all parts. Point 9 is "break down barriers between staff areas." Everyone within an educational technology service center must have an appreciation for the job of each department or functional area. The more complex and varied the services offered, the more this is necessary. Everyone must understand the aim of the organization. If the aim is to make the boss look good or to increase the number of patrons served each year, then the organization is in deep trouble and a short course in resume writing is in order. Chapter 12 expands on determining the aim of an educational technology service center.

People must be able to talk to each other and work cooperatively toward the aim of the organization. A principal barrier to cooperation is the system of merit reviews and annual appraisals found in most companies and almost universally in government and education. Dr. Deming rails against such activities as being one of the single greatest barriers to developing pride of workmanship and promoting cooperation between workers. There is no incentive for one worker to help another if someday the other worker may get a better rating. In a merit review situation the poorly rated worker is an asset to the highly rated worker. It makes her look good.[9]

Each employee must understand his or her function within the system as a whole and "view it as a catwalk," in the words of Dr. Paul Batalden, quoted frequently by Dr. Deming. As work flows from station to station it creates a stream of the process. At each point where the work changes hands, a relationship exists. The relationship is that of customer and supplier.

Every employee is both a customer to the previous process and a supplier to the next.

This is a fundamental requirement for understanding systems and one which all employees should be taught.[10] Optimization is a management process whereby every component of the system operates in harmony with every other. The aim is to optimize the system as a whole, not each individual component. Dr. Deming uses the example of an orchestra to illustrate this point. The orchestra does not need to consist of the best musicians in the country to produce a high quality performance. It must be managed (conducted) so that the efforts of all the musicians interact in harmony to produce an optimal performance by the whole orchestra.

In any system there exists a series of customer/supplier relationships. The system as a whole may have an ultimate customer, but each component of the system that produces the service or product also has a customer. In a traditional organization each component of the system, like a department or some other functional area, does its work in isolation from the others. When its work is done, the product or paperwork is passed on to the next unit. In engineering it is called "throwing it over the fence." Anyone who has ever refinanced a home has experienced this phenomenon.

For nearly one hundred years the American automobile industry designed and manufactured cars this way until Ford Motor Company began using the work of Dr. Deming in the early 1980s. The Ford Taurus/Sable line was the first American car designed and manufactured using Deming management principals. A design team was established that for the first time brought together employees from design, engineering, tooling, assembly, marketing and sales. A major effort was made to interview customers to learn what satisfied them most about their cars. Ford even worked with autobody collision experts to learn how the car could be designed to make fixing it easier if it was in an accident.[11] Did a commitment to quality make a difference? In 1980 Ford had 17 percent of the U.S. auto market and the letters FORD stood for Fix Or Repair Daily. By 1993, Ford held 25 percent of the U.S. auto market, five of the top ten cars and trucks sold in the United States were Fords; and the Taurus was the best selling car in America.[12] Ford learned the lesson of breaking down barriers between departments and getting them all involved in the design and manufacturing process. The same can be done for any enterprise.

Just because a university, school or other educational technology center does not make a tangible item like a car doesn't prevent it from designing its services to create maximum benefit for the end user. At the same time the internal systems that produce the service can be optimized to reduce loss due to waste, rework and errors.

An educational technology center is a system. Like any system, it is made up of many components or subsystems. Each component represents a stage in production or a process toward producing the finished product or service. The service offered by an educational technology center is the result of the interactions of all of the components within the system working toward the common aim. *To do this it is not necessary for each individual component to operate at full capacity, maximum effort or at the highest level of production.*

Take a moment and read the last line again.

Dr. Deming refers to this as the "obligation of a component." "The obligation of a component is to contribute its best to the system. Some components may operate at a loss to themselves, or be 'suboptimized,' in order to optimize the whole system."[13] This is the basis for good team-work. The individual musicians in the orchestra example are not there to perform virtuoso solos, but to work with the other members of the orches-tra.

The Deming method requires that management foster an atmosphere that promotes teamwork, cooperation and communication between all components of the system. One department may not be able to work at full capacity if that will overwhelm the next with too much work. A video duplication center may be able to turn out 100 tapes a day and swamp the clerks who cannot keep up with the flood of labels to type. Better communication between the departments could even out the work flow, reduce the stress on typists and improve the productivity of the system as a whole.

Can it happen overnight? No. It takes time to change a system be-cause systems are built of people. To get people to change requires a knowledge of psychology—part four of profound knowledge.

Understanding some psychology

Profound knowledge is made up of four parts, all interconnected and linked. Understanding one part is not possible without understanding the other three. Knowledge is only possible by applying information to theory. There is variation in all things. This includes people. The study of psychology helps us to understand the differences between people. It also helps us understand how people change, what their motivations are and how they interact with each other. In the study of a system there is recognition of a basic customer/supplier relationship. The relationship is created and developed by the interaction between people. These people may be workers in the same department or different departments. The relationship may also exist between people who are the ultimate customers of the service center and employees of the center. The technology center is also a customer to the many suppliers that help it deliver services. All of these interactions and relationships can be strengthened by understand-ing some psychology.

How people learn and how people are motivated are viewed by Dr. Deming as the two most important aspects of psychology to know about.

Managers must remember that people learn in different ways. Ironically, managers in educational institutions, many of whom are former teachers, tend to treat their employees as if they are all the same, forgetting the principles of instruction that allowed them to reach the diverse learning styles of students in their classes. Employees are similar to students—except they punch a clock and are adults. Some catch on quickly. Others take more time. Some must be shown a job several times and others can learn by seeing it done but not by reading about it. Others need pictures, videotapes, practice or some other combination of instruction.

Understanding motivation can be a challenge to many managers. In his four day seminars Dr. Deming explains why it is important to recognize the difference between intrinsic motivation and extrinsic motivation. Traditional Western management has relied on extrinsic motivation almost exclusively for 100 years. Money, rewards, fear, coercion, posters like "Do Your Best Everyday," slogans and numerical goals are examples of extrinsic motivation. Deming management relies on intrinsic motivation. He taught it to the Japanese in 1950. American corporations only began listening to the prophet from their own country in 1980—thirty years of wasted time—perhaps the greatest crime of omission in modern times.

We are all born with intrinsic motivation. Intrinsic motivators include the desire to do a good job, the desire to learn, natural curiosity, the desire to take pride in work, the need for love and self esteem. Over time the forces of Western society slowly beat these things out of us.

Grades in school, competing for a place on a team, competition among peers, competition for artificial goals and competition for recognition both at school and at home wear away at intrinsic motivation. Children quickly learn that they are in a system that creates more winners than losers and that survival can depend on how well you cope with losing. Why do we insist on recognizing the valedictorian in a graduating class? Is there only one good student per class? What is the message we send by ranking our students?

Figure 4-1 shows three actual bumper stickers that illustrate the destructive nature of well-intentioned recognition of excellence. The first is commonly used by parent-teacher groups to recognize good students. The second can be purchased in many novelty stores and is a direct result of

The Effect of Ranking People
(The Bumper Sticker Effect)

I HAVE AN HONOR STUDENT
AT XYZ MIDDLE SCHOOL

MY KID JUST BEAT UP
YOUR *HONOR* STUDENT !

At ABC Schools We Honor
ALL Our Students !

Figure 4-1

the resentment that ranking breeds. The third takes a little more enlightened approach and reminds us that there is honor in all work and that all children need to be valued.

As an adult, the decline of intrinsic motivation continues. Ironically, in the human spirit, hope springs eternal. We start a new job fresh and on top, ready for new challenges, ready to learn our new role and full of the hope that we can make a difference. Remember back to your first job out of school. It may have been as a teacher or a librarian; at twenty-three or twenty-four years old you were ready for a new beginning. How quickly did the reality set in? What were the politics? Who was the right person to know? You learned what made the supervisor or principal happy, and the forces of destruction slowly set in. You got by and made it to June.

You learned how to play the game and survive within the "system." In what other business are the professionals in a building allowed access to only one or two phone lines between them? What other profession locks its employees out of the office after 4:00 p.m. and challenges them if they are in the building working on Saturday? What other organization subjects the work force and the customers to an environment where the heat is turned on at 8:00 a.m. and off at 2:00 p.m.?

Consider the school district that refuses to purchase lined writing paper of the correct size for elementary students until the supplies of narrow lined paper ordered mistakenly were used first.

To solve this problem the staff engaged in some creative thinking. They photocopied the last sheet of elementary lined paper to make sure their students had the writing supplies they needed. In an effort to be economical with the writing paper, the business department created an $11,000 photocopy bill for all the copies of lined paper made by the teachers at five cents each. This is a perfect example of suboptimization of the system, heavy financial losses and unknown destruction to morale.

How many of us know 35-year-old educators who are coasting until retirement? Is it any wonder that roughly 40 percent of all beginning teachers leave the profession by the end of their third year?[14] The intrinsic desire to make a difference has been beaten out of them by the system.

Only management has the power to combat the destructive forces in the work place. It is the job of management to create a work place that allows workers to experience joy in work and pride in their contribution to the mission of the organization. Deming's Point 8 is "drive out fear." It is a good place to begin an appreciation of the psychology required to transform an organization.

Our discussion of a system of profound knowledge is by no means complete. At best, this is an introduction to a philosophical approach to management from which the application of the 14 Points logically flow. And, like the 14 Points, we cannot pick and choose which parts of profound knowledge we will accept and which we will ignore. If we try to manage with only three of the four parts, the function of management will be suboptimized. We need not be an expert in each of the four components, but each must have a place to optimize the system of quality management. Further study about the nature of profound knowledge is available through a videotape on the subject in the Deming Library available from Films Incorporated, Chicago, and in Dr. Deming's book, *The New Economics For Industry, Government and Education,* MIT Press, 1993.

[1] Quoted in *Volume 1: The Fourteen Points. The Deming Library.* Videotape. Films Inc., Chicago, 1989.

[2] Dr. Deming quoted in a four-day seminar, St. Louis, October 6–9, 1993.

[3] Levy, Stephen. "The Case Of The Purloined Productivity." *Macworld,* March, 1993. Pg. 57.

[4] Deming, W. Edwards. *The New Economics for Industry, Government and Education.* Cambridge. MA: MIT Press 1993. Pg. 106.

[5] Dr. Deming quoted in a four-day seminar, Philadelphia, February 17, 1993.

[6] Contributed by Brian Blecke, Manager of TQM Marketing, Films, Inc. Chicago.

[7] Deming, pg. 98.

[8] Tidman, Kieth R. *The Operations Evaluation Group: A History of Naval Operations Analysis.* Annapolis, MD: Naval Institute Press, 1984. Pg. 9,12,13. See also Ackoff, Russell and Maurice Sasieni. *Fundamentals of Operations Reasarch.* New York: Wiley & Sons, 1968.

[9] Op cit., *The Fourteen Points. Vol. 1.*

[10] Deming, pg. 31.

[11] Walton, Mary. *The Deming Management Method.* New York: Perigee Press, 1986. Pg 140.

[12] Clements, Michael. "Ford Sees Record Mid '90s Car Sales." *USA Today,* December 2, 1993. Pg. 1.

[13] Deming, pg. 100.

[14] Darling-Hammond, Linda F., and Arthur Wise. *Effective Teacher Selection.* Santa Monica, CA: RAND Corporation, 1987.

Chapter 5

LONG RANGE VISION AND THE DEMING METHOD

AMERICAN MANAGEMENT IS DESTRUCTIVELY SHORT-TERM ORIENTED. This attribute of business and industrial management pervades most government, university and educational agencies as well. Not necessarily out of conscious choice, but because we know no other way to run things. It is the American business paradigm and it defines how we traditionally run things.

Once an organization embarks on the road to quality using the Deming method it will eventually have to confront the problem of short-term thinking, which the paradigm of quality management will not tolerate.

Short-term thinking almost always comes directly from results-oriented management, management by numbers or management by objective. Results-oriented management is characterized by an annual ritual of developing numerical goals for each department and work unit within an organization. The college recruitment goal might be ten percent over last year. Purchasing might try to cut photocopy paper costs by 15 percent. Computer operations may be told to cut overtime hours by 20 percent. The department head generally goes through the same routine with each supervisor within the department and they in turn do the same with the people under them. At the end of the year the results are checked against the numerical goals.

Results oriented management places a heavy emphasis on goals and measurement but rarely contains a method through which the goals can be met. Improving the quality of service in a technology center requires emphasis on the methods that will bring about improvement, rather than measurement or numerical goals.

Management by results reinforces the traditional chain of command and leaves little room for improvement of processes that might cut across several departments. It also pits one department against the other when the attempt to meet a goal in one area is in conflict with the goal in another. Purchasing's attempt to cut costs by buying lower grade paper may increase the amount of time it takes to get documents duplicated. The duplication department, with its own goal to reduce turnaround time, may experience more delays due to increased photocopier jams, smudged copies and more service calls. Competition between departments for the resources of the organization is heightened and there is virtually no basis for cooperation. As long as an organization remains divided against itself, there will never be a strong focus on the customer.

Management by results focuses the attention and energy of the organization on a specific goal, generally a number. Over the years, managers have learned not to set a deadline for reaching a goal too far in the future. If it is, the worker may see the goal as unattainable or out of reach and become frustrated. Managers know that frustration reduces productivity and they strike a careful balance between the goal to be reached and the time to get there. In quality management there is no way to say when an organization has reached the state of quality. It is not a place to be arrived at, explains David Langford, "There is no there there."

Focus on Process

Organizations that have adopted the Deming philosophy no longer rely on results-oriented management. The energy and focus is always on improving the process that creates results. Are results not important? Of course they are. Results provide a sign post of what an organization has done. Past tense; what *has* been done. Of far more importance is the aim of the organization, the overall vision of what the organization is to become in the future.

- Last year we repaired 235 computers, 115 monitors and 375 VCRs
- Last month we circulated 4,300 videotapes
- Last year we sponsored 27 satellite conferences
- Last year we assisted over 5,000 students in the computer lab
- Last quarter MIS answered 1,200 requests for data from administration

These are all statements of fact that may be useful in an annual report to a board of directors, a university president, or to the administrator of an educational technology unit. They are useless for judging the quality of service, explaining how to improve or predicting what might happen in the future. For this reason, although they may be demanded by higher administrators, such statements of result carry no importance when working to improve the process of production and service. They contribute nothing toward the aim of the agency.

In traditional American management any of the above quoted statements may be turned into a goal for the following year. Just as sales managers set new and higher goals for their commission sales people, it is not uncommon for educational technology center managers to set higher goals. Sometimes the goals are set from above, sometimes we impose them on ourselves. Increase circulation by three percent, repair 15 percent more computers, sponsor 12 more satellite conferences, assist ten percent more students, cut costs by eight percent, reduce recalls on repairs by 50 percent, the list can be endless. As managers become more comfortable with the Deming philosophy, they will stop imposing goals on themselves and the unit they manage.

The only goal that is necessary is continuous improvement of the system. It is a goal with no end. Remember the words on the chalk board in the rental center quoted in the introduction, "In the race for quality, there is no finish line."

We like to think that goals are imperative for the progress of an organization. We must have something to shoot for. In practice the opposite is true. Short-term goals only encourage short-term thinking and destroy any motivation for long-term planning. What is required is a long-term vision of the organization that is shared by management and worker alike. Numerical goals are reached out of fear or by juggling the numbers to fit the expectation. If you want to cut costs by three percent, find something in the budget that totals three percent and don't buy it. It will make you look like a financial genius.

Do you want to raise productivity? Eliminate a position and do the same amount of work with fewer people. The labor cost per service rendered, or item produced, is lower and therefore productivity is higher. With management by objective and management by numerical goal, the focus is on the goal and finding someone to blame if the goal is not reached. Out of self-preservation a way is found to make the goal. Has the system of production and service been improved? Not at all.

Dr. Deming points out that there are certain facts of life that are not goals or even aims, just facts. For example, the threat of a technology center being closed unless costs are cut is a fact of life. Dr. Deming says that this fact may be translated into a long-range goal only if a method is provided for its accomplishment.[1]

"By what method?" is a constantly repeated question from Dr. Deming. If you are going to have a goal then a method must be provided to accomplish the goal. But quality goals are not numerical targets. Quality goals have a direct connection with the mission of the organization and focus on the needs of the customer. When quality goals are set, they are set for improvement of the organization as a whole, not for each individual department. This is done to ensure cooperation between all departments and focus improvement efforts on higher-level ideals.[2]

What is Required?

What is required is leadership. Point 2 of the 14 Points is "constancy of purpose." The aim of the organization provides the constancy of purpose: the vision, the long-term and sustaining mission of the organization. Vision comes from leadership that must be provided by the top management of the organization. Becoming a visionary is a difficult leap for most people. It is made more difficult because it requires giving up old short-term, goal-oriented methods in favor of methods to which no tangible outcomes can be immediately ascribed. It also requires that managers give up the old notion that their job is to direct the activities of others. They must now be willing to ask others, "Will you follow me?"[3]

Providing a vision for an educational technology center is no easy task. To start, it means no longer being reactive but proactive, anticipating the future. Developing a vision for an agency forces attention outward, toward the future. If a technology service agency is running on a survival mode, management may feel it is hopeless to look beyond next month or next year. To avoid taking the long view will guarantee continued heavy losses and a perpetual struggle against the forces of destruction. It is no wonder that Dr. Deming's 1986 book is titled *Out of the Crisis*.

Leadership with vision requires creativity, hope and inspiration not bound by precedent. Not bound by the old paradigms of what audio-visual or educational technology is "supposed to be." Leadership comes with an obligation to constantly ask the question, "what service would be useful to our users in the future?"

A vision can be a very durable item simply because it takes a long-term view. It can also be dashed against the rocks if there is continual change of leadership. Dr. Deming describes it as one of the seven deadly diseases, "mobility of management," that must first be cured before the movement toward quality can begin.

Given stability of leadership, the certainty of long-term vision can be a powerful factor in developing a cohesive sense of mission among the employees of any organization. Instead of being distracted with short-term, numerical goals, they can be unified by the same long-term view. They are then free to focus on how their jobs may be done better to improve the system of production and service. Focus comes from knowing "why" a job is being done. The "why" comes from knowing the mission and vision of the organization. Goals can only tell us "what" is to be done, never "why."[4]

Staying Ahead of the User

If you really want to stay ahead of your users, then your agency must have an aim. By definition an aim is in the future. We would like our aims to be as far into the future as possible. The following questions might help change the focus of an educational technology service center from the present to the future. If an organization is always fighting fires, redoing projects, looking for lost items, handling complaints and counting errors, there may be very little time for thinking about the future. But it is imperative that leadership make the time to look ahead. Not to next week, but into the next decade or more.

- What kind of organization do you want your agency to be in the future?
- Who are your users?
- Who will they be in the future?
- What are their needs now?
- What will their needs be in the future?
- What issues will affect the design of services in the future?
- How can your agency be ready for these issues as they emerge?
- How can your agency lead users to the new services you will offer?
- What would happen if your center ceased operation tomorrow?
- Why are we here?
- What business are we really in?
- What business should we be in?

All of these questions should be considered when constructing the aim of your organization.

If you cannot tell why your organization exists in 25 words or less then you may not understand the aim of your own organization. Most American managers do not know what their job is in the new economic age and do not know what their aim is. They do not know because they have never been allowed the opportunity to think of such things. They do not know that there is an alternative to the way things have always been done. Management consultant and author Joel Barker calls it "paradigm paralysis."[5]

As a manager it is your obligation to create the future of your organization and communicate it to your employees and your superiors. Dr. Deming explains that there was no ground swell of consumer demand asking for the electric light, the telephone, television, microwave oven or VCR. These things were developed by people with vision who saw them as developing into something useful that consumers would want in the future. We may do the same in our own technology centers.

Becoming more future-oriented means that evaluating and assessing the relative merits of new technologies and new approaches to education can be done over an extended period of time. It means being aware of new developments from the first time they are made public. Even if there appears to be no current use for the new approach at the local level, the media and technology manager needs to be aware that the technology exists and is in development. By being future-oriented, media and technology managers create the time to make connections between local user needs and the capabilities of new technology. Since not every innovation can be adopted, managers are in a better position to make decisions on what should be added to the resources available through their center and have a high degree of confidence that the users will be pleased with the addition.

District and regional centers that followed the development of videodisc, saw it as a viable instructional delivery system and invested in it early were ahead of their users when demand for it began to rise. Compact Disc-Interactive presented the same opportunity in 1993. Media centers with a vision of the future began exploring its possibilities and prepared themselves to lead users to another tool for education.

Today a campus computer lab can offer students the ability to write term papers more easily. In the future it may offer students the ability to create multi-media term papers with color photographs, video clips and a voice narration.

Today a multi-district regional center can offer videotapes and building level collections of materials. In the future it may offer video on-demand with an asymmetrical digital subscriber line (ADSL) system.[6]

Not too long ago the only way to send requests for delivery of materials to a regional or university media center was on paper forms by courier or mail. Today they can be ordered by fax or through direct, 24-hour-a-day, on-line user access by telephone. New developments and service improvement such as this came about through the vision and planning of the software supplier, not the overwhelming demand of end users.

Virtual reality technology is presently limited to high level medical and military applications and some arcade games. Will it have a place in a regional or district media center? How might VR improve the level of instruction in a college or university? The questions may be unanswerable at present, but they need to remain active because they represent one possible future of many for media and technology in education.

If you want to demonstrate to other managers what it means to be long-term oriented, try turning in a 23-year plan for your educational technology center. Why 23 years? Because it is an odd number and peaks curiosity. And why more than ten years? To really break out of the traditional planning box, take the organization into the next generation of employees and consider what kind of an organization you will be leaving for them.

To understand the value of being future-oriented, it is useful to dig out a copy of *Megatrends,* written in 1982 by John Naisbitt. Nearly every trend and shift described in the book has come to pass and they now influence our daily lives and how we manage our work. The ability to be future-oriented is a skill that has become more important in the last ten years. The accelerated rate of change demands this. Any new technology or innovation now progresses from idea to application in a far shorter amount of time than in the past. It took 35 years to progress from the creation of a vacuum tube to a radio. It took 12 years to get from a crude cathode ray tube to a workable television. From the invention of the transistor to the first integrated circuit took five years.

The importance of vision is to make a connection between the development of future services or technologies and the anticipated needs of the user. Real needs and real services that will materially improve the quality of life for the user. The annals of educational technology are littered with false starts, innovations and three-year projects that disappeared when the funding ran out. How many of them really improved the ability of a teacher to communicate? How many of them improved the ability of a student to retrieve and use information? How many of them created any lasting change to the system of educational communication? How many of them produced lasting, systemic improvement in the way students learn? The reader may decide. The point of this book, and using the Deming method, is not to find a way to install quality in our educational service centers, or justify the use of technology to improve education. It is to find a way for improvement of the system of technology service on a continuous basis.

Strategic Planning

In a government agency, education or similar non-profit organization, strategic planning has three distinguishing characteristics. First, it delays action that may actually improve things. Second, the plan tends to focus more on current problems than on developing a vision of what is required for the future.[7] And third, the resulting document generally represents everything that the members of the strategic planning committee are least inclined to argue over. The result is a maintenance of the status quo and institutionalized mediocrity.[8]

The personal experience of the author with strategic planning activities for two national associations, an intermediate unit, several school districts and a state department of education, in addition to anecdotal information from colleagues and personal examination of several more plans, tends to bear out this observation. A discussion of planning for quality service can be found in Chapter 12.

Strategic plans result in a pile of short-term goals and objectives that, for the most part, can be met with little effort. If anything usable comes out of a strategic planning activity it is the mission statement. This may be a good place to start when building the vision of an agency. Beyond that, there are few strategic plans that have actually resulted in improved performance of the organization. Things are still done much the way they have always been done. The same problems still arise and the same fires need to be put out. Why? Because the plan was superimposed over the same old system. Unless the system is changed, the subject of Chapter 6, we will get only what the existing system is capable of; nothing more.

Instead of investing time in strategic planning, use the time to look beyond the boundaries of the agency and envision what your users will expect from your services years from now. Such an exercise can provide guidance for the actions that must be taken to meet user needs. Then begin to develop the cooperation that is required and provide the leadership that will move the organization into the future.

[1] Deming, W. Edwards. *New Economics for Industry, Government and Education*. Cambridge, MA : MIT Press, 1993. Page 42.

[2] Ishikawa, Kaoru. *What Is Total Quality Control? The Japanese Way*. Englewood Cliffs, NJ: Prentice-Hall, 1985. Pg. 61.

[3] Senge, Peter M. *The Fifth Discipline*, New York: Doubleday, 1990. Pg. 215.

[4] Macher, Ken. "On Becoming a Visionary," *Association Management*, Feb. 1987. Pg. 43.

[5] Barker, Joel. *Discovering the Future: The Business of Paradigms*. St. Paul, MN: I.L.I. Press, 1985. Pg. 72.

[6] ADSL, Asymmetrical Digital Subcriber Line, developed by Bellcore and Bell Atlantic for on-demand broadband video delivery and interactive video systems on common copper wire phone systems.

[7] Hamel, G. and Prahalad, C. K. "Strategic Intent." *Harvard Business Review*, May-June, 1989.

[8] Sagor, Richard. "The False Premises of Strategic Planning." *Education Week*, April 1, 1992. Pg. 28.

Chapter 6

THE SYSTEM OF SERVICE

WHAT BUSINESS ARE WE REALLY IN? IF YOU THINK YOUR AGENCY is in the business of delivering video tapes to schools, you're in trouble. If you think the business of a campus computer center is to give students a place to do term papers, you're in trouble. If you think that the business of your technology repair unit is to fix equipment, you're in trouble. If you think the business of management information systems is to run computers for administration, you're in trouble.

"We Make Window Shades"

In the early 1900s a certain window shade company wanted to make its business grow. Everything it tried failed to make the business any bigger. They brought in a management consultant, to look over what they were doing wrong. After a few days of study the consultant took the board of directors into a bright, sunny room. She (yes, she) went over to the window and pulled down all the shades. She asked what had just happened? The board responded, "The room got darker, of course."

"Gentleman, your problem is that you think you are in the window shade business," she explained. "Your real business is lighting control."[1]

Armed with that revelation, the company was now liberated to see new business opportunities where there were none the day before. The company could now see beyond the product line and see the *result* of the product. How many educational technology service agencies are limited by seeing only their product or service? How much creative energy is lost and how many opportunities have escaped by the failure to see beyond the tangible? This is another example of what Dr. Lloyd S. Nelson, Director of Statistical Methods for the Nashua Corporation means when he says, "the most important losses are unknown or unknowable."[2]

To begin improvement, Dr. Deming us to define the aim of our organization. In the Deming method, there is no reason to create a system if the system does not have an aim. In an educational technology center our aim is not to deliver videotapes or hook up classrooms to a downlink. The aim of an organization is never defined by an activity or method. It is always defined in terms of how the organization improves the quality of life for its users, customers or clients.[3] You may work in a regional media center, a university instructional technology center, a high school media center, a community college TV service, a medical education center or any place that provides educational technology resources to teachers and learners. What these centers do may vary greatly in scope and method, but their aims may all be the same. How do the activities of these technology centers improve communications in the classroom? How are the *interactions* between student and teacher, and student to student improved?

On an almost universal level, educational technology service agencies are in the business of helping their clients improve the quality of interaction between teacher and student to improve the quality of instruction and learning. If that is the aim, then how is it to be done—by what method?

System Output Is Always More Than the Sum of the Parts

Although our processes may differ from one center to another depending on our setting and client base, all of the processes are embedded in a system that produces the ultimate service of our agency. Understanding systems is one of Dr. Deming's four components of profound knowledge introduced in Chapter 4.

A system is a network of interdependent components that work together to try to accomplish the aim of the system. A system must have an aim. Without an aim, there is no system. The aim of the system must be clear to everyone in the system. The aim must include plans for the future.

W. Edwards Deming.[4]

"The performance of the whole is never the sum of the performance of the parts taken separately, but it is the product of their interactions. To manage a system effectively you must focus on the interaction of the parts rather than their behavior taken separately," explains Dr. Richard Ackoff, former Dean of the Wharton School of Business at the University of Pennsylvania and a long-time associate of Dr. Deming.[5] For this reason, the output of the system is always greater than the sum of the parts. The interactions between individual processes are the multipliers that produce the outcome of the system.

In American management we frequently fail to see the work flow within an organization as a system or to recognize that the interaction between processes is important. The phrase, "improve the system of production and service" occurs throughout this book and in other books on the Deming method. For whatever reason, many educational administrators have trouble with the "production" part. This is where they protest that, since education doesn't really produce anything tangible, the Deming method does not apply. It might be fine for making cars, but not for running the educational establishment.

Production also applies to the processes required to provide a service. An obvious example could be a campus television studio. A department might seek the services of the technology center to produce a videotape on a particular subject. There will be a sequence of planning, writing, approval and preparation to be followed prior to going into the studio. A process of blocking shots and technical rehearsals prior to taping various sequences will be followed. The actual taping will follow another series of processes. And post-production editing will combine other elements such as sound effects, music, field taping, voice overs and graphics to create the final product for delivery to the client department.

Did the technology center produce a product—the videotape? Or did it provide a service by filling the communication needs of the client?

A regional media center that serves as a central resource of instructional materials for several thousand students provides a service. Materials required to assist in the instructional process are ordered by teachers for delivery on specific dates. The regional center provides a service in selecting, storing, maintaining and delivering resources. The processes involved with providing the service constitute a system of production, the end result of which is the service used by the teachers. The elements of "production and service" are inseparable when examining the management of a system.

What Does a System Look Like?

Traditional Western management relies on an organization chart to graphically represent the structure of an enterprise. Corporations and government agencies that have begun to use quality management principles rely on flow charts. The difference is profound and represents a paradigm shift of how managers view their organizations. Educational technology service centers can begin to accelerate their involvement with quality management by looking at their center as a "system of service" instead of as an organization chart.

An organization chart shows lines of responsibility. It describes who reports to whom; what department is under what manager. It may also show who controls department or project budgets. As shown in Figure 6-1, an organization chart primarily tells us whom to blame when something goes wrong.

A flow chart shows the progression of information and material that is required to produce a product or service. A flow chart does not care about boundaries between departments or who reports to whom. It focuses only on the processes within a system and the flow of work through them.

In 1950 Dr. Deming put on a blackboard for his Japanese hosts the drawing in Figure 6-2. It is referred to as the Deming Flow Diagram and is used in all of his seminars. It illustrates the fundamental flow of materials and information needed for the production of a product or service. Although the core of the diagram looks like a typical production line, the significance is the place of the customer in the flow. Customer and user feedback must go beyond, "Are your satisfied?" Dr. Deming explains that the most important part of the system of production is the customer. [6]

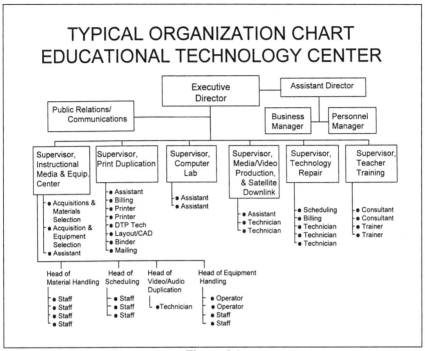

Figure 6-1

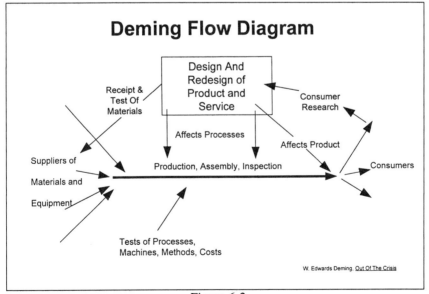

Figure 6-2

The system actively seeks user input on the design of new products and services, and on the improvement of others. Figure 6-3 adapts the Deming Flow Diagram to educational technology services. The reader can pick and choose various supplier and customer elements to match the mission of a specific kind of technology center. The diagram represents the continuous cycle of a system that provides services to the clients of the center. The diagram can be applied to any process within the larger system as well.

Customers and Suppliers

The feature of the Deming Flow Diagram that makes it different from a typical process flow chart is the inclusion of the customer as an influencing factor on the design and redesign of the process and product. Only by staying in touch with our customers, our users, can we begin to anticipate their needs for the future. The process of assessing the possible needs of our users in the future also requires a certain amount of operational research. The aim of the research is to consider many alternatives and test new approaches that may fill future user needs. The research may include informal reviews of literature, focus groups with clients, keeping current with new developments and attending professional conferences. We cannot lead our users to new materials and technologies if we do not have a method of gathering and assessing information about new developments and ideas. We cannot intelligently assess the information we have about alternate methods and new technologies unless we know how our clients use technology. We need to know how our customers make use of our products and services in the field. What obstacles do they face? What developments in educational technique will affect their use of media and technology? What aspects of their system can they control? What are the dynamics that create interaction in their classroom? When was the last time you watched a teacher use a videotape or computer program in a real classroom?

The anticipation of need leads to development of new services or offering of new technologies. Agencies that know their users' needs are in a better position to lead their users to these new services and new technologies. They position themselves as leaders and as catalysts for change

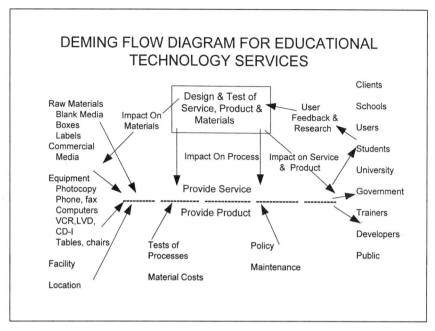

Figure 6-3

and improvement. Centers that merely wait until there is demand or until the new technology is generally accepted will never move ahead. The relationship and interaction between the technology center as supplier and the client as customer is crucial to understand.

Suppliers are considered essential parts of the system of production and service as well. For and educational technology service center, incoming raw material may be blank tape, blank floppy disks, video boxes, laserdisc boxes, label stock, information, commercially produced programs for computers or video, photocopy paper, printer ribbons, computer paper and anything else that is consumed or goes into producing our ultimate service. As a supplier of a service, we must work with our customers, we must also recognize our role as customer to the suppliers we rely on. Our service can only be as good as the raw materials used in the production of the service. It is also essential that we work with our suppliers to get the quality we need to furnish our services.

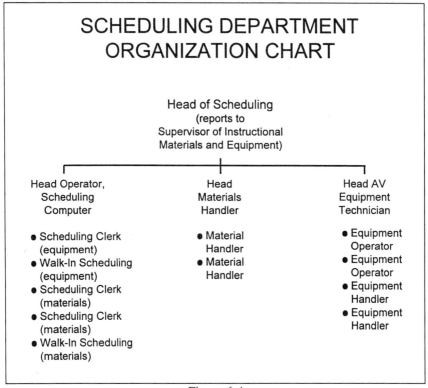

Figure 6-4

Whom to Blame or Whom to Serve

Figure 6-4 shows a typical organization chart for the media and/or equipment scheduling operation in a large technology center. We now know who answers to whom and what the job titles are. We have no idea what their places are, or what function they serve in the system that provides service to the users of the center. Organization charts reinforce traditional management styles that place an emphasis on lines of authority and compartmentalization of activities. This creates a silo or chimney effect in an organization. Although the flow of the process, scheduling materials in this case, passes horizontally through the organization, the focus of the people in the system is vertical; up and down the lines of authority. The hierarchy of the organization chart drives the internal culture of the staff. It results in working more to please the boss and avoid being blamed for problems. Both of these efforts focus energy up and down the lines of authority. How can these efforts improve the system? They can't.

The effect is also extended to communications between departments and functional areas. Information about problems, new ideas and improvements tend to flow up one line to the top of the department chart, like smoke up a chimney, before they can flow down the organization chart in another department.[7]

How much does this promote communications between departments? Not much. Every link in the organization chart is a potential barrier or a place for misunderstanding to emerge. It is sort of an institutionalized game of "whisper down the lane." Over time, employees learn that it is fruitless to try to get ideas through such an arrangement and they stop trying. To lose its most important asset, the intellectual capital of an employee, is a heavy loss for any organization.

Dr. Deming's Point 3 is "drive out fear" and Point 9 is "break down barriers between departments."

The creation of flow charts can be of material assistance in meeting these two points within an educational technology center. The act of creating them can foster communication and team work. Once a flow chart is complete, it is then used to find appropriate points to begin quality improvement efforts. Look closely into the central line of flow in the diagram in Figure 6-3 and visualize some service the center provides.

Each process in the system that produces a service in your center also has a customer/supplier relationship. How is a request for service handled? A request for a piece of equipment, a videotape, a print job, a computer repair, down-link time or a consultation might begin the chain of events that leads to fulfilling the request and providing the service. Where does the paperwork go? Who gets what information and in what order? Is there a priority to each request? How do we know if the service was rendered to the satisfaction of the client?

Flow Charting a System, Don't Try This Alone

Learning how to flow chart a system is an essential first step to finding areas for improvement within a system. Most managers have never thought of graphically representing the flow of a process within their center and it is a skill that requires some practice and patience. The exercise of flow charting can serve several important purposes.

First, the idea is to show the process *as it exists right now*. Do not try to correct or redesign the process while you are flow charting it. The end result should be a good representation of how the process is actually being handled. Second, as mentioned earlier, flow charting can be a tremendous team-building activity. Do not try flow charting alone. Work in pencil and bring in everyone who has anything to do with the process you have selected to look at.

A word of caution about flow charting, or about any of the charts used to improve quality: don't get hung up on the look of chart. The K.I.S.S. principal must be in effect at all times. Keep It Simple. It is not necessary to run out and buy a flow charting software program for your favorite computer. Don't worry about the shape of the boxes either. Just be sure everyone you are working with has a common understanding of the symbols you are using. Three shapes are all that are really needed: a rectangle to show an activity, a diamond to indicate a decision point and a circle to indicate a yes/no answer to a condition question.

The act of flow charting helps start people talking to each other about what their jobs are and allows them to see where they fit into the total system. Even in very small organizations and departments, some people have no idea how their work contributes to the aim of the system. For the typical employee the system "is everything but him."[8] To see the whole system for the first time can be a revelation.

If one of the missions of your agency is the circulation of instructional materials to schools or other users, you might want to trace the entire process from the time an order is received until the material is returned from the user and checked in.

A process within the system, like entering orders into a scheduling system computer might be a good place to begin flow charting with the staff as well. Remember to involve other people and help them begin to think about the whole of the organization. No individual knows, really knows, all of the steps involved with the system of production and service in any organization. That is why we work in pencil. It is very easy to have the flow chart of a process *look* complete. Yet another person may

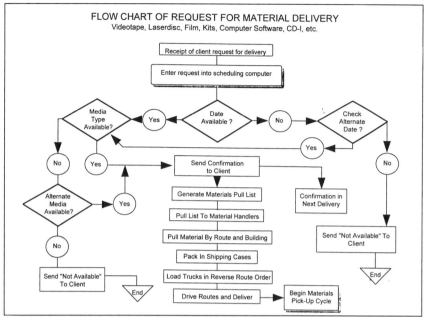

Figure 6-5

look it over and point out another sub-routine or exception that must be factored into the chart.

Figure 6-5 illustrates the flow of information and material required to fulfill the request for delivery of a videotape to a school served by a regional media center. The request arrives one of several ways, each of which requires a different handling method. Once the request is accepted into the scheduling computer another series of processes takes over. On the appropriate date a computer routine will assign a specific print for delivery. A pull list will then be generated that will tell the staff which title and print number to pull for delivery. Later a packing list will serve as a paper record of which titles go to which teachers in which schools. The load for a school will be packed in a box and loaded onto a van for delivery. On the requested date the box will be delivered and the teacher will have the material required to support that week's lessons.

An easy to understand and highly instructive book on flow charting is *Deployment Flow Charting,* by Myron Tribus, published by Quality & Productivity Incorporated, Los Angeles, CA.

Error, Variation and the Potential for Chaos

Every place the process changes hands or the information is touched is a potential place for errors to occur. And errors *will* occur. It would violate the laws of probability for a system never to have an error or variation. Anything can happen in the course of handling a client request for materials to be delivered. The order can be keyed into the computer wrong. The wrong title number or print number can be pulled. The item can be packed in the wrong box or delivered to the wrong school. Minor errors in one part of the system can have a profound effect on the system as a whole.

Even if there is an error rate of only one tenth of one percent in a given process, the error will compound itself as it moves through the system. A relatively small error created somewhere in the system becomes amplified over time to the point where the performance of the system is no longer predictable and will break down completely—chaos. This is an example of chaos theory at work and illustrates Dr. Deming's axiom that all systems must be managed.

As part of our study of variation it might be useful to understand the impact of non-linear dynamics, or chaos theory, on a system. Largely because of the work of Sir Isaac Newton, we tend to look at most events and activities in a linear fashion with a direct cause and effect. Our assumption is that if we set up a system to perform a specific function, like distribution of educational media, it will perform pretty much the same way day to day and week to week if it isn't tampered with. The fact is that since the system is influenced by a number of variables, it will almost never perform the same way twice. Variation in the system will always exist.

A Stable System?

Some variation is regular and predictable, other variation is unpredictable and totally random. There is a difference between variation attributable to random events and variation attributable to chaos. Chaos will show a cyclical plot that may not be readily apparent until observed over a long period of time and will fall within stable limits. A plot of random variation will never show a repeated pattern or stability. The ability to predict the behavior of a system is important to management.

A system can be chaotic and stable at the same time. A plot of typing errors created by a secretary can be shown to be stable, falling within mathematically derived limits. For example, no fewer than one error per day and never more than five per day. But the variation in the number of errors created each day will not be predictable. We have no way to predict that tomorrow the secretary will make two errors, we only know that over an extended period of time the number of errors will not exceed five per day. The system is locally unpredictable but globally stable.[9]

The use of control charts to analyze the performance of a system works the same way. The system can be shown to be stable, and its performance predicted to continue into the future, even if there appears to be chaotic variation day to day.

Pour a little cream into a cup of coffee and observe the swirl of milk and coffee as they mix. The pattern is unpredictable and will not be duplicated from one cup to another, but the end effect of what looks like a chaotic process is perfectly predictable. "We might have trouble predicting the temperature of the coffee a minute in advance, but we would have little difficulty forecasting it an hour ahead," explains Edward Lorenz, the MIT meteorologist who rediscovered the chaos effect in 1962.[10]

The phenomenon of the chaos effect was actually first arrived at in 1892 by the French mathematician Enre Poincare while studying Newton's Laws of Motion. He plotted mathematical models for the motion of three moving bodies and found that the linear nature of Newton's work with two moving bodies did not hold up.[11] It was impossible to predict the motion of the three bodies into the future. Certainly there is no process in an educational technology center that does not involve the motion of at least three variables.

Poincare's work led him to develop a concept now known as "sensitivity to initial conditions." In effect, it says that small errors in knowledge about the beginning conditions can create errors (changes, variation) in the performance of the system totally out of proportion to the size of the initial flaw. The logical response to this is: the more we can know about the conditions at the start of a sequence, system or cycle, the higher confidence we have of predicting the performance. The fact is that we cannot possibly know enough about the beginning conditions to accurately predict performance over time. Minor or overlooked conditions will manifest themselves in unknowable ways far into the cycle.

It was not until 1962 when MIT meteorologist Edward Lorenz began modeling weather patterns while trying to find better prediction methods that chaos began to be recognized as a science. Lorenz started with a simple convection current and established three values for the beginning of a weather cycle.

He then let a computer run a plot of the model for several months of the cycle. Then, to study some aspect of the cycle more closely, he stopped the cycle and reinserted the initial values at a point several months into the plot. He expected the new plot to follow the original plot exactly, and it did for a time. Then the new plot line began to diverge from the original line, gradually at first, and finally creating a totally new and unrelated plot line. What happened?

The values for the initial model were arrived at by computer and carried out to six decimal places. The values for the second plot were taken from a print-out that had rounded the numbers to only three decimal places. The seemingly minute and imperceptible differences between the beginning condition of a number carried out to six places to the right of the decimal and the next plot carried out to three places were enough to set the system into a state of chaotic behavior. He called the phenomenon the "butterfly effect," because, carried to the extreme, it is possible for the beat of a butterfly wing to alter a weather pattern that may occur several days in the future.[12]

Even the apparent chaotic nature of a dripping water faucet has a cyclical pattern that can be plotted and shown to be a stable system, undesirable perhaps, but stable. What about errors in the performance of a delivery system for an educational media center? Most errors are the result of the variables inherent in the system itself. Dr. Deming calls these common cause errors. There will be a predictable range of variations within specific limits arrived at through mathematical formulas. The rate and range of variation for these errors will remain stable until one of two things happens. The natural forces of entropy (discussed later in this chapter) slowly degrade the performance of the system, creating more and more errors, until there is no confidence that the system will produce anything correctly. Or, the system is improved in such a way that the cause of the variation is eliminated or the range of variation narrowed. Remove the improvements and the system will revert to its previous level of stability. In any case the system must be managed. Just to overcome the degrading forces of entropy requires maintenance and repair.

Deming explains that a system must exhibit stability before it can be improved. An unstable system is not predictable, so any change designed to bring it into a stable state will be based on educated guesswork. The performance of an unstable system, once acted upon, will change and continue to proceed in a new, unpredictable direction even after the cause of the change is removed. A stable system will always return to its original state once the outside influences, interferences and changes are removed. A pond will return to being calm after the rings from the splash of a pebble subside.

To move a system from a stable, but undesirable, level of performance to an improved level of performance requires application of profound knowledge and the 14 Points. One way to begin this process is to improve the interaction between components, since that is where most errors creep into the system.

The Interaction of Components

The product of the system is the result of the interactions between the components of the system. Each process within the system includes the people who carry out the work of the process. For the interactions to be successful and contribute toward the aim of the system, cooperation must exist.

A flow chart can be constructed for almost any function in a technology service center. A few examples of flow charts that might be useful to plot follow:

- Selection of equipment for purchase
- Selection of media resources for purchase
- Purchase order flow
- Billing flow to clients
- Material handling, shipping and return cycle

- Requests for equipment repair
- Requests for video production
- Requests for consultation
- Requests for equipment delivery
- Requests for print production
- Cooperative purchasing
- Catalog production
- Newsletter production
- Orientation / training of new staff
- Orientation / training of new users

To pick a system to flow chart, start with a process that is either the most critical to the organization or one that has the most complaints (either internal or external). Use a big newsprint tablet and plenty of pencils. Start with a general flow of the steps involved in the process and then invite anyone who has contact with the various steps to help fill in the functions at each point. Don't forget all the "if /then" alternatives. If a form is missing information, where does it go? If a title number doesn't match a packing list, then what? If equipment is returned broken, what happens?

Be prepared to do a lot of erasing and redrawing. If the chart can be hung up on a wall or left on a table for several days so that everyone can have a chance to study it, you increase the likelihood that it will be made as complete as possible. Be sure to remind people that the intent is to plot what the process looks like *right now*. If improvements or changes come to mind during the exercise jot them down on self-stick notes and put them at the appropriate places on the chart.

Once everyone is reasonably satisfied that the process in question is accurately charted it can be copied over into final form showing the current procedures of the process.

Where to Improve?

Now that we have a flow chart, or several flow charts, what are we looking at? We have a clear picture of how information and material travel through the system of production and service. We have a clear picture of how information and materials *change* in each process of the system. And, each employee can see his or her place in the flow and in the system as a whole.

Staff can now clearly see where their work comes from and where it goes. The exact relationship with their internal suppliers and internal customers is now defined. Dr. Paul Batalden, President of the Health Services Research Center, Minneapolis explains, "Anyone needs to see the process as a catwalk, a flow diagram. Until you see your job as a catwalk, you will fall off [of it] and fail." The worker now knows who to interact with both up stream and down stream in the system, without regard to barriers between departments.[13]

Managing the Spaces Between the Boxes

As we look at our new flowchart, two aspects of the chart must be examined. Most obvious, the processes represented by the boxes in the chart. Each process can be individually flow charted if necessary. Less obvious is to look at the spaces between the boxes. Remember the quote from Dr. Ackoff, "Performance of the whole [system] is never the sum of the performance of the parts taken separately, but it is the product of their *interactions.*" [Emphasis added].

Flowcharting begins to let us see our agency, department or technology center as a system that must be managed. It also begins to help us ask, "what can be improved?" The simple answer is, "the interactions between processes." We must look at the flow between processes, not the flow up and down the hierarchy.

The most basic interaction is people to people. To manage and improve people-to-people interactions requires some knowledge of psychology, a component of profound knowledge.

Next is people-to-machine interaction, and finally, machine-to-machine interaction. Managing either of these requires some knowledge of psychology, an understanding of variation and an understanding of a system of knowledge. All the components of profound knowledge are necessary to effectively manage interactions within the system.

Opportunities for Improvement

At each point where an operation changes hands or information is passed on from one process to another, there is opportunity for improvement. These are the same places where there is opportunity for errors to creep in. As the exercise of flow charting the process progresses, people begin to spot places to improve the system, sometimes by eliminating unnecessary steps, sometimes by changing procedures. Sometimes the simple act of being more cooperative with the preceding and following steps of the process yields improvements.

Now is the time to begin redesigning the work flow and assess the impact of the suggested changes. Alternate methods of improvement need to be weighed against each other and against their effect on the system as a whole. Once an improvement is selected for implementation, it is important to document the change and monitor its effect on the process. Obviously changes that lead to a deterioration of the process must be eliminated and alternatives tried. Changes that reduce errors, improve productivity and reduce rework should be institutionalized and made standard operating procedures.

The flow charting process described here is actually a very basic way to begin on the road to continuous improvement. But it illustrates the benefit that can be accrued, with a very small investment of time, to improve the system of production and service.

Without spending additional money and with the same staff, a typical process might see a 25 percent reduction in errors and a 30 percent reduction in time needed to complete the process. The combined savings could be much higher depending on how much time was spent correcting the errors that have now been eliminated. Look for small improvements, not sweeping innovations. It is the small and continuous improvements that will be sustainable over the long run. The Japanese concept of *kaizen* (ky' zen), focuses both management and worker on continuous improvement through many small gains, each of which build on another. How small? At Nissan Motor Company the smallest unit of time-saving that will be considered for an improvement project is 0.6 seconds, or 1/100th of a minute. It is equivalent to the time it takes to reach for something or take half of a step.[14]

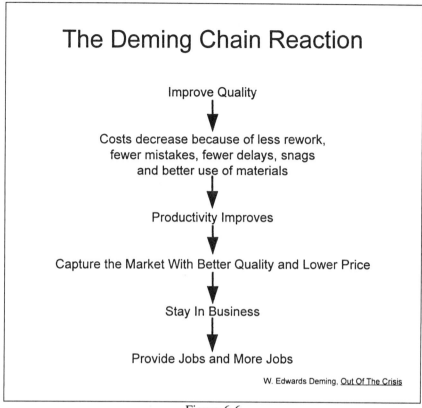

Figure 6-6

Dr. Deming cites the benefit of better quality as a chain reaction:

Dr. Deming adds that in place of "capture the market," a government agency should "delivery economically the service prescribed by law or regulation with an aim toward distinction of service."[15]

The reduction of rework caused by errors can save any organization thousands or millions of dollars each year. The typical American company spends 18 to 22 percent of its revenues in finding and fixing errors. Motorola estimates that it saved $750 million dollars in 1990 alone by improving quality and therefore reducing rework and warranty costs.[16]

Figure 6-7 illustrates the benefits of the Deming Chain Reaction to educational technology services. In a government agency the chain reaction produces a valuable asset: time. Time is created to give better service

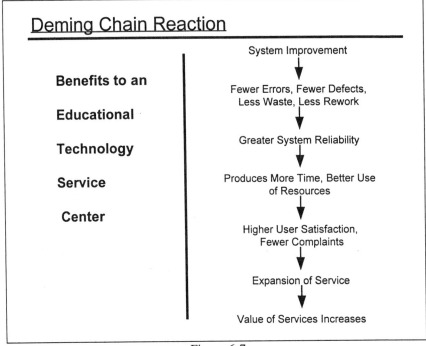

Deming Chain Reaction

Benefits to an

Educational

Technology

Service

Center

System Improvement

Fewer Errors, Fewer Defects,
Less Waste, Less Rework

Greater System Reliability

Produces More Time, Better Use
of Resources

Higher User Satisfaction,
Fewer Complaints

Expansion of Service

Value of Services Increases

Figure 6-7

to users, communicate better with educational decision makers, expand professional development programs and create new services to meet changing user needs. Time means more resources are available for other uses because there are fewer defects, fewer errors to correct and fewer fires to fight. As less time is spent on rework, correcting defects and chasing errors, time is created for new services and better service to clients.

As the commitment to quality management moves forward, the Deming chain reaction begins to accelerate. The result is greater system reliability and higher user satisfaction. User satisfaction creates more users and expands utilization. Expanded utilization increases the value of the service. The effects of the chain reaction become readily apparent and the challenge then becomes sustaining the momentum of continuous improvement with *kaizen*.

It becomes too easy to realize dramatic gains early and then be sat-

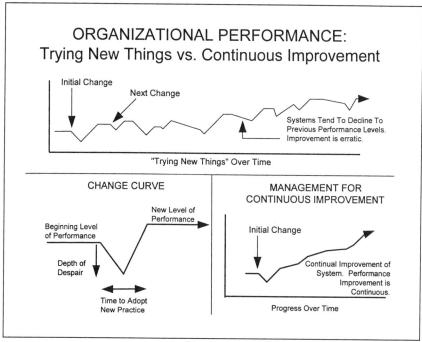

Figure 6-8

isfied with the improvement. In a conventional change curve there is movement from one level of production or service upward to another. The improvement is caused by some change in the way things are done. But the improvement becomes merely another plateau which, if left on its own, will slowly begin to degrade back toward the original level of performance as shown in Figure 6-8. A certain amount of management is needed just to maintain the new level of performance, but management for continuous improvement is required if the system is to move forward and stay ahead of user needs.

The Containing System

All systems are connected to other systems. Sometimes the connection is that of supplier or customer. But there is also a connection to a bigger system. This relationship is said to be with a "containing system." The scheduling process of a university media center is a subsystem or process contained in the system of the university media center. The university media center is a subsystem of the university itself. The containing system of the media center is the university. The containing system of the university could be the state department of higher education, in the case of a state institution.

A containing system is the bigger system that the educational technology service agency is a part of. It is from the containing system that "system imposed" requirements—those things we have no control over which must be complied with as a fact of life—are encountered. As soon as a manager runs into something that is beyond his or her capacity to control, the containing system has been encountered. Do not waste time and energy trying to change that which you cannot change. This might include civil service rules, union rules, or irrational policy decisions from above. Focus instead on the identification of what can be controlled that will effectively improve the processes at hand. This is called taking short-term action with a long-term aim. Improve the quality of the system by working on things that you can control right now.

Recognize the containing system and what must be done to operate effectively within it. As a manager it is your job to provide your people with what is required to meet the aim of the organization. Management's job is to work ON the system of production and service so that all employees can contribute effectively to the organization. Recognize that there are simply some things that are beyond your ability to control from your position in the system.

Service Is Everything

Service transcends all products. Service will make or break a technology center. A center may have the finest collection of up-to-date resources, the best computer facilities, the finest teleconferencing facilities, an efficient print shop and get the best deals on cooperative purchases and it all means nothing if the user gets poor service.

The quality level of service in any organization depends largely on training of the staff. Training should address both the mission and aim of the agency as well as training for the job of servicing the client. User service starts with the point of first contact. How is a telephone answered? How do the delivery drivers deal with their building contacts? How is the service desk handled? How do computer lab assistants interact with users? What does an order form look like? What does the newsletter or the catalog look like?

If our technology service centers are to be effective, they first must be inviting and able to draw people in to sample what we have to offer. Only the most naive government bureaucrat still believes that their agency will continue to exist simply because it is a government agency. Our continued success, then, depends not just on the return business of satisfied users, but on the users' bringing a friend. It is not enough that users be satisfied with the service they get, they must be able to brag about it.

The Effect of the Unknowable

What you cannot measure is always more important that what you can quantify.[17] Worrying about meeting a numerical goal for the year is a waste of energy when the most important numbers are unknowable. How can we measure the contribution of teamwork and pride of workmanship to the quality of service? Training shows up as an immediate cost, but the future value of it to the organization is unknown and immeasurable.

What is the cost of a dissatisfied user? Although it is impossible to know, the *effect* of the dissatisfaction must be factored into the management of any enterprise. An unhappy customer typically tells 22 other people while the satisfied customer tells only eight. In the world of commercial products, over 90 percent of dissatisfied customers never return, but only four percent of them actually complain.[18] Brian Joiner suggests that this is a huge source of untapped information on what would please the customer and how to improve service. To get at this information requires establishing a system that invites user comments, complaints and suggestions. Users have to know how to complain, by what means they can be heard. And they must know that they will be heard. In a closed or limited customer base such as a university, school district or regional technology center service area, encouraging complaints sounds destructive, but it is an important step toward better customer/supplier relations. (See also Chapter 8.)

If the research holds true and only four percent of your users actually complain, or about one in 25, then it is safe to say that every one complaint your agency gets actually represents 24 other people. Never again allow yourself to be lulled into thinking everything is all right because you only handled four complaints last month. Recognize now that you handled four but "heard" from 100 dissatisfied users.

If each happy user tells only eight people, and each dissatisfied user tells 25, you will need at least three satisfied clients for each dissatisfied user, just to stay dead in the water. What your center really needs is users who will *brag about using your services*. This effect will arrive as waste, errors and rework begin to drop under a policy of continuous quality improvement.

Goal Setting

Goal setting is generally not a bad practice. The trouble comes when *numerical* goals are created as the management tool for an organization—especially at the individual level through management by objectives. As described under Point 11 in Chapter 1, the focus then becomes the number to reach instead of improvement of the process. A goal of becoming a "world class" technology center is a noble aim. So is the goal of creating a service that clients will brag about using. Although goals such as these can quickly drift into becoming slogans, they can be valuable long-term quality goals.

Given any sort of goal, Dr. Deming always asks, "By what method?" How will our organization change to become something people will brag about? It won't happen by asking people to do a better job; they are already doing the best they can. It won't happen by buying a bigger computer, setting numerical goals, renovating the office or changing the look of the newsletter. It can only happen when the system is changed, and only management can change the system.

Measurable, numerical evidence of improvements to the system will emerge as time goes on. Some in weeks, some in years. But setting numerical goals is always futile. As the statisticians Dr. Donald Wheeler and

Dr. David Chambers of the University of Tennessee explain, there can be no basis for setting a numerical goal because:

> . . . on an unstable process, one cannot know what it can do. Likewise it is futile to set a goal for a stable process—it is already doing all it can do! The setting of goals by managers is usually a way of passing the buck when they don't know how to change things.[19]

For example, regional or campus video/film centers routinely inspect the condition of returning materials by means of electronic inspection equipment. Films are checked for torn sprockets, wrinkles, bad splices or breaks. Video inspection equipment looks for edge damage, wrinkles and excessive signal drop out. In an effort to keep up with the volume of returning materials, the department head might establish a minimum number of tapes or films that must be inspected per hour. This is a frequent practice and is a direct result of the management methods advocated by Frederick Taylor at the turn of the last century.

The signal from management to the worker is clear: numbers are more important than quality. The intent of the worker then is to please the boss and therefore the *number* becomes the job instead of the process. Let's assume that management has set the quota at 35 items per hour. In a few months, management wants the workers to "do better," so the quota is raised to 40 items per hour. Either the inspection system will break down out of sheer frustration, or the new number will be met by skipping some items, allowing marginal materials to slip by, or by hiding tapes so they by-pass the inspection process entirely. In any case, the imposition of an arbitrary quota will bring heavy losses to the video/film center later in the form of complaints about defects and lost material due to breaks and jams that could have been prevented. Further losses from employee frustration and declining morale are important but unknowable. In a technology center that is customer-oriented, employees responsible for inspecting returned materials know that their job is to ensure that the next user gets material that is of the highest quality possible, not to process 35 items per hour.[20]

Why would the quota be raised from 35 to 40? "Because that's what I think they are capable of doing," says management.

Does the inspection quota take into consideration tapes (or films) of different lengths? Does it factor in the number of showings between cleaning/inspection? Does it take into consideration the age of the inspection equipment or the speed at which it operates, or the lighting in the work area, or the flow of materials, or the arrangement of the work area? If the workers were not running on fear, how many pieces could they reasonably inspect in an hour and do a good job? Was a chart ever constructed that would reveal this information over a suitable period of time? It is doubtful that the quota would have been set in the first place if management had been enlightened enough to ask these questions.

Dr. Kosaku Yoshida, a long-time colleague of Dr. Deming, postulates that goals are routinely raised in increments of five or ten because that is how many fingers we have.[21] The point is that setting higher numerical goals is done in absence of profound knowledge: the knowledge of variation and the knowledge of systems. Performance improves only by improving the method. But management, "in default of knowing what should be done, can only do what they know."[22] "How could they know?"[23]

Stable and Unstable Systems

Quality management requires prediction. If we have a high degree of knowledge about the past performance of a system we can predict that it will continue to perform at a specific range of variation. We cannot predict that the output of the system will improve because there is no way for a system to improve itself. Only if people work to improve the processes, and the interaction of the processes, within the system will the performance of the system change for the better. But without knowing if the process under consideration is stable or unstable, there is no way to predict if the changes will improve future performance. The only way to identify the stability of a process is through statistical process control or SPC. This requires understanding something about variation and how to compute predictable ranges of variation derived mathematically from data gathered on performance of the system.

Further information on the use of control charts and SPC can be found in *Out of the Crisis,* by Dr. Deming; *Understanding Statistical Pro-*

cess Control, by Drs. Chambers and Wheeler; and in *The Deming Route,* by William Scherkenbach. For now, however, adhere to Dr. Deming's Point 11, "eliminate the use of numerical goals."

A System Left to Itself Will Degrade: Entropy

Anything, left on its own, will begin to deteriorate. This concept is known as entropy in scientific circles but it has equal application to the management of a system. The force of entropy can never be eliminated from a system. Entropy causes processes to decay, parts to wear out, breakdowns and failures. Carl Von Clausewitz described the breakdown of combat efficiency in a fighting force due to wear and tear caused by common factors such as weather, heat, cold, mud, dust or poor food as "friction."[24]

An automobile must be maintained to keep it running. If the oil is not changed and the engine is not tuned on a regular basis it will run rougher and rougher until it will not run at all. An automobile is a system.

If patrons are allowed to return their books to the shelves of a library, soon no one will be able to find anything. A library is a system.

What happens to a classroom when the teacher is called into the hallway for a moment? How soon does the order of the classroom begin to break down in the teacher's absence? A classroom is a system.

The results of a system are produced by the interactions between the component processes of the system. If the interactions are not managed, entropy sets in and the system degrades over time. Even an apple on a table is a system. If it is not managed, that is, put in the refrigerator, it begins to rot as a result of its interaction with the air and warm temperatures.[25]

The effects of entropy must be factored into the management of any system. Knowledge of a system must also mean the ability to recognize the signs of breakdown and deterioration before they begin to have a negative effect. In equipment recognition can be fairly easy and a program of preventive maintenance can be instituted. In a service process such as handling orders or packing material for shipment, tracking performance of the system might be done with control charts or check sheets. (See

Appendix A.) Knowing what the effects of entropy on a service process look like gives time to "repair" the system.

This assumes that the worker has been trained, knows what to look for, and is aware of the negative impact on the process if corrective action is not taken. If the natural tendency for a process to degrade over time is not managed, the effects will eventually dominate the system, creating chaos and heavy losses.[26]

Systems Must Be Managed: The Secret of a System

"A system must be managed. It will not manage itself," Dr. Deming tells us. So many innovations of management, or improvements to a system, fail because the system is not managed. It is not enough to simply improve the service or product. The improvement will eventually degrade if its interaction with the rest of the system is not managed. So the real secret to a successful system is, "*cooperation* between components toward the aim of the organization." This kind of cooperation allows everyone to gain.[27]

Road Map for Improvement

Flowcharts show where an agency is as a system. For unless you know where you are right now, it doesn't much matter which direction you go. This is also known as the Lewis Carroll school of management.[28] The act of producing flow charts and putting them to use as a catalyst for improvement can be a powerful way to help technology managers accomplish the shift from a results-oriented to a process-oriented organization. Improve the process and the results will come. Focusing on results alone never produces lasting improvement.

[1] This story was related to the author during graduate level work in issues management. John Naisbitt identifies the consultant as Mary Parker Follett in *Megatrends,* page 85. A similar story appears in the videotape, *Discovering the Future,* available through Films Incorporated, Chicago.

[2] Deming, W. Edwards. *Out of the Crisis.* Cambridge, MA: MIT Press, 1986. Pg. 121.

[3] Deming, W. Edwards. *New Economics For Industry, Government and Education.* Cambridge, MA: MIT Press, 1993. Pg. 52.

[4] Ibid., pg. 51.

[5] Ackoff, Richard. Quoted in *A Theory of a System. The Deming Library.* Videotape, Chicago: Films Inc. 1993.

[6] Deming, *Out of the Crisis,* pg. 5.

[7] Rummler, Geary A., "Managing The White Space," *Training,* January 1991. Pg. 55.

[8] Deming, *Out of The Crisis,* pg. 318.

[9] Gleick, James. *Chaos: Making A New Science.* New York: Viking, 1987. Pg. 48.

[10] Ibid., pg. 25 &48.

[11] Ibid., pg. 145.

[12] Ibid., pg. 23.

[13] Deming, *New Economics,* pg 31. Also quoted by Dr. Deming February 17, 1993 in a four-day seminar Adams Mark Hotel, Philadelphia, Pa.

[14] Imai, Masaki, *KAIZEN, The Key to Japan's Competitive Success.* New York: Kaizen Institute, McGraw Hill, 1986. Pg. 30. KAIZEN, when in all capital letters, is a registered trademark of The Kaizen Institute, Ltd.

[15] Deming, *Out of the Crisis,* pg. 6.

[16] George, Stephen. *The Baldrige Quality System: The Do It Your Self Way to Transform Your Business.* New York: Wiley & Sons, 1992. Pg. 25.

[17] Fellers, Gary. *The Deming Vision: SPC/TQM For Administrators.* Milwaukee, WI: ASQC Quality Press, 1992. Pg. 73.

[18] Ibid., pg. 72.

[19] Wheeler, Donald, and David Chambers. *Understanding Statistical Process Control,* 2nd Edition. Knoxville: SPC Press, 1992. Pg. 187.

[20] This example is a composite of two actual situations. Names and places have been omitted to protect the guilty.

[21] *Made In Japan "Whole"-istically.* Videotape. Los Angeles: Quality Enhancement Seminars, 1989.

[22] An observation made by Marshal Maurice de Saxe in 1757 in a philosophical analysis on the nature of military leadership. Quoted in *On Strategy* by Harry G. Summers, Jr., pg. 243.

[23] A question frequently posed by Dr. Deming in seminars and books.

[24] Von Clausewitz, Carl. *On War*. Anatol Rapoport, ed. New York: Penguin Books, 1968. Pg. 160. Originally published, 1832.

[25] An observation made during a collaborative inquiry session by Michael Quinn, New Jersey Department of Education, Academy for Professional Development, March 19, 1993.

[26] Wheeler, pg. 16.

[27] Deming, *New Economics,* pg. 51.

[28] Carroll, Lewis. See *Alice in Wonderland*.

Chapter 7

INTERNAL AND EXTERNAL CUSTOMERS

NOW THAT WE KNOW OUR AGENCY REPRESENTS A FLOW OF INFORmation and material from one process to another, we can look at how improving interactions between processes in the system is the first place to start improving quality and productivity. For an organization in crisis, the actions taken to improve internal processes will automatically address the cause of many user complaints, thus raising reliability and user confidence. For the stable agency, improving interactions between processes can yield new gains in time, reduced rework and produce opportunities for the development of added services. In either case, the initial temptation to placate user problems and complaints without a system for reducing the causes in place will result in continual fire fighting with no time for system improvement.

Chapter 4 refers to the four aspects of Dr. Deming's System of Profound Knowledge. Understanding systems is one aspect. To implement improvements will require working with people, and that requires some understanding of psychology, another of the four aspects of profound knowledge.

Internal Communication

People are the most important asset of any system. The quality of how people within the system interact with each other can determine much of the effectiveness of an organization. This book does not propose to set out rules of group behavior that will make people get along better. Nor does it propose a method of counseling for cases of chronic staff dysfunction. What we will discuss here is how a better understanding of the system and the aim of the organization by all employees can lead to better communications and a higher level of cooperation.

During the discussion of flow charts in Chapter 6, an analogy was made that the flow of work in a system is like a catwalk. If everyone in the process knows their place on the catwalk, then they know with whom they must communicate. They can also see their place in the system as a whole. The interactions between workers is an important part of the production process. The best quality-oriented manager in the world will not be able to improve a system if there is inadequate communication between workers or between management and worker.

The Next Worker

Anytime one worker passes material or information on to another worker, a customer/supplier relationship exists. This is an "internal customer" relationship. The concept of internal customers extends through all levels of an organization. We can think of each process as being the customer of another, or one department as a customer of another. Look at the system of education in general and consider the internal customers.

Before beginning to explain this concept to the staff in general, practice what it means with the people you come in contact with most frequently. Next time you ask your secretary to type a letter, think of yourself as the supplier and your secretary as your customer. What can you do to please the customer so that the end product will be produced efficiently and with the most desirable level of quality? What level of quality material do you supply to your customer? Can the secretary read the first draft? Is it full of abbreviations and personal shorthand that might be open to interpretation? Is the deadline clear? Does the secretary know who the ultimate customer of the letter will be? Sending it back for revision and correction is waste and rework. Being interrupted by the secretary five or six times to clarify what you really meant to say is waste and rework too.

Managers also have a customer/supplier relationship with their immediate subordinates. In an educational media and technology center this could include department supervisors for equipment repair, video production, materials circulation, staff development and the professional library. Much of the customer/supplier relationship in this case deals with the quality of information passed down the line. Under existing management technique, upper management decides what supervisors need to know. In a quality organization, management has to hear what supervisors say they need to know to allow their departments to contribute to the overall aim of the organization. That can be a traumatic shift for long-time managers.

Driving out fear and breaking down barriers starts with better communication between department heads and between department heads and the agency director. Current competition and suspicion between one department and another has to be eliminated. Open discussion of long-range plans and agreement on the overall aims of the organization are essential elements of better communication.

As a manager begins the long road of continuous improvement the process of teaching the staff about quality can begin with a few questions. Each employee can ask two questions: "Who is my customer?" and, "What does my customer expect of me?"

Define your terms first. As part of the staff training that will lead up to these "homework" questions, employees must learn that the customer referred to here is their "immediate customer," the person who gets the work next. Of course, in many educational technology centers, staff may carry out multiple functions that connect with five or six different processes. If this is the case, then there will be five or six different "immediate customers" depending on the process in question. Sometimes a multi-function employee will pass work on to two or three people, each of whom is also multi-function. When this is the case, it is important for an employee to identify the process that is being discussed and the person involved because the same person may be named more than once, but for a role in several different processes.

If the employee now knows who the customer is, the second question begins the dialog with the person who receives the work next. Define your terms again. What does "expect of me" mean? What makes my work more desirable to the next person in the process? The level of desirability depends on what the output of the person will be used for. For example, a video library that ships materials on a daily basis to many schools will use a list generated by a computer that tells which titles should be packed for which school. An employee operating the scheduling computer prints out this list every day and passes it on to the workers who actually pull the tapes from shelves and pack them.

The immediate customer in this case is the material handler. The material handler's raw material is the "pull list." What are the requirements of the immediate customer?

To the employee who generates the pull list each day only a few customer requirements may actually be in his or her control. The process of sorting out what can and cannot be controlled at the shop floor level is instructive. It allows the worker to find the answer to the question, "What can I do to make my work more desirable to the next person?" It also shows the workers what is *not* within their power to control. The scheduling operator can get the pull list out on time, put it in the right

---

Material Handler Requirements for Pull List

(customer requirements)

- Ready at same time each day.
- Can always be found in the same place each day.
- Readable: dark lettering, letters large enough to read easily.
- Printed on 8.5″ × 11″ green bar paper.
- Arranged in order by school.
- Arranged by media type within school.
- Arranged by title number within media type from low numbers to high.
- Multiple copy numbers distinguishable from main title number.

spot each time, make sure it is printed on the right size paper and that the printer cartridge is changed on a regular basis.

Depending on the training of the operator and the kind of scheduling system, the other requirements may or may not be in his or her control. Customer requirements can change over time as well. Continuous feedback loops from all internal suppliers and customers can allow changing requirements to be accommodated when necessary.

What about customer requirements that cannot be controlled by the scheduling operator? It falls to the manager of the process to take action that will bring the performance of the process up to the requirements of the material handlers. It may require changing the print-out format or ensuring that there is enough green bar paper and printer cartridges on hand. Although these things sound simplistic, they are examples of how a manager can help people do their jobs by providing them with the appropriate materials and tools.

Communication Flow

In a traditional organization work flows from one process to another but communication does not. As we have seen in Chapter 6, communication in a traditional organization tends to travel up and down the chain of command, while the work is moving across the white spaces in an organization chart from one process to another. The task of management in an organization that wishes to be transformed is to bring communication into line with the flow of the process.

In an educational technology center, even a small one, the misalignment of communication and work flow can be a prime source of rework, scrap, wasted energy and time. Some university and regional media centers pride themselves on the cohesiveness of their work force and the level of cooperation they have achieved. Client needs are taken care of and there is a solid flow of information about the performance of the system between workers. This sounds good on the face of it, but consider two other factors.

First, at the same time normal and routine matters are being taken care of by workers closest to the solution, there is still a constant flow of information up line to the department head or center director. Out of fear on the part of the worker or insecure paranoia on the part of the manager, or a little of both, the old communication system remains. Effort is duplicated and the manager is still linked back to the daily reportage of activities and normal problems within the system.

The question is, Why is certain information continually passed up to management? As long as the work force continues to feel that it must ask "permission" to help out a special request or deliver on the expectations of the client, there is fear. Over a long period of time and with continued training, the reporting up line may eventually take the form of progress reports in stand-up meetings. "This is the problem that came up, and this is how we handled it." Or, "This is the result so far of the improvement we implemented last month." The object is to free the manager from extensive briefings about routine activities or problems that have already been taken care of. Information on how the system is functioning is more important.

Second, what has happened within the process when a problem has been resolved? We know the workers in the process have talked to each other (which is good) and we know that the manager or department head has been informed (which may not be so good), but what else? This is not to suggest that workers stop communicating with department heads or directors; far from it. The issue centers on *why* such information is being reported to management. In a traditional system, the reporting is done to explain a problem and what was done to correct it. This is also know as "report and resolution." But what was done to keep the problem from occurring again?

Report and resolution is fire fighting. A quality organization has mechanisms in place to look for the cause of problems and classify them into random causes (called special causes) or reoccurring causes inherent to the system (called common causes). So the purpose of communicating between the shop floor and management becomes part of an established and agreed upon system for quality improvement. The system allows for cause to be determined and the creation of improvements that will eliminate or reduce the number of problems in the future.

This is where quality teams and quality circles enter the picture. How is the staff organized to deal with problems created by the system?

How can they tell if the cause of the problem is random, and therefore useless to try and correct, or likely to reoccur with predictable frequency?

Customers of Functional Areas

As staff training progresses, entire functional areas or departments can begin to work as a team to look at questions that help define the customers of their department. Large educational technology centers in universities, regional media centers and city-wide districts frequently have many functional areas. These can include:

- Video/film & media circulation
- Print duplication
- Video and audio tape duplication
- Technology repair
- Professional development programs
- Technical support
- Video production
- Management information systems
- Cooperative purchasing
- Distance learning operations
- Equipment circulation
- Delivery services
- Computer lab
- Systems and building design consulting
- Professional materials/curriculum library

Add to these the business office, mail room, security and central administration.

Additional areas could be added and specialized functions listed, especially for technology centers connected with hospitals, medical teaching centers, public library systems, government agencies, military bases and law enforcement.

Each functional area should have a list of immediate customers, many of which may overlap.

Processes Within a Functional Area

The processes within each of the functional areas also have a series of customer/supplier relationships. Look at technology repair, for example, in Figure 7-1.

Computers, printers, VCRs, television sets and other equipment are gathered from numerous locations: around campus, around the district, or, in the case of a regional multi-district center, from many schools. Incoming equipment is handled by an intake associate, logged in, tagged and sorted. Notes are made on the reason for repair and the presenting symptoms, rather like triage in an emergency ward. Equipment is then sorted to specialist technicians for repair. The repair process itself might trigger a sub-process to order a special part not kept in stock. When repairs are complete an invoice is prepared and sent to the business office for billing. The item goes back to the delivery department for return to the client.

Who is the internal customer of the intake associate? When the repair is complete who is the immediate customer of the repair technician? When the secretary prepares the invoice and the equipment is ready for return, how many internal customers must she contact? The answer to the first question is "the repair technician"; the second, "the department secretary"; and the third, "two: the business office and the delivery department."

Flow charting is a tremendous aid to untangling the processes in any department and is discussed at length in Chapter 6. It makes it clear where the internal customers are. It does not solve the problem of communications between departments. If only one department in a large educational technology center has a quality-oriented manager, there will be severe limits on the quality improvements that can be made. Dr. Deming stresses that quality leadership and a continuing commitment to quality must come from the top of an organization. In a multi-tiered bureaucracy such as a large university or intermediate unit, support may not come from the very top. But the farther up the traditional lines of authority the commitment comes from, the greater the success in the functions downstream. Dr. Deming insists that quality begins at the top and that it can be "no better than the intent."

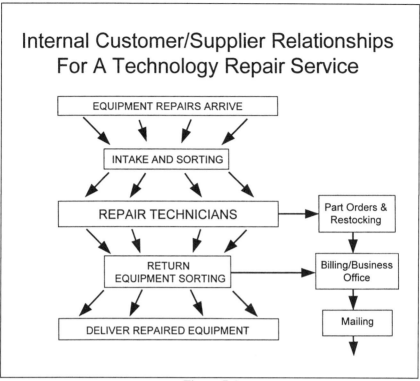

Figure 7-1

Isolation of Departments

The manager alone in a system with other managers who have never heard of Dr. Deming, can become exceedingly frustrated. Remember that the output of an organization is a result of the *interactions* between the components.

In an actual case, the director of a media center experienced first hand the breakdown of these interactions.

This particular center continually experienced long delays with delivery of materials and equipment that were required prior to the beginning of the school year. The director completed all bid activities and delivered the purchase orders to the business office before classes ended in June to ensure prompt processing. In August, the director called several suppliers to see if the material had been shipped. Discussions with the vendors revealed that they had not yet received the purchase orders. In some cases so much time had passed that the quote was no longer valid and the price had gone up. Following normal procedures, the director called the head of the business office to trace down the orders. After several days waiting for a reply, the media director paid a visit to the business office and struck up a conversation with the secretary who processed incoming purchase orders. She explained that she had just come back from vacation, that the orders had "really piled up" and she was doing them as fast as possible. She also showed the director the ten-inch-high stack of purchase orders yet to be processed. The purchase order at the top of the pile carried a recent date in August. With permission of the secretary, the director began thumbing through the stack and, almost at the bottom, found most of the purchase orders from the media center.

The secretary was working through the pile from the top down, and each day, new purchase orders were placed on top of the pile. Department heads who had planned ahead and done their ordering early would never get their materials on time because the orders remained permanently on the bottom of the pile. Departments that waited until August had their orders processed promptly. Before the media director left the office he scooped up the pile and turned it over, putting the oldest orders on top. He asked the secretary to put new ones at the bottom and continue working from the top down. Now the first in would get processed first.

By the time he returned to his office there was a heated phone call from the head of the business department waiting for him. She ranted on, complaining that the media director had exceeded his authority meddling in the affairs of a department he knew nothing about. She was very irritated. Explanations from the director that the material was needed prior to school opening and that purchase orders prepared in June were still at the bottom of the pile, while those cut recently were being handled first, were to no avail.

A subsequent report to the chief school administrator pointed out that the failure to process orders in the sequence they arrived had, in just this one instance, cost the district and the media center over $12,000 in price increases. The same business manager had caused the district to spend 25 percent more for a large projection lamp order because the alternate vendor didn't have a state contract number, even though they had better prices. The superintendent responded that he had full faith in the abilities of the business manager and that the media director should stick to his own department.

At the time, the media director had never heard of Dr. Deming. Perhaps there was a better, more-productive way to approach the situation that would have led to long-term improvement in the relationship between the media department and the business office. But, not being equipped with the teachings of Dr. Deming, how could he have known?

All the people involved were doing the best they could. They were functioning exactly as they had been trained or had been taught by observing others' behavior. They would know no other way. The superintendent backed up the actions of another central office manager. The business manager focused on why someone from another department would presume to speak to someone in her department *and* tell her how to do her job.

The media director, concerned only for his own operation, took matters into his own hands and did unknowable damage to any possible future communications with the business department.

All of them thought they were doing their job. Yet none of them really knew what their job was. All of them operated in isolation within the system. The purchase order clerk did not know that how she did her job mattered to anyone else. She saw only a pile of papers in a basket that had to be taken care of "as fast as possible." The focus was on speed and clearing the basket. She had no idea who depended on her work.

The business manager focused on chain of command, proper channels and the problem of someone meddling in her department. She, too, had no idea how the processes within her control affected other departments. The superintendent, equally isolated, abdicated any interest or responsibility for the communication problems between two departments, opting simply to back-up the business manager and tell the media director to stay in his place.

The contrast becomes more pronounced if only one department is quality-driven and the rest operate with traditional management attitudes.

The incident speaks volumes for implementing a plan to improve communication between functional areas and train all levels of personnel to understand the internal customer/supplier relationship.

External Customers

Organizations that seek to improve their operations appear to have a natural tendency to look first at the attitudes of their external customers. Every organization, profit, non-profit, educational or government has an "ultimate customer." The ultimate customer, or the external customer, actually uses, buys or perceives the benefit of the product or service created by the organization. It can be a fatal flaw to look first at the external customer or user, especially for the organization in crisis. The place to begin improvement is with the internal processes as discussed at the beginning of this chapter.

To take this a step further, it is a good idea for management to take care of improving its own internal communication and processes before approaching the hourly work force.

Do we ignore the needs of our ultimate users while we work on internal improvements? No, not at all. Successful agencies and organizations always work with their users and scan the future to develop services and products that their users may find useful. The resulting information gathered this way must first be applied to internal processes. As the processes develop and the interactions between processes improve, the user will benefit.

The fatal mistake comes when management of a failing organization, in an effort to create a visible sign of change and improvement, launches a new product line or service without developing the internal processes to support it. A regional or university technology center criticized as not moving toward new technologies might purchase quantities of videodiscs and make that known to its clients. It might install a new computer lab or CAD/CAM center because university management thinks it is a "good idea." This is reactive management. The user complains and management reacts. What does the user really need? What are the instructional needs of the client? What are the internal processes required to support the new product or service?

In the case of the videodisc collection, assuming the titles selected are usable, questions will arise about the infrastructure required to handle them. How and where will they be stored? How will they be packaged? How will damage be prevented? What mnemonic will be used as a media type code? How will they be shown in the media resources catalog? If they are Level III, what software system will be kept in stock, Hypercard, Link Way or both? What will the circulation period be? There may be other questions. The manager who launches new services without a plan for implementation, constructed with the collaboration of the workers who must work in the system, does so at the peril of the media/technology center. Process issues such as these and the activities required to plan for quality service are addressed in Chapter 12.

The Deming Flow Diagram in Chapter 6 shows the customer or user as having a place in the continuous process that produces a product or service. Their place in the total process is the vital link between the service provided by the media/technology center and the requirements of the user. It forms one of the significant points for interaction between client and center. There are many other points for interaction with external customers, all of which may promote two-way communication and provide a source of information to answer key quality-oriented questions. Some of the functions that can provide interaction between the agency and the external customer are:

- Office Reception
- Answering Telephones
- Delivery Drivers
- In-Service Programs
- User Newsletters
- Administrator Newsletters
- Scheduling Materials
- Reference and Information Inquiry
- Attendance at Professional Meetings
- Needs Assessments
- Focus Groups
- Material/Equipment Condition Report Forms

- Involvement With Administrative Committees
- Annual Reports
- Fax Numbers
- 800 Numbers
- Open Houses
- Technical Consulting

No one of these functions will provide agency management with all of the information it needs to develop long-range improvement plans. It requires an extensive mix of these and a significant amount of time to analyse the information and synthesize usable results. Now we are defining user needs and characteristics of service that the user values. Later we will examine the management process of setting a quality policy for the organization that takes into account user need and satisfaction. But what are we looking for right now?

What Does the User Really Want?

We are looking for answers to two basic questions: *What is it that users find valuable in our service and products?* and *What product or service might they need in the future?*

The first question requires defining indicators of quality. Sometimes the indicators are not directly quantifiable but show up as a frequency response. Documenting those things that satisfy (or dissatisfy) users can be done to a certain extent with user surveys. But informal collection and open-ended methods can add significant weight to the findings.

User comments during phone calls with secretaries and scheduling staff, on material condition reports and in casual conversations with delivery drivers are important. An informal feedback mechanism to capture that information should be established. Drivers, secretaries, receptionists and student employees are the front-end contact the agency has with most users. They should be encouraged to communicate positive and negative comments through the feedback system. They could use a check off card or a few lines written out on a slip of paper. It does not have to be complicated. Comments both good and bad can be compiled to provide a profile of user response to the service provided by the media/technology center.

A random sample survey conducted by a large regional media center contained two open-ended questions. "What part of the RMC service requires most improvement?" and "What does the RMC service do best?" Compiling the hand-written responses revealed a high frequency of certain words and phrases that surprised the management of the agency. The two highest categories of positive response, accounting for more than 40 percent of the responses, were "collection variety" and "convenience." The significance of "variety" altered management's plans for future collection development. The director had been considering a shift in purchasing patterns for the video/videodisc collection that would have eventually created a collection with fewer titles but many more extra copies to satisfy demand. But the users said that they valued variety. Purchasing continued to emphasize variety of titles.

A key concept in the continual improvement process is to avoid eliminating what the customer values during the effort to improve the service or product. Ford Motor Company implemented this concept in the early '80s during the design phase of the Taurus. Ford went out of its way to find out all the automobile characteristics that owners found *most* desirable. It then sought to make sure those characteristics stayed in the next generation of car. The conventional approach to satisfying customers in the past had been one of eliminating objections and complaints. The fallacy of this approach is that it assumes whatever appears to replace the objection will de facto satisfy the user. This is a dangerous assumption.

Eliminating one service to make way for another can be equally damaging. A multi-district intermediate unit that begins satellite teleconferencing services and allows the video library to decline through fiscal neglect may be destroying a loyal base of user support. The educational technology tool box requires variety to meet the varied communication needs presented by our users. Supporting one service at the expense of another is sub-optimization of the system.

The Appearance of Quality

There is a danger to confusing quality improvement with public relations. Following Point 1, "constancy of purpose," includes how you communicate with your employees, users, superiors, stake holders and the public-at-large. Any discussion of quality improvement, service satisfaction or warranty must be matched with consistent action or the credibility of the technology center will suffer. There must always be congruence between what your agency says it will do and what it actually does. Credibility is a difficult thing to rebuild once it has been lost.

Good public relations is a valuable asset to any organization and technology centers have highly visible ways to build the image of a quality organization. But if the visible indicators of quality are just on the surface and there is no substance within the organization, then they are not worth the effort.

Assuming that your technology center has begun to make significant strides in quality improvement, there are a series of things that can be done to make the value of the agency more visible and communicate better with users, administrators and stake holders.

Having an agency logo is important. Keep it simple and readable from a distance.

Put the logo on everything, not just letterhead and purchase orders. The logo need not be a graphic design, but it should be highly identifiable with your technology center. It belongs on everything that goes out of the office: video boxes, envelopes, order forms, complaint forms, bills, newsletters, catalogs and delivery vans. More on the design and use of an agency logo can be found in Chapter 9 in the subsection on printing.

Communication with users and administrators through newsletters is effective if you can keep the content focused and consistent. Newsletters to users are an important way to explain new services, highlight new materials, publicize policy changes and answer questions about the service. Your users get a lot of mail, so the newsletter has to be a "quick read." A single sheet, printed on both sides, will have a much better chance of being read completely. Unless your center has a great deal to say, three issues a year should be sufficient.

Consider publishing a newsletter just for administrators. Use it to keep them informed about trends in technology that can affect education on a policy or budget level. For a consistent source of information on how to communicate effectively with your employees and users, consider a subscription to the monthly newsletter "Communication Briefings." Subscription information is available at 800-888-2084.

Indicators of Service Quality

Clients of a media and technology center might use any of the following as indicators of quality.

Service	Products and Materials
on time	defect free
prompt	up-to-date
convenient	accurate
friendly staff	timely
helpful	interesting
dependable	easy to use
easy to use	variety of titles & subjects
accessible	available

Customer Expectations

The second question determining what the user wants asked, What product or service might they need in the future?

What do our users say they want? and What might our users need in the future? are two different questions.

"Customer expectations are about 99 percent nonsense," Dr. Deming declares.[1] "The customer (user) expects only what you have led him to expect," he continues. Dr. Deming points out that through history the customer has rarely created anything new. Innovations like integrated circuits, television, home computers, fax machines, electric lights, automobiles, Federal Express, videotape and the telephone were never the result of customer demand.[2] Yet modern society would now have a hard time existing without them.

All of these developments were the result of prediction based upon a perceived future need and potential use. Dr. Deming points out that a measure of luck is also involved. The successful educational media and technology center will always have an eye on the future. By virtue of its role as a technology resource it is more likely to be aware of new developments and emerging technologies that may have application for the clients of the center. The planning role of management is to make an appropriate match between client requirements and existing or new technology, then lead the user. The success and satisfaction of the user with the new product will depend on a variety of factors. But it is management's responsibility to ensure that the center is organized and supported to increase the possibility of success for the greatest number of users.

Introduction of new technologies is only one part of meeting user requirements. Continual improvement of existing services is also required. Broader access to a resource collection has become a standard expectation of technology users. Clients of media services are also users of automated teller machines (ATMs), voice mail, fax machines, 30-minute pizza delivery and computers at work. They have come to expect the multiple options that are standard features of modern American society. They expect no less from the media service agency.

Improvements for users of district, university and regional media services ordering materials now include fax orders, on-line telephone access, catalogs on CD-ROM, remote key word search access and ordering via modem and a personal computer. Availability rates are increased through the purchase of duplication rights. The results are more flexibility and greater possibility for user satisfaction provided the infrastructure that supports the access is organized for quality service.

Regional course-sharing via fiber optic networks, CD-ROM data access, satellite links, video site collections, Compact Disc-Interactive, videodisc with computer and barcode access, computer labs, are all options that have made the educational tool box bigger. What users are led to depends on the communication problems they are attempting to solve and the interactions they are trying to improve. The local educational technology director may be the only person equipped to look beyond the apparent need to see what is *really* required to fill the need and satisfy the user.

[1] Deming, W. Edwards. Quoted in Four-Day Seminar, Philadelphia, February 16, 1993.

[2] Deming, W. Edwards. *New Economics For Business, Industry and Education*. Cambridge, MA: MIT Press. 1993. Pg. 7.

Chapter 8

WASTE, REWORK AND WARRANTY

IN THE MID-SEVENTIES IT WAS ESTIMATED THAT 15 TO 40 PERCENT OF THE cost for most items produced in the United States was directly related to the waste and rework required to produce the product.[1] Handling damage on the shop floor alone may run from five to eight percent of the production cost.[2] With the exception of a relative hand full of United States corporations, this figure is no doubt still accurate. As this book was written the author's agency experienced a four-week delay in receiving new computer furniture. The original shipment arrived in seven cartons and required assembly. Two were damaged in transit because of poor packaging and had to be returned for replacement. A third carton was in good condition but the contents were dented. This item was also returned. During assembly it was discovered that the screw holes for a privacy panel did not match the pilot holes in the desk. To make it fit, the holes had to be redrilled in new locations—a process referred to as "field modification." In the process of making phone calls to have the damaged pieces returned, the company omitted one piece from the reorder and additional calls had to be made explaining that all three returned pieces were to be replaced. Did the company make any money on this? Probably not. Did it build customer confidence and good will?

This is such a common example of waste and rework that normally there would be no reason to mention it. This sort of thing is not unique. It happens all the time. It is to be expected. That is precisely the point. Why should this be common and why should it be expected? It shouldn't be, but this is what we have come to expect and this is what we allow to happen.

The percentage of loss related to waste and rework has a direct bearing on the level and cost of service offered by regional, university, district and other educational media and technology centers. In the case of the damaged furniture, the center lost time correcting or replacing defective parts and poor packaging. It also lost time and productivity while computer operators used half-finished, poorly arranged work spaces for four weeks. This internally wasted time should have been directed toward the mission of the agency and serving customers. But it is internal waste and rework that rob a service center of the edge it needs to be seen as an outstanding provider of media and technology support.

Being government agencies or affiliated with government bureaucrats has had a numbing effect on the sensitivity to rework and waste within a government organization. The general press tends to show $300 hammers or costly weapon systems that fail to perform as examples of government waste. When politicians speak of cutting waste in government it generally results in arbitrary budget cuts or new regulations that govern spending. The mandate to "do more and more with less and less" given to most government service agencies has become a cliche. Dr. Deming's fundamental question arises once again, "By what method?" How shall we do more with less? For a system of production and service such as an educational technology center provides, the waste and rework factors can be very subtle yet provide the key to answering that question.

Ironically, the politicians who expect to reduce waste and save money by cuts in funding for multi-district and university educational technology centers create even more losses for the system of education as a whole. They force individual districts or departments to start their own media libraries and technology support centers. A monopoly can produce maximum service, but requires enlightened leadership. If an individual district begins its own technology service, both it and the regional center will incur heavy losses because of higher individual operating costs. The same applies at the building level. If each department tries to build its own video collection, each will operate at a higher cost than a single video library. Dr. Deming points out that the same thing happened after

Bell Telephone was broken up in 1984. Before, we had a telephone system, he explains. Now we just have phones.[3]

The failure over the years to account for the impact of errors, rework and false economies on a system of service can be devastating in unknowable ways. The good news is that something can be done about it.

Answering Complaints Is Not Enough

Most organizations have no standard method for tracking errors in production or missed opportunities for service. Likewise, most managers are blissfully ignorant of the extent to which the failure to satisfy customer needs adversely effects the performance of the organization. This is not to be confused with the process for handling complaints. Years ago department stores and corporations typically had a complaint department. Now it is called "customer service," but the function is the same. Companies have customer service representatives, and warranty offices that try to take care of customer problems. Even some university and regional media centers have policies that prescribe how complaints are to be handled.

These efforts are rarely part of a larger, organized effort to use such consumer feedback in a constructive way to improve the system. Correcting problems found by the user or client becomes a matter of fire-fighting and individual attention on a case-by-case basis. Some sort of paperwork may be generated by the case to explain what was done to correct the problem. In corporations it is referred to as "report and resolution." However, it is doubtful that any of the thousands of "routine" complaints handled by any given organization are ever documented, much less tracked. Complaints are bad news.

Nobody wants to be the bearer of bad news, so the job is to get the customers satisfied and hope they go away. Information about the nature of the complaint or problem is never passed on to the department where a change could eliminate the problem in the future. Few companies, including educational media and computer software producers, have real customer service representatives. They just have to handle complaints. However, since company management may not know what servicing a customer means, the worker does the best he can. (See Appendix B for an illustration of the losses caused by the customer service representative of a media producer doing what management expects instead of what the customer expects.)

Chapter 6 refers to unhappy customers and to how many people they will tell their tale of woe. A report done by the United States Office of Consumer Affairs shows that of customers who were dissatisfied with a product, nearly 70 percent did not complain. Of those who did complain, more than 40 percent were unhappy with the response they received from the supplier. The report further explains that customer loyalty is enhanced when a customer is fully satisfied with the corrective action. More than 70 percent of clients with complaints who have been taken care of properly will continue to buy the product or use the service.[4]

It costs the same amount of money and time to produce a defective product as a defect-free product. The added cost is in the rework and time spent making things right. What is really needed is a system of service that prevents errors from being made in the first place. But until we have designed and developed such a system for our centers, the errors that get through to our users will have to be addressed.

Adequately addressing our users' complaints is not enough. A system is required to track and assess the problems and provide constructive input to the redesign of the service. That system must include:

- Employee training on how to handle people
- Training in how to initiate corrective action
- A system to record, track and assess complaints by type, source and frequency
- An active program to gather complaints that are otherwise unreported
- A program to inform clients of potential problems

Training your staff in basic telephone and greeting techniques is an essential part of good customer service. But more training is required when dealing with irritated and upset clients. The angry teacher, who has had lesson plans ruined because the wrong videotape arrived, has no interest in dealing with an indifferent, sullen or bored employee. A study of why people stop using a particular store or supplier found that 68 percent switched because of the indifferent treatment by one of the employees.[5] How much does quality cost? In this case the failure to have quality contact with customers can be immense. The cost, or more correctly, the investment, in training for good telephone techniques is modest.

The program to inform clients of potential problems, listed above, is rarely standardized, although many media managers may do this out of courtesy or intuition. One of the best ways to undermine user confidence in an agency is to fail to keep them informed—about the bad as well as the good. If you expect delays in the delivery of materials, tell people up front. Don't gamble that it might arrive in time and risk the complaints when it doesn't. If your media scheduling system is about to go through an upgrade, don't limit the story in the newsletter to all the wonderful new features it will have. Include a side bar that there may be delays, that the confirmation form printout may look a little different, that the phones may not be answered promptly for a week while some staff are in training. Let users know what to expect and the level of complaints will be reduced. But fail to inform users of a potential situation that you are aware might happen, and they will feel betrayed.

In the mid-1970s it was revealed that Oldsmobile routinely used Chevrolet engines in some of their models. There was a major outcry from owners claiming that Oldsmobile misrepresented their product. It didn't matter that Oldsmobile and Chevrolet were both GM products. Owners wanted an Oldsmobile engine in their Oldsmobile. It took a long time for Olds to recover from the bad feelings it created with the buying public. Keeping potential buyers informed up front could have prevent the backlash.

Witness the difference in August 1993 when Saturn, a company founded and operated on Deming's principals, decided to recall over 350,000 automobiles, or nearly every car it had built since startup, for a minor defect in the electrical wiring. Dealers put up "welcome back" signs and balloons and laid out food for the returning buyers. Saturn sent individual letters to owners explaining that the wire replacement would take about twenty minutes, which included a car wash. The recall was positioned as a follow-up service to their buyers; part of the process of keeping them informed. Saturn reasoned that consumers would rather be informed of a potential problem and have it corrected by a cheerful dealer than have it glossed over. They were right. By December Saturn sales were up 21 percent.[6]

Every complaint costs a government or institutional media service center. It may not show up in the budget but it is a cost that must be factored in. Just the time to take the phone call and handle the problem takes people away from their work. If the resolution requires a letter, more time and people are involved. Some complaints sound simple but the cost to correct the problem to the satisfaction of the client can be staggering in relationship to how the error was created in the first place. (See the discussion of chaos theory in Chapter 6.)

Anything that can be done to eliminate the cause behind most of the complaints reduces waste two ways.[7] First, staff time to respond to the complaint is reduced, creating time to do other things. And, second, the waste of having to do things over again on the shop floor or in the office is reduced.

Two of the most obvious examples common to educational technology services are equipment repair and the circulation of materials used for instruction. What do you do about a piece of equipment that has been repaired by the repair service and returned to the client school or department only to be returned the following week? How often does it happen? What kind of equipment is returned most? What is the most frequent cause of the return?

Fix the System

Of course if all you do is resolve complaints and fix errors that have made it into the client's hands you will be out of business very quickly. Most of the staff will be so busy with rework that normal service activities will cease to function. You have to work upstream in the system to find the cause of errors and problems. But it's important to know which causes are worth fixing, and to look at the total system of service.

Must the cause of *every* error be fixed? No, not at all. The idea behind continuous improvement is to create a system that keeps the number of errors to a minimum and narrows the variation produced by the system. Correcting user complaints does not do this. Fixing the system does.

First, you have to know what the system is capable of producing. This can only be done by tracking the performance of the system over an extended period of time and applying statistical process control techniques that will determine if the system is stable or unstable (discussed in Chapter 6). If the system is stable, the control limits derived from the data will show two kinds of errors; common cause errors and special cause errors. They will also show that if the system is left alone, the variation will continue within the control limits into the future: prediction of performance.

Common cause errors fall inside the control limits and are caused by something within the system. They represent normal day-to-day variation that no amount of hard work will overcome. They are problems caused by the system itself, not the employees. Special cause errors lie outside the control limits and may signal a need for corrective action if the error is likely to recur. A single point outside the control limits does not automatically trigger action, but a series of two or more outside points on the same side of the control chart requires investigation.

Control charts to plot performance and the use of statistical methods, quite literally, allow the system to talk to you.

Common Cause Errors Are Reduced Only on Improvement of the System

In the normal course of operations in a technology service center all sorts of things can go wrong. In the case of a materials delivery system, the wrong title can be pulled from the shelf, the wrong copy pulled, the item can get into the wrong shipping case and go to the wrong user, a video box can be returned with the wrong title inside or the item can miss being pulled altogether. It is necessary now to construct a process for sorting through all of the information gathered about complaints and rework.

For whatever process you decide to address first, there must be a standard and systematic way of collecting data on both errors and rework. A complaint from a customer needs to be recorded, but so does an error caught by a worker even before it makes it out the door. Employees must be trained in using the gathering system and they must be fully informed on why the data is being collected and what it will be used for. The people closest to the work will be expected to gather the needed information and record it. The control chart for recording the errors should be convenient to the basic work area and accessible to everyone. Hanging a clip board on a wall or posting a chart to a bulletin board are common methods. The chart should never be in a drawer and no employee should ever have to ask to see the chart. It should always be out for everyone to see.

Gathering error and rework information can be a threatening activity if not handled correctly, with an understanding of the psychological effect it can have. (See profound knowledge and the need for understanding some psychology in Chapter 4.)

A great danger presents itself if this kind of activity is among the first visible signs that the agency has begun a continuous improvement process. Management must remember the 14 Points and the admonition to "drive out fear." Much groundwork must precede the implementation of a system to track error data. Management, supervisors and workers must trust each other. Workers must have confidence that the new methods are not being used to justify layoffs or to evaluate performance at review time. Management must have a high degree of confidence that the figure on the control charts won't be "fudged" to make a department look good.

All departments need to be involved in training for systems thinking, and trained in knowledge about the aim of the organization. Then, with the aid of reliable data, a cooperative effort can be made to begin activities that will result in continuous improvement and furtherance of the aim of the technology center as a whole. This requires that management demonstrate its commitment to the new philosophy by visible action, not just lip service. If conditions of trust and cooperation are not present, the data gathered may be suspect.

The prime motivation of any practice in quality management is to find *cause* and not blame. The result of knowing cause is to be armed with knowledge that will help improve the system.

Calculating the Cost of Errors

As managers and workers we have all experienced the frustration of having to do a job over again. It may be that 5,000 workshop fliers had to be reprinted because the date and time were wrong. It may be that

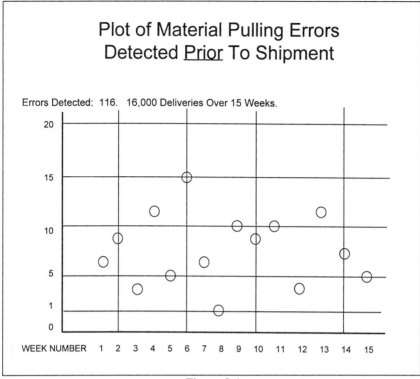

Figure 8-1

a rush request for 20 budget reports has to be redone because the last person left blue paper in the copier. Or it may be the hurry to find a technician to drive across campus at 4:00 p.m. to set up a sound system for the dean of students because the request form she put in three weeks ago got misfiled.

As said before, anything that causes users to get something other than what they expect holds the potential for heavy losses to the organization. The intangibles, such as how many people they will tell and how many unhappy users are not heard from must be factored in. But can we really assign a dollar cost to errors and rework?

The Cost of Rework

Federal Express developed a simple set of figures that represents the cost of rework based on where the problem is discovered in the system. It is not too complicated to use, but you have to understand that it costs just as much to make a defective item as it does to make a good one. It costs the same to pack the wrong tape in a shipping box and deliver it as it does the pack the right one. It costs the same to install a replacement disk drive that doesn't function as it does to install one that does. It costs the same to duplicate 10 videotapes of the wrong title as it does to duplicate 10 tapes of the correct title. The added cost, and thus the loss, is from the rework.

In a typical American company, 18 to 20 percent of revenue is eaten up by inspection and fixing internal and external mistakes.[8] Imagine the growth on national productivity if just the Fortune 500 companies were able to cut this in half.

Federal Express developed the 1–10–100 rule to explain the cost of system mistakes. It states that if an error or defect is caught and resolved at the time it is made, it cost a factor of 1 to make it right. If the defect is caught before it gets out of the plant, it cost ten times the first factor to fix it. And finally, if the defect gets into the hands of the user (customer), it will cost 100 times the original cost to make it right and satisfy the customer.[9] Obviously it is more desirable to catch and correct errors as they happen than to wait to catch them later in the process. Ultimately, that is the aim of continuous improvement: to work up-stream in the process to find the cause of errors and eliminate them by improving the process.

Prior to implementing Dr. Deming's methods many corporations relied on end of the line inspectors to catch problems. The fallacy of this method is that it is too late. The mistake has already been made. Once a defect is caught the material is sent to a rework shop where corrections are made before it is shipped. Unfortunately this system is frequently coupled with piece work and quotas systems. Many times partially assembled products are rushed off the assembly line to meet a production quota and then technicians are sent to the customer site to complete the assembly work.[10]

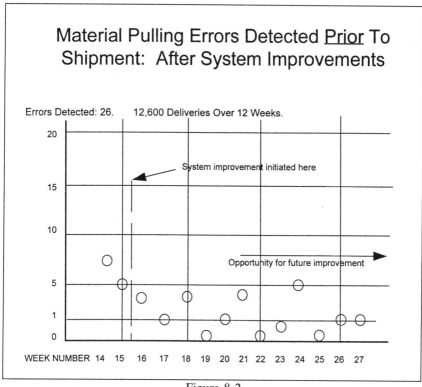

Material Pulling Errors Detected <u>Prior</u> To Shipment: After System Improvements

Errors Detected: 26.   12,600 Deliveries Over 12 Weeks.

System improvement initiated here

Opportunity for future improvement

WEEK NUMBER 14 15 16 17 18 19 20 21 22 23 24 25 26 27

Figure 8-2

For a video/film center that routinely circulates large numbers of items to a variety of locations, the 1–10–100 formula has specific application. Typically media materials are stored on long rows of shelving or racks and each item is assigned a unique item number. Associates responsible for materials handling use the number to locate the correct item for shipment to a client. The item is pulled and then packed for delivery. In many centers this is a one-step process; the item is placed directly into a shipping case or bag and then closed for loading. In some centers it is a two-step process where all the items for a given delivery site (a school) are pulled and stacked waiting for packing in shipping cases sometime later in the cycle.

If an error is caught by the puller checking her own work, the cost is a factor of one. Just put the wrong one back, pull the right one and move on. If an exception to the packing list is detected by the packer there is a bit more of a delay. The title numbers are compared again and then he goes back to the racks to return the item and pull the correct one. The cost in time and delay to the process is a factor ten times greater than if the puller found the error initially. Still, it is better to find the errors prior to delivery of the materials to the client schools than after, when the cost to correct the problem will be 100 times the initial cost. An improvement in the method for handling the pull and pack process may include instituting what Philip Crosby calls a "make certain" accuracy check. Accuracy for both pulling and packing is essential to create a system where delivery errors are kept to an absolute minimum.

A corporation familiar to the author assembled printed circuit boards before the advent of large scale integrated circuits. If a component was accidently plugged in wrong, the assembler generally found the mistake prior to soldering and made the correction. One day the shop foreman decided that the pace of assembly should be increased and established a daily quota of so many boards to be built per person.

Within a week one of the assemblers was pulled off the line to work full time fixing incorrectly assembled boards prior to shipment, a function that had been previously unnecessary. The foreman, lacking profound knowledge, could do no better.

Responding to Complaints

What happens if an error does slip through the system and makes it into the classroom? Actually it depends on the system as a whole. Go back to the beginning of this chapter and the section on keeping customers informed and customer complaints. The same Office of Consumer Affairs study also found that one of the principal reason that displeased customers did not complain was because they did not know *how* to complain. And you thought everyone knew how to complain.

If the system of service includes a process for handling complaints and the client base is informed about how to use it, what it can do for them and what its limitations are, then you are more likely to actually hear from a larger percentage of dissatisfied users. Otherwise, fall back on the rule of thumb that for every one person complaining, there are four others who didn't call.

It is time to flow chart again. What happens when a call comes in that the wrong item was delivered to a client school? There are only a few options:

- Apologize and explain that it was the only error this week out of 1,200 pieces shipped.
- Apologize, check to see if the correct item is still in-house and ask if a courier from the school can come in and pick it up.
- Apologize, check to see if the correct item is still there and explain that it will be dropped off at the school the next morning.
- Check the shelf and find that the correct item is missing, and then:
- Apologize, initiate a search for the correct item, which by now could be any where. Chaos strikes and needless staff time is invested tracing a needle in a hay stack.

The first two options are not recommended. This is your mistake, don't ask someone else to be inconvenienced to correct it. Don't make excuses either. Your teacher (customer) has had her lesson plan ruined. Her students won't get to see the content of the tape. She made an act of faith with your center that has now been breached. When you sent that confirmation to her six weeks ago that said the item would be delivered on a certain date, that is exactly what was expected. It doesn't matter that the other 1,199 items that week were delivered correctly. It doesn't matter that this teacher may have received 500 items correctly in the last 12 years of teaching. She doesn't care. *This* is the one that will be remembered. And some research suggests that she will remember it for the next two years.[11]

The third option is the best course of action but may not always be practical. Some regional centers cover three, four, five thousand square miles or more. It may take two hours to get to the most distant school in the region and back. It also may not be practical from a cost perspective unless the manager knows how to predict the cost of warranty for a full year and makes it a budget item.

Cost of Warranty

For educational technology centers of any size, cost of warranty is an almost totally foreign concept. The author has brought this up in casual conversation with colleagues over the years and it is generally met with a blank look and a quick change of subject. Technology repair work has a little more concrete base on which to develop the concept of warranty. If the repaired item doesn't perform, is the school charged for the work? Who absorbs the cost of the rework and correction? In repair centers where overhead is covered by a flat rate or some other arrangement, the client is only charged for the parts involved. It still raises the question, How do you make good on defective repairs?

For the media delivery service some accommodation may have to be made for driving out to schools on a special run to deliver the correct item. With the exception of the few regional centers and multi-type library systems that deliver daily or twice a week, the next regular run will be seven days later. Someone has to go to the school, and it is going to cost money. Extra hours, gas and depreciation on the delivery van have to be factored in. If it is done by an employee in a private automobile, the reimbursement rate and lost time have to be considered. But how can we know how many times a year such a run will be necessary? What if all of them are to schools more than an hour away?

There are several approaches to this problem: Ignore the whole issue and hope it doesn't make much difference; guess; pick a number that sounds reasonable and multiply it by the cost to drive out to a school that is an hour away. Or you could gather data for a year on misdeliveries, plot the probability that any of the buildings they occur in will be less than an hour away and calculate the potential cost of warranty.

All of the above are correct answers, although the last option is likely to result in a more accurate budget and a better determination of whether providing warranty service is possible. Make decisions based on data.

It doesn't require a background in statistics to look at a map of your service region and note the geographic distribution of your buildings, their volume of utilization and their relationship to the location of your technology center. On a college campus this is a moot exercise, except for the time involved in constantly sending someone across campus with the right material.

If a pattern of distribution is apparent or it is obvious that the great bulk of the school locations are within a given radius of the center, you can be very safe in predicting that most of the sites you will have to drive to during a year will fall within a given circle.

How Many Errors?

Next, find out how many wrong deliveries were made last year. If you go out onto the shop floor or ask the scheduling clerks how many misdeliveries there were last year, whatever answer is given will be wrong, unless someone has been diligently recording this information already. Human memory is very poor, especially about things that have a negative connotation to them. And, after all, if the wrong tape was delivered, it means that someone screwed up, and if someone screwed up, then collecting data about that can be used for only one thing: heads are going to roll. Your efforts to improve service by making good on delivery problems can be confounded by employees who are fearful and are trying to protect themselves.

The odds are that any number given for wrong deliveries will be on the low side. An accurate record will be necessary for next year. But for the first year a safe place to start might be the error level most American factories function at, which is about 6,210 errors per million opportunities, statistically referred to as Four Sigma.[12] That translates into 6.21 delivery errors per thousand circulations or 62.1 per ten thousand. So a typical regional media center circulating 30,000 items a year could reasonably expect to misdeliver 186 items. That is an accuracy rate of 99.379 percent. A center with uniform labeling, good lighting, adequate staff, readable pull sheets and a stable process might be around .52 errors per thousand or 5.2 per ten thousand, a 99.948 percent accuracy rate. By comparison Motorola Corporation, which popularized the Sigma concept, runs close to Six Sigma which is 3.4 defects per million opportunities. L. L. Bean, which ships over 130,000 packages a day during the Christmas season, typically makes 1 error in every 500,000 shipments. By comparison, Dove soap bars, advertised as 99.44 percent pure, have roughly 5,600 impurities per million parts.

Making Things Right

In any system there will be complaints. In quality management, complaints are used as a source of information about how well the system is operating and how well we are serving our clients. But the immediate need is to respond to the complaint and try to make things right.

The authority to correct errors that have reached the end-user should rest with the staff actually handling the complaint. Clerical staff, schedulers, maintenance technicians, expediters and anyone else who is in a position to know what is required to satisfy a customer's complaint should be able to do so without having to check with someone or ask permission of a supervisor.

If a repaired VCR is still not working when it is returned to a building, the caller should not have to wait for a repair technician to get permission to send out a loaner or authorize a recall. If the wrong videotape is shipped to a client school, the scheduling clerk handling the call should know how to make the situation right and put the required procedures into action.

To operate this way requires staff training and a system of service that already has a high reliability rate. Front line staff have to be trained in how to handle complaints. This means some knowledge of psychology (a component of profound knowledge) in order to smooth the ruffled feathers of irate callers, and knowledge of systems (another part of profound knowledge). Training needs to cover phone techniques, questioning strategies and the capacity of the system to actually rectify problems. Staff cannot promise remedies that are beyond the capacity of the system to an irate client. They must know how to get to the root of the complaint and know what realistically can be done to correct the situation.

Some large technology centers may have tremendous flexibility in both funding and human resources to spend time fixing problems. Of course the point of quality management is to eliminate the sources of potential errors throughout the system so rework becomes unnecessary. Then the center can begin to offer extra, unexpected service assistance that will delight the user. But until that time some sort of warranty is required. Warranty service requires careful design and planning or it can quickly destroy user confidence and bankrupt an organization.

In a center with a primary mission of making available various types of resources to teachers at many locations, the effect of delivery errors can be devastating. To the teacher who ordered the material for use on a specific date, the lesson plan is ruined and their confidence in the materials service shaken. It will not matter that every item ordered for the last three years has arrived on time and in good condition. The failure to perform at the expected level of service is the event that will be remembered.

The effect of the error can be devastating to the center internally, as well. Most large city, campus and regional centers rely on the efficiency of their systems to function at a certain level of staffing, which is generally limited by funding. A call that the wrong videotape has been delivered to a school sets off a chain reaction of events, shown in Figure 8-3, that can consume a tremendous amount of time and may involve several people. The multiplier effect of these factors is completely out of proportion to the apparent significance of the incident. And because of that, many centers make their apologies and wait for the next complaint.

This attitude is not acceptable. It should not have been acceptable in the past, but it was. Users deserve some sort of warranty against defects. They have come to expect it with cars, toasters, television sets and pest control. They expect to be satisfied when things go wrong—don't you?

Calculating Cost of Warranty

In order to begin a real warranty program against incorrect deliveries, management must have some hard data on hand about the current performance of the system. This will require tracking delivery errors over an extended period of time. Ten to fifteen weeks of deliveries should give a solid base line on which to judge performance and decide if warranty is affordable. Gathering such data and having a high degree of confidence in it are two different things. The data can only be recorded by the staff receiving the complaints, and they must feel secure that the information will not be used to discipline or blame someone. Point 8, "drive out fear,"

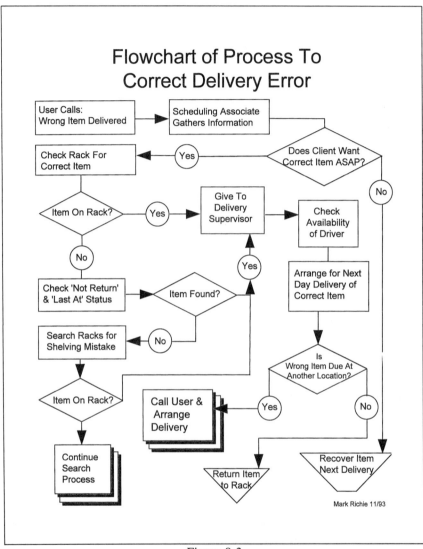

Figure 8-3

must be firmly in place long before this kind of data can be assembled with any kind of confidence. Everyone must understand that in a quality organization, hunches and gut feelings are not used to make decisions on system design. Decisions are made based on data and facts. And they must be collected to get them.

One large Midwest regional media center with a service base of more than 85,000 students in 250 schools started a delivery warranty program in midyear. It announced that it would make good on any misdelivered items by driving out the correct item within 24 hours. In six months the center spent nearly $1,500 in salary time alone correcting 60 wrong deliveries. At the time it was averaging 2,000 circulations per week and averaged over six months the accuracy rate was 99.8 percent. When benefits, mileage, depreciation and internal staff time are factored in the cost per correction approached $50. The cost of warranty was actually closer to $3,000 for the six months. The service was dropped and never mentioned again.

Two things were learned. The first was that the level of errors was much higher than previously assumed. This was because users now had a mechanism for complaining and a promise that the error would be corrected. Users who may previously have suffered in silence now picked up the phone. The second lesson was that launching a new service without a method for predicting the potential cost is dangerous. Management had no clue how much such a warranty promise would cost. It was implemented based on the delusion that the service was already reasonably accurate and that it would be good public relations to say that the delivery service was guaranteed. On the surface, being 99.8 percent accurate may look pretty good. But in real terms it translates into two errors per thousand opportunities. With a circulation of over 80,000 per year, that is a potential of 160 errors per year at a cost of close to $50 each to correct, or $8,000. This assumes that there exists a stable system in which two defects per thousand is a predicable level. Management is prediction.

Calculating the cost of fuel, drivers time, depreciation and internal activities to correct a misdelivery for the author's regional center worked out to roughly $40 per error. In 1985, if the budget could have handled it, the cost of warranty would have been $2,300. In 1992–93, the cost of warranty was $800 on correcting 20 misdelivered items. Everyone is still working just as hard as they did in 1985. The difference is the system that produced the errors has been improved over the years and the errors have been driven down to a level where warranty is financially possible. The result is higher system reliability, greater user satisfaction, less time spent on rework and a lot fewer apologies.

So then how do we warranty our work? It is clear that a blanket warranty for any service: media delivery, equipment repair, print duplication, video duplication, is out of the question for most educational technology centers at this time. Unless there is a highly refined and stable process, with an error and rework rate so low that warranty costs are affordable as a budgeted item, announcing a warranty program is foolish. Few media centers: campus, regional district or otherwise, are in that enviable position. If a center was to begin adopting the Deming philosophy this week and leadership made a major commitment to becoming a quality organization, a warranty could be offered in perhaps two to three years.

Case-by-Case Warranty

Until then case-by-case warranty may be a good compromise. Each technology center must assess the relationship between the error received by the user, the total cost to correct it and the mission of the center. For example, a campus video/film center may very well be able to offer on-campus warranty of video deliveries—if the center has enough student or part-time workers to make special trips out to exchange the wrong item for the correct one. If it is a regional media center servicing several thousand square miles the situation is different. On a case-by-case basis it could offer to drive out correct material to schools that are relatively close to the center and thus provide some management to the losses. But if the problem is in a school at the most remote corner of the region, warranty service may be totally out of the question.

In the case of equipment repair, factors such as repair complexity, kind of equipment and availability of loaners will help determine the level of warranty that can be offered. Perhaps loaners can be arranged for certain types of printers or monitors, but loan of a large screen video projector might be out of the question. The lesson is: don't offer warranty service unless you are prepared to deliver on the promise.

A case-by-case warranty is an internal policy function of the agency. It means that, as far as possible, the center will make every reasonable effort to correct errors that adversely effect the client. It is an internal function that will not be generally announced for the reasons covered

above. It requires that the technology center manager and the area supervisors have a very clear idea of exactly how much warranty capacity they
collectively have. It also requires that front-end associates: scheduling
clerks, receptionists and repair technicians, be trained in how to handle
complaints. Complaining clients are better served if the first person they
talk to is equipped to resolve their problem. Don't make users more aggra-
vated by putting them on hold while seeking permission or asking someone else what to do next.

For this to work, front-end employees must know what the capacity
of the system is for resolving errors. They will destroy the service if they
offer more than can be reasonably delivered. They must also know what
powers they have to resolve problems and exercise them without fear of
being second-guessed by management or reprimanded later.

Good warranty service is only possible if we have driven out fear
and broken down barriers between functional areas inside our own agency.
Management must construct a training outline with the help of area supervisors that determines exactly what it is possible to do to help a client in
a wide range of situations. Then each employee who encounters clients
must be trained in how to work with the client and how to put appropriate
corrective measures into effect. Such training must be a continuing function. As time goes on, employees will develop better judgment for deciding when and how much corrective action to offer. Open sharing of sit-
uational information between front-line associates, in the form of quality
team meetings, will contribute collectively to the effectiveness of the warranty service. These meetings also serve as a place to collect information
on where the system of production and service is breaking down with an
eye toward improving the processes that allow errors to occur. The aim
is to reduce the amount of warranty work that must be done by improving
the system.

Remember, too, that errors fall into two categories: those that are
attributable to common causes and those that are from special causes.
Chapters 4 and 12 cover this concept in more detail. Common cause errors
are due to some function of the system and are unlikely to be eliminated
unless the system is improved. A videotape delivered in the wrong box
may be a common cause error.

Special cause errors are due to some other cause outside the system that may never occur again, or only once in a great while. A flat tire on a delivery truck creating late deliveries is a special cause. In warranty terms, it does no good to waste time and energy trying to fix common cause errors. The fact is that in a stable delivery system, a few errors will be made. Make good on them as quickly as possible. Some percentage of equipment repairs will be returned for rework; some for common cause, some for special causes. Knowing which is which will help put p ᵔr'e to work toward constructive activities that will improve the system in..ʈead of chasing down special causes that may never recur.

The most difficult part may be knowing when to say yes and when to say no. Part of the training will have to include general internal guidelines on when to say "yes," and for how much warranty to provide. Distance may be a limiting factor. System limitations may mean that only locations within 30 or 40 minutes driving time can have a replacement driven out. Equipment stocks can limit the ability to provide loaners for extended periods of time as well.

Position of the user with the complaint may well be an appropriate criteria. Ideally, everyone with a complaint should be treated the same. But realistically, the politics of any organization and its containing system dictate certain types of warranty actions. A building principal an hour away who was intending to use a tape during a staff development program, only to find she has received a tape about rocks and minerals, is likely to have the correct tape driven out to her. A campus media center is far more likely to render extraordinary warranty to the university president or a department head as well. Only individual judgment can determine the most appropriate course of action.

Will all of this attention to warranty and sources of errors preserve your level of use and keep users coming back? No, non-linear dynamics and Murphy's law will always be in effect. Customers are subject to changes in conditions that will effect their previous patterns. A long-time user may suddenly stop coming around. Staying close to your users may reveal the cause behind many of these defections. It may be a local rental store, it may be a new curriculum or a new principal who doesn't want his teachers "wasting time with all that video stuff." It may be a change of teaching style to more hands-on, more field trips or more individualized instruction.

The good media manager will be aware of some of these changes before they happen. But by providing a service that is accurate and dependable, management can eliminate two highly visible reasons for user defections.

[1] Feigenbaum, Armond, V., "Quality and Productivity," *Quality Progress,* November, 1977.

[2] Deming, Edwards, W., *Out of the Crisis.* Cambridge, MA: MIT Press, 1986. Pg. 12.

[3] Deming, Edwards, W., *The New Economics.* Cambridge, MA: MIT Press, 1993. Pg. 77.

[4] Juran, Joseph M. *Juran On Quality By Design.* New York: Free Press. 1992. Pg. 80-83.

[5] George, Steven. *The Baldrige Quality System.* New York:Wiley & Sons. 1992. Pg. 128.

[6] McWhirter, William. "Back On The Fast Track." *Time,* December 13, 1993. Pg. 70.

[7] This assumes the cause is traceable to a "special cause" error that is likely to recur. "Common cause" errors are triggered by the system and will continue to recur until the system itself is improved. See Chapter 6 and 12 for a discussion of stable and unstable systems. Also Chapter 12 on control charts.

[8] George, op cit., pg. 24–25.

[9] Ibid.

[10] Aguayo, Rafael. *Dr. Deming: The American Who Taught The Japanese About Quality.* New York: Simon and Schuster, 1986. Pg. 27.

[11] *Fundamentals of Total Quality Management.* Compact Disc-Interactive. Self-Paced Interactive Continuing Education Program. (SPICE) Atlanta, GA: AMPED, 1993.

[12] George, op cit., pg. 115.

Chapter 9

SOURCES OF SUPPLY

DR. DEMING'S POINT 4 IS "END THE PRACTICE OF AWARDING BUSINESS on the basis of price tag alone." To an educational technology service center that is part of a government structure or one that is part of a private university bureaucracy, Dr. Deming's commandment may appear impossible to implement. Government agencies are hamstrung with outdated regulations requiring competition on the basis of the lowest price or multiple suppliers for each item purchased. Purchasing agents in business and industry for years have chased after the lowest price for materials and never hesitated to switch suppliers if a lower price was found elsewhere. Their counterparts in government and education have done the same.

To some degree Dr. Deming urges that we not be too hard on ourselves or buyers in general for using price tag as the deciding criteria. After all, he laments, it has been their job, and we can't fault someone for doing his job.[1] But buying on price alone is no longer good enough. If the transformation of an educational technology center into a quality organization is going to be guided by the 14 Points of Dr. Deming, then the issue of buying on price tag must be dealt with. The transformation requires buyers of equipment, material and supplies to shift from looking at the lowest initial cost to lowest total cost.

Buying at the lowest price is a short-term activity. If photocopy paper is $2.20 a ream this month and next month another supplier can sell it for $2.10, the order goes to the new supplier. If your duplication center can buy a case of T-30 video tapes at $1.63 apiece and a case of T-120 tapes at $1.25 apiece, the conventional wisdom says the T-120s are the better buy. If the criterion is only initial cost, this may be true. But in a quality organization, total cost is the deciding factor. Are T-120 tapes more likely to jam in school machines when subjected to heavy circulation, wide swings in temperature and humidity, chalk dust, poorly maintained machines and indifferent handling? If there is an 18-minute program on a 120 minute tape, is it worth the extra time required to run all the excess tape through a tape inspection machine? If a T-30 tape weighs 1.1 pounds and a T-120 weighs 2 pounds, how much extra unnecessary weight do material handlers have to move around in a day? Can these little differences matter? On a weekly circulation of 1,000 items the weight saved would be 900 pounds for each movement. A typical tape might be handled 13 or 14 times in a full pull/pack/deliver/return/check-in/rerack cycle. The total weight movement saved would be about 11,700 pounds. If only half the collection had been duplicated onto the less costly T-120 tapes the time saved on video inspection during a typical week would amount to almost 17 hours. Calculate total cost of ownership and use.

Buying with lowest total cost in mind is a long-term activity. Long term thinking can be difficult at first for something as routine as buying copy paper or blank media. As time goes on and you become more comfortable with operating a technology center as a quality organization, long-term thinking will become quite natural. Most of the Deming philosophy requires a shift from looking at the near-term to looking as far into the future as possible.

Total Cost

What does total cost mean? Simply, it is the total cost incurred on a system by the purchase, use and upkeep of an item. The item can be consumable like paper and videotape, or durable like a VCR, satellite dish or delivery van. The failure to consider total cost can be the source of heavy losses in business and unimaginable losses in education and government.

Education and government agencies are typically constrained to operate under very specific state bid and quote laws. A typical state law may require bid specifications, advertisements, performance bonds and sealed bids for purchases over a specific dollar amount. Quotes, informal or written, may be required at some other range of spending limits. These are system-imposed requirements that none of us can control. They are, as Dr. Deming refers to them, "facts of life." Ironically, very few bid laws require awarding business to the lowest bidder. In most cases, if all other factors are relatively equal, the contract goes to the lowest bidder anyway, but it is generally not a requirement. Consult the bid and quote laws in your state for exact regulations. Federal government agencies may be under obligation to purchase from mandatory supply schedules and should be careful not to violate Federal Property Management Regulations.

To operate effectively with the bid and quote laws and still factor in total cost may require actually writing it into the bid or quote specifications.

Some factors of total cost that might be written in are:

- Cost of annual service contracts
- Yearly estimated maintenance costs
- Fuel economy
- Mean time between failure
- Response time by repair technicians
- Ease of user service
- Cost of operating supplies: toner, fax paper, cartridges, ribbons, etc.
- Delivery time
- Availability of loaner equipment
- Distance to carry-in service center
- Assembly requirements
- Installation requirements
- Availability of on-site training
- Availability of 800 service number; 10 hours, 15 hours or 24 hours a day
- Delivery costs
- Energy efficiency rating

- Estimated repair costs on life of unit
- Average down time per month (year)
- Availability of continuing training

Some combination of these factors and many others must be considered when selecting vendors for supplies, material and equipment. To further control the problems that can be caused by poor supply sources, Dr. Deming calls for the establishment of long-term relationships with single suppliers.[2] To some extent, this aspect of Dr. Deming's method may have to wait until more enlightened minds take over the government bodies that make bid and quote regulations—a process that may take a very long time. But to the extent possible, an effort must be made to limit the number of suppliers for any given item of material. This can be done partially by assessing each piece of material used by the center and determining name brands, models and grades that work best in a specific application.

Standardizing on specific brands of computer paper, floppy disks, blank video tape, empty video boxes, shipping cases, storage racks, computer furniture, masking tape, ball-point pens, pencils, felt-tip markers, self-stick notes and envelopes (among other items) does several things. It simplifies inventory and reordering internally, which saves time. It makes going out for quotes, when required, easier because everyone is quoting on the same thing. If there are multiple suppliers for office supplies and they are all quoting on the same items, then the competition is on service factors such as delivery time, delivery cost and inventory availability as well as price.

Cooperation for a Standard

Dr. Deming and others demonstrate that cooperation between corporations that normally compete with each other is highly desirable. Some of the more obvious examples include a standard spacing between rails among railroads all over North America, standard paper sizes, standard light bulb sockets, standard battery sizes and standard videocassettes.

The educational video/film industry could do a great service to itself and to its customers by agreeing on a standard style of video box and a standard style of videodisc container. Some companies use a clear video box which requires the tape to be inserted with the door toward the hinge. Most producers use a box that requires the cassette door to face the opening side of the box. In both designs, the video box will not close and latch properly unless the tape is in the right way. Untold hours are spent each year opening returned video boxes and turning the tapes around so that the box can be closed properly. The present solution is: when ordering titles from producers who package in boxes that do not conform to the standards of your center, request no boxes at all and ask for a credit on the packaging. When the product arrives, package it in your own standard video boxes. Trying to repackage titles otherwise creates a tremendous amount of rework and wastes a lot of video boxes.

There are at least five principal styles of videodisc boxes commonly used by producers. Each of the five has a different height and width, making the efficient use of standard shelves impossible. Three of the designs have no effective way of preventing the disc from falling out if the box accidently opens. At least two of the designs have no secure way of keeping the box closed even under normal handling conditions. One of the most durable and safest designs has no provision for placing labels on the spine, which complicates the storage system and greatly slows pulling and shelving activities. A medium that could have allowed for storage of a rather large resource library in a space much smaller than a typical video/film collection now requires has defeated itself. Short of repackaging (waste and rework) every videodisc in the collection as it arrives, media centers are forced to suffer with wasted shelf space to accommodate different width and height boxes.

In the print shop of a regional technology center pressed for storage space, it may make more sense to pay a slightly higher price for photocopy paper from a vendor who can promise next day delivery than save $100 and have inventory stacked in the hallways.

Standardization of supplies follows one of the principal tenets of quality management: that uniformity reduces cost. With fewer suppliers, there is less paperwork. With fewer types of material to order, there is less paperwork, easier inventory and less space required. Standardization of video equipment brands can simplify repairs, allow for interchangeability of parts and may lead to lower rates on service contracts.

Example: Computer Paper and Printer Ribbons.

The scheduling operation of a regional media center at one time kept six kinds of pin-fed computer paper on hand. In a typical week the paper in the printer had to be changed 15 to 18 times. One kind of paper, 11 × 14″, was only used once a month, while another, blank two-part 8½ × 11″ was only used twice a year. Over a period of time, most of the paper in stock was used up. Internal process requirements were reassessed and the regional center settled on the need for only two kinds of paper, one-part blank and three-part blank. Inventory became much less complicated and placing orders for new stock was simplified.

The next step was to purchase a second printer and a dual printer stand. Each printer is now loaded with a different paper stock. Using an A/B switch arrangement, operators flip a switch to change between paper types and printers. Paper is reloaded into the printers only when the paper supply runs out. A rough estimate is that the new arrangement saves 45 minutes a week or about 27 hours each school year.

Most large scale technology service centers generate a tremendous amount of paper for internal operations—monthly and weekly reports, routing lists, print assignment lists, pulling lists, packing lists, user confirmations and the like. Millions of characters produced each week means that printer ribbons reach their capacity for producing legible lettering relatively quickly. Yet many technology centers will use ribbons until the image is too faint to read or someone complains.

Who uses the print-out? Users read their confirmations. Faint, hard-to-read confirmations send a message about how the center is managed. Clear, crisp, dense confirmations send a different message. Material handlers use pull and packing lists. The accuracy of packing and delivery of materials depends on the ability to quickly and correctly read the item number to pull from the shelf and which location it is intended for. Save money, budgets are tight, do more with less, we are told. With that in mind, the business administrator buys lower-cost ribbons and the operator lets the ribbon run longer in the printer than it should. Does this save money? Where are the losses factored in from rework correcting mispulled items because the pull list was hard to read? Where do we factor in the time lost while the staff slows down to read faint lettering in attempt to do their job right?

Hourly materials pullers are trapped in the system. They cannot order better quality print ribbons or order them changed on a regular cycle. That is a function of management.

Should management budget $500 a year or more for printer ribbons? Perhaps it should. What is the cost of warranty? (See Chapter 8). Has anybody ever gathered data on the lost time and rework caused by unreadable internal documents? Dr. Deming would probably ask. "How could they have known?" Now you know.

It may seem excessive to spend five paragraphs on something as mundane as computer paper and printer ribbons in a book about quality management. However, this is where it starts. Banners, news releases, reports to the board of directors, training, reading books for self-study and strategic plans combined mean nothing until action is taken to improve the system of production and service. Improvement is a combination of millions of little things, that when focused toward the aim of the system yield material gains in quality.

Internal Price Tags

There are two aspects of Point 4 that need to be considered. The first, detailed above, deals with what we commonly think of when we talk about "doing business on price tag"; buying things. But there is another aspect to doing business on price tag that affects the internal operations of an organization. It has to do with the way decisions are made everyday about common operational details. It can take simple forms like whether to use frosted or cellophane tape in a particular situation. The purchase of printer ribbons discussed above is an example. More examples follow.

Example: Quality Blank Videotape.

Purchase decisions with more costly consequences might involve buying no-name, less expensive videotape or name brand blanks. Unfortunately that is no guarantee of quality because there is no universal standard in the videotape industry to define "Grade A" or "Grade B" tape. The only way you can ensure uniform quality with blank videotape is to get an independent testing sheet on the product and see that it has fewer than ten dropouts per minute after 100 plays. The quality of the shell influences the durability of the tape over time and, like the tape itself, there are no industry standards to define a "Grade A" shell. Simply insisting that the shell bear the VHS logo is no guarantee either. JVC Corporation, owner of the patents for VHS tape and shells, has an active program to take legal action against unlicensed loader/duplicators.[3]

Example: Overnight or Ground?

A well-known computer systems manufacturer was awarded a contract to supply and install a multi-terminal system for an educational service agency. Part of the contract required on-site installation and training over a three-day period by a company technical representative. The equipment was shipped in several boxes and arrived well in advance of the installer's visit. The packing slips on the boxes matched the contents of the boxes. The installer arrived on a Tuesday and in the process of installing the system realized that a key cable for a remote terminal, specified and included in the price, was missing. Also missing was a speaker for the computer sound system. The installer made a call to the home office, two time zones away and asked for the cable and speaker to be Federal Expressed overnight.

The next day 10 a.m. passed without a Federal Express shipment. A call was placed at 11:00 a.m. to the home office to get the package waybill number so a tracer could be placed on the package. The conversation went something like this:

Customer: Hello, we were supposed to get a package with an important cable in it this morning and it didn't arrive. Do you have a package waybill number so a trace can be put on it?

Company: Oh yes, I sent that out yesterday, but it shouldn't arrive for several days.

Customer: Did Mr._____(vice-president of the company) ask you to send that out?

Company: Yes he did.

Customer: How did he ask that it be sent?

Company: Well, he said to send it overnight, but it is so expensive to ship things overnight that I sent it ground. Was it really that important?

The secretary was only doing her best, but she did not understand the aim of the company or the losses she created. "How could she know?" as Dr. Deming is likely to ask. If she has never been told, never been trained in the aim of the company, she will not know. Of course that assumes that management knows what the aim of the company is: quality begins at the top.

The customer and the technical representative spent additional wasted time calling computer stores and driving around to buy a speaker and a cable (too short) to get the system running. Time spent finding material to make up for what was not shipped when it should have been, and not shipped overnight, as requested, cut into training time. The customer loses and the company loses.

The secretary did what she thought best. She has heard things in the office that color her judgment. The vice president told her to send it overnight. But she knew that cash flow is tight. Watch the photocopies and count the paper clips; ground rates are lower, it will save the company some money. When the customer goes to a state or national technology convention will he brag to other technology center directors about how great the service was? Will the customer take pride in making a smart decision to do business with this company? Will the customer tell this story to 18 to 24 people? Will the story end up in a book?

Who was responsible for making sure the shipment of parts and equipment was correct? Who makes sure that the system is delivered on time, installed correctly and that training is done to the satisfaction of the customer? Not the salesman. He has already received his commission from the first installment payment and is working on his next quota. No one in the company is responsible for seeing the sale and installation through to the end. The aim of this company is to meet quota and pay the rent. The customer is a necessary nuisance to that activity.

A series of examples related to various aspects of doing business on price tag alone and their effect on educational technology centers follow.

Example: Projection lamps.

In 1979 a high school media specialist discovered that a vendor of projection lamps routinely beat "state bid" prices by an additional 15 percent. Seeking to share the savings, he coordinated the lamp purchases of the other five schools in the district and realized a net savings of nearly $400 per school (big bucks in 1979). The superintendent refused to sign the purchase order because it did not have a state bid number on it (not required by law incidentally). The district lost $2,000 up-front plus any other savings from future projects the media specialist might have tried. Realizing that there was no pay-off for trying to save money, the media specialist never attempted it again.

Example: Photocopiers.

A local government purchasing agent bought the same model photocopier for all departments in the government. Paper for the copiers is purchased by the skid and is the lowest grade at the lowest cost. An educational technology center with its own purchasing system shares space in a complex of government buildings. On a regular basis, workers from neighboring government departments ask to use the photocopier in the technology center because the government-purchased copier is out of order. One day the technology center's copier experienced a chronic series of paper jams. Cause? The cheap (low bid) paper left in the machine by one of the government employees.

Example: Fax Machines.

The department of education for a heavily urbanized state on the east coast delivered a fax machine to the superintendent of schools' office for each county. The department of education explained that it would improve communications by allowing the county office to quickly pass important messages on to local districts. Each county of this state may have up to 50 local districts. The model of fax machine provided to the county offices for this important mission did not include a multi-number dialing feature.

To fax an urgent one-page document to 40 locations requires the labor of a secretary keying in each number individually and passing the page through the machine for each transmission, a process that takes over an hour and a half, if there are no busy signals.

With a multi-number capable fax machine the process takes about one-third less time and does not require more than ten minutes of staff time to start the transmission.

What was the total cost? The machine was the standard, state bid fax machine, specified for the lowest initial cost, that is, no frills and obtained from the lowest bidder. The purpose for which it was to be used was never considered and therefore the *total cost* for the machine inflicts heavy losses on each county office. There is unnecessary extra time spent with the machine by the clerical staff and needless delay of faxing through genuinely urgent messages. The burden to the supply budget is increased since the machine depends on special rolls of fax paper to operate. A plain paper fax machine with multi-number dialing that might have cost twice as much initially could have paid for itself in the first three months in staff-time saved and the ability to use readily available photocopy paper, simplifying inventory at the same time.

The source is lost, but someone once said that in education, "we would rather spend $10 four times than $25 once."

Whether you buy outright or lease a photocopier, get the highest capacity model you can afford with the most features. A document feeder and collator are "must have" features unless you have an abundance of staff able to devote time to making copies. Small operations in particular should get a collator and document feeder. Although smaller media centers may not be in the financial position to afford these extras, every effort should be made to obtain them. The fact that they are operating with very few people means that the advantages of the added features will create a multiplier effect on staff productivity.

Example: Delivery Vans.

Delivery vans available through state purchasing arrangements are typically equipped with the minimum level equipment and features. This is done partly for reasons of economy (initial cost) and partly to simplify the job of the purchasing department by avoiding the complications of bidding on extra features. Generally, there is nothing that compels local government agencies, state universities and educational service centers to buy only what is offered on state contract. It may be a matter of policy on the part of the local governing body, but it is highly unlikely for it to be mandated by law. Bid and quote laws may only prescribe that purchases over a certain level be sent out for competitive bid.

Most regional, university and large city media and technology centers have occasion to purchase delivery vans. When doing so, take some time to assess the requirements of the driver, the kinds of deliveries that are made, frequency of stops, length of route and condition of roads encountered. A straight, off-the-shelf van may very well be the most desirable. (Note that we are looking for what is most desirable, not what is acceptable; see Chapter 10 for an expansion of this.)

Consider the requirement for light inside the van so that the driver can read labels on boxes and equipment to be delivered. A van with full windows all around adds a lot of cost. But specifying windows down the passenger side only and in the back doors meets the requirement. It provides plenty of light and the added safety of visibility down the right side of the vehicle. Take a good look at a phone company van. Most of them only have windows down the right hand side. Ford calls it a "display van" option. With no windows on the driver's side, shelving can be installed if needed.

Step bumpers are an option sometimes not found on the standard government-purchased van. Yet some drivers find them a great assistance for getting in and out of the back when both hands are full. Ask potential bidders if oversize mirrors are an option and specify a right-hand outside mirror as well. Save some money on the specifications in the paint and chrome area. Chrome bumpers, rear view mirrors, grills and hub caps are the standard in most cases. You can specify that they be painted instead, generally gray or argent. Full length floor mats can be factory installed, and as a bid item, generally for less than having them put in after purchase. They help absorb road noises, keep things from sliding around and make the van a little more valuable on trade-in because the rear deck isn't scratched and worn down to bare metal. Should there be a radio? Even a common AM/FM radio is frequently not found in a state contract delivery van. Maintaining driver comfort, fighting boredom and getting traffic reports all contribute to the effectiveness of a delivery service.

What about suspension systems, fuel tanks and batteries? Videotapes don't really weigh that much. Even loaded with deliveries for 30 schools and a variety of repaired equipment to be returned, most loads don't come close to the rated payload of a basic van. But the suspension system is what takes up the impact from the road and affects the overall durability of the truck. As a rule of thumb, getting the upgrade option to heavy-duty shocks and springs will make the truck last longer, help hold the wheel alignment longer and extend the time between shock replacement. Larger-size tires generally come automatically with the heavy-duty suspension option as well.

Specify the larger fuel tank option, if there is one, even for urban driving. Going from a standard tank to a 35-gallon option cut the number of fuel stops required per week in half for one regional media center. This resulted in less time spent getting gas and fewer fuel invoices to process.

A heavy duty battery option is a good investment. Delivery is the life blood of many educational technology centers. Having materials scheduled, packed and ready to go on time doesn't do any good if the truck won't start. Even centers fortunate enough to have garages should specify heavy duty batteries. Cold weather and restarting the truck 25 or 30 times a day can create problems for a normal battery.

If possible get high-backed seats, at least for the driver's side. Standard truck seats in many makes do not have head rests because federal regulations do not require them. In the event of even a minor rear end collision, the head rest will protect the driver from a potential whiplash and possible extended time away from the job. High-backed seats are a good investment in safety as well as comfort for a worker who may spend as many as seven hours a day in the truck. Get an airbag if it is available. High-backed seats and airbags are now standard in Ford vans even though the government does not yet make that a requirement.

Investing in a mini-van for a media center delivery vehicle may be an exercise in false economy. The initial cost alone may approach a full-size van on bid. While the cargo capacity in terms of weight may be usable, the diminished interior cubic footage can create a problem. Drivers must be able to move things around during a delivery run and, frequently, they must climb over boxes and read labels. Stooping over in a full-size van is much more comfortable that the confined height of a mini-van. Agencies with deeper pockets might want to observe United Parcel

Service's practice and their package delivery cars (UPS' name for their trucks). Everything is on shelves and the driver can stand up in the back.

Example: Videotapes.

A large regional media center, in an attempt to "buy American," began purchasing videotape for duplication from a mid-western manufacturer. The tape and shells were made and assembled in the United States. The center ordered 500 tapes at a time during a mass conversion project. In the process of conditioning the tapes for use in a video inspection machine, it was discovered that more than 80 tapes were short-loaded. A further 135 tapes were found to have many defects in the last ten minutes of the tape. The problem appeared as two closely spaced vertical lines that moved through the picture at regular intervals. Close inspection revealed pairs of folds or ripples in the tape.

The sales representative made appropriate arrangements to have the defective tapes returned and replacements sent. The company sent the staff a nice cheese wheel and a letter of apology for the problem. Of the 215 replacement tapes received, 48 contained the ripple defect in the tape. Phone calls directly to the plant manager were fruitless. A test pattern was recorded from a laser disc onto several of the defective tapes and sent, along with a letter describing the problem, to the plant manager's attention. More than three months later the manager called to ask why the tapes had been mailed to him. The sales representative never called again and the center now purchases imported tapes that have proven reliable and don't have to be inspected prior to use.

Example: Computer Support.

Good computer system support can be like having an extra staff member. Bad customer support can wipe out the credibility of an entire technology center.

Dr. Deming urges cooperation with suppliers and customers. Educational technology centers that rely on specialized computer scheduling and inventory systems should have an interest in seeing that the company they purchase it from remains strong, profitable and customer-oriented. On the one hand it means resisting the temptation to get a "special deal" on every upgrade and enhancement. But on the other hand it means working with the company to get the kind of support that will truly enhance overall service to users. When the system goes down for no apparent reason, there is nothing worse than to hear the computer service representative respond with, "Gee, I never heard of that happening. I'll have to check with someone who knows about these things and get back to you."

Your users don't care what your center's problems are. The customer support people in the computer company must know how vital it is to find a prompt remedy to a system failure. If they don't know, their customers have an obligation to make their needs clear to the computer company and the company should respond. Cooperation begins this way.

Example: Office Supplies.

Poor inventory management of office supplies can eat away at staff time and consumable materials budgets. From an internal point of view, the more different types of things in an office supply inventory, the more complex ordering and stock control are. Do we really need to stock three different sizes of paper clips? Are two different types of packaging tape on three-inch cores absolutely necessary?

Reducing inventory to what is truly required for the job is not a particularly American management trait. In Japan, a machine tool maker, prior to modernizing one of its plants, had every tool used in the current process laid out on tables. Engineers were then asked to justify the need for each tool. At the end of the session the number of tools required had been reduced from 672 to 46. The typical American solution to the same problem, according to Hriday Prasad, Manager of Industrial Control Systems at Ford, might be the creation of a massive computer program to manage the tool inventory.[4] The lesson transfers to office supplies: simplify by reducing the number of things to order and inventory.

From an operational view, poor office supply management can create heavy losses through waste and rework. Office suppliers frequently recommend substitutes for specified items on their quotes: generally different brands and at a lower initial cost.

Well-intentioned business administrators have sometimes unwittingly caused great losses to the organizations whose interests they are supposed to be protecting. They will scan bids for lower cost alternatives to what was specified by the department head and place the order.

Unwilling to fight the powers that be to reject the substitution, the department accepts the lower-quality material and the losses commence. Masking tape used to label shelving edges curls and falls off after three weeks. Generic self-stick notes fail to work if reapplied more than twice. Cellophane tape used to secure packing lists to boxes loses its grip when the humidity changes. Sometimes it won't adhere to the surface of a shipping box. Correction typewriter ribbons stick to the paper and constantly jam. Computer ribbons, a dollar cheaper then those specified, must be changed every three weeks instead of every five. Generic staples jam in the electric stapler. These little things that office workers put up with everyday and consider to be normal frustrations of the job are actually signals of losses within the system.

Most supply-related problems in an office can be eliminated by working back through the purchase stream and comparing requirements for the job to the performance of the product. It may be that unbranded paper clips work just fine and an alternate brand computer ribbon may give just as good performance as a name-brand ribbon. But the only way to tell is by testing and evaluating results. Even details like paying attention to which side of the paper should be run though the machine first when making double-sided copies can reduce rework from paper jams or smeared copies.

PDSA, The Plan-Do-Study-Act cycle covered in more detail in Chapter 12, gives us a tool for making decisions based on facts, not hunches. Take some petty cash and buy one or two samples of the item that is to be substituted. Use it in actual operations and record the changes and results of its use. Compare all aspects of the performance and look at the total cost. The PDSA cycle will show us if the performance is equal to or better than the original item and at what cost. It also provides us with a mechanism to standardize items to be ordered in the future. Standardization of materials and processes is a key competitive advantage used by the Japanese. We should profit by it, too.

Example: Media Storage Systems.

Standardization of shelving systems allows for interchangeability of parts and greater flexibility of room and shelving arrangements as collections grow and change. It is a worthwhile investment to slowly replace non-standard shelving throughout a center until there is uniformity.

Many technology centers, because of initial cost, use common flat shelves for videotape storage and arrange the tapes much like books on a shelf. A method more likely to reduce errors is the use of individual slots for each tape. Most large educational video/film centers use racks with replaceable wire separators. The one-inch spacing racks used for 16mm film cans can be replaced with 1¼" space racks that will hold most common video boxes. Although more expensive than flat shelves, providing an individual slot for each tape has a number of significant advantages.

There is instant and positive visual inventory of items. If any item is missing, an open space shows up without having to read title number sequences. With conventional shelving, tapes fall over and get pushed together to make room for returning items. Shelving requires many extra motions and more reading of title numbers to put the tapes back in the correct spots. With individual slots, the shelving process goes faster and is more accurate because there is a specific location waiting for each returning item.

Commonly available media racks come either three or four feet long and nine shelves high. This assumes storing the tapes with the spine, and therefore the title, facing toward the aisle. But, if the item number is placed on the short side of the video box with labeling tape and the box is stored with the spine facing up, a tenth shelf can be added to the rack to make better use of the floor space. In a three-foot shelf this adds 22 more slots for tapes and with a four-foot shelf it adds 32 more. A ten shelf, four-foot unit configured this way will hold 320 tapes in four square feet of floor space.

Uniformity lowers cost. To save money, many centers resort to labeling items with felt tip pens. Hand written numbers on the edge of cans and boxes leads to misread numbers. Typewritten labels are too small to be read quickly without causing eye fatigue over time. Use a standard labeling system for all media and clearly mark video boxes, disc packages and film cans. A 20 point or larger type from a computer printer or labeling system like Kroy or Brother produces large, highly visible labels that can be easily read from several feet away.

Readability studies show that black lettering on a white background is most effective. Institute a conversion project to relabel everything in the collection with the same style and size numbers. Tape for these lettering systems appears expensive, but uniformity and large easy-to-read numbers are key elements in the effort to drive down the number of potential errors in both pulling and shelving activities.

Some computer systems can generate labels with 20 point or larger numbers that might be usable. The principal drawback is the label stock, which should be checked for durability first.

Floor space is at a premium in most technology centers. Racks, drawers and shelves of some kind are used to store tapes, discs, films, kits, models and software. Every linear foot of storage space requires access with aisle space. The minimum aisle space recommended for stacks is 38 inches.[5] So each linear foot of 12 inch deep shelving needs approximately 1½ square feet of floor space if the shelves are arranged to face each other and create a 38 inch aisle. The amount of aisle space required for each storage unit must be factored in or a tremendous amount of floor space can be wasted and employees made to walk much farther than necessary to get to all parts of a storage area.

There is a double-sided video storage rack on the market with individual slots that will hold up to 448 tapes. It is four feet long and one foot deep. The tapes are stored long side up with the spine facing the aisle. This means that it requires a total of 28 square feet of floor space, four under the rack and 24 in the aisles. Now consider the ten-shelf-high rack described above in which the tapes are stored short side toward the aisle. Two of these racks back to back hold 640 tapes. Including the aisle space required, they need 32 square feet of floor space. The two one-foot-wide racks placed back to back require 14 percent more floor space but have a 42 percent larger tape storage capacity.

Example: Printing.

Quality printing could be the subject of an entire book. For our purposes it pertains to print services that are required for the operation of an educational technology center. These requirements include letterhead, catalogs, newsletters, labels, stickers and forms of various descriptions.

Technology centers and any organization can find great benefit in knowing how to work with a printer. This includes the in-house print shop of larger educational technology service agencies. The same technology manager who cuts corners on generic self-stick notes and low-quality blank cassettes will expend every nickel of the savings by requiring a special-order paper stock for a newsletter.

Once you have found a printer you can work with, learn what the printer needs to made a good print job. Find out what kind of mechanicals he will accept, what kind of desktop publishing software he can handle and what paper colors and sizes are commonly kept on hand. Learn the language of the printer. Find out how to specify fold, paper weights and what the cost factors are for colored inks and multi color jobs. Ask for an estimate of lead time requirements and give the printer warning on when to expect your job and when you will require it to be delivered. In-house print shops are afflicted with numerous last minute jobs from a variety of sources. Some of them consist of a pile of hand written pages and a sketch of what the finished publication should look like. The deadline is always yesterday.

Stick with basic colors and paper sizes. Amateur publishers get into trouble because there are so many choices of colored paper and ink. For paper stay with white, cream, beige, light blue, light green and light yellow. All of these colors test well for readability with black ink. Avoid at all costs goldenrod-colored paper. It is highly visible but ranks low in readability. And, after all, we would like our publication to be read. Also avoid running text and headlines over illustrations and photographs. This technique also destroys readability.

Work with the printer who handles your materials catalog. Good printers will have suggestions for producing it at lower cost while still keeping it usable. Specify how many overruns you are willing to buy. This is an inexpensive way to get extra catalogs for new teachers and people who lose them. Video/film centers might consider publishing a supplement every other year in place of a full catalog. Make the supplement include everything new received in the last three years instead of just the most recent purchases. This creates a catalog that highlights the newest and most up-to-date titles while avoiding the downward swing in circulation that generally accompanies publication of a resource supplement.

Create an agency logo. Most regional media centers and campus technology centers have some sort of identifying mark or logo. If your center does not, it is a good investment of time and perhaps money to have one designed. Keep it simple both in lettering and graphic design. It may also include a legend that adds a description of what your center does or what it stands for. Corporate logos for years have carried the position of the company. "We bring good things to life." "We try harder." "The quality goes in before the name goes on." "Fly the friendly skies." These are all familiar examples of corporate legends that go with the company name.

Care should be taken with creating both the logo design and the legend. The center has to live with it for a long time. Do not reduce this activity to a contest or farm it out to a friend who is "artistic." Several good books on graphic design are filled with information about creating a solid logo that will be distinctive and easily recognizable.

Recognition is the primary reason for using an agency logo. For a company, it is a product recognition device. For a campus technology or district media center it is a statement of product origination. It tells everyone who sees it who supplied the material that is being used.

Once a logo and legend are settled on, use them on everything that leaves the center. Many centers with very fine corporate logos limit their use to letterheads and newsletters. Put it on everything. Order video boxes with the logo and agency name stamped on the box. Order directly from the manufacturer to save a few dollars on the initial set up fees instead of paying mark ups to a middleman. Plastic Reel Corporation has offered regional media centers deep discounts on custom printed video boxes for many years.

The logo belongs on purchase orders, annual reports, invoices, checks, envelopes, memo pads, shipping labels, newsletters, brochures, resource lists and the side of the truck. Consider producing a 15-second trailer to edit into the beginning of every videotape showing the media center logo and stating, "this program is provided by_____media and technology center."

Quality management includes the perception users have of your organization. Uniformity and consistency of style help shape that perception. A newsletter that has a consistent look issue to issue and a logo that clearly identifies the source of materials and information helps raise credibility.

Example: Postage.

Postage can quickly eat up budget dollars with very little effort. A postage machine may help many large centers control and track costs. Moderate and smaller centers might do better buying prestamped envelopes from the post office instead of paying the fees for a postage machine. The postal service also offers prestamped envelopes with a preprinted return address of up to four lines. Or the envelopes can be run through a printing press to put the agency logo and return address on as well.

How Satisfied Are You with Your Suppliers?

Part of the process of working upstream and eliminating problems before they get into the system requires developing a cooperative relationship with suppliers. It might be useful to assess how satisfied you really are with the suppliers to your center. Satisfaction with a supplier usually involves the quality of the product and, perhaps, delivery time. Consider as well, all the potential areas for waste and rework created by problems in accepting delivery on materials. Tracking the following indicators provides valuable information.

- Percent of deliveries arriving late
- Percent of orders arriving with back orders indicated
- Time span between arrival of first packages and last in a single order
- Percent of boxes arriving with damaged contents
- Percent of orders arriving with short count

- Percent of orders arriving with wrong part/wrong title—actual number wrong

- Percent of packing lists that do not match the invoice

- Percent of invoices that do not match the purchase order

- Percent of packing lists that do not match either the invoice or purchase order

A report by McKinsey and Company found that a typical company gets about 33 percent of its orders late and rejects about 1.5 percent of deliveries. Quality companies that have developed better internal practices and working relationships with suppliers get about two percent of their orders late and reject just 0.0001 percent of deliveries.[6]

A Pareto chart can show which errors are the most common. It can also show which companies have the highest incidence of delivery problems over an extended period of time. Using the chart, the media manager knows which companies are in need of special help to better understand your needs, and which companies to avoid in the future. Calculating the cost of looking for missing items, matching packing lists with invoices, deciphering unintelligible invoices and making phone calls to straighten out problems with the company provide a clearer picture of the "total cost" of doing business with a specific supplier.

Making It Stick

Gains from learning how to buy on total cost instead of initial cost can be wiped out very easily. Constancy of purpose is required. The purchasing process must be standardized and operated with an agreed-upon set of procedures. Requests for new or different supplies must be justified and supported with data from tests of the material in actual use. This is quality management at the nuts and bolts level. The system of service we provide, no matter what the setting, is the result of the interactions of all the processes that go into providing the service. The processes can only be as good as the material we use. Failure to apply the principal of total cost at the initial stage of the process, buying materials, will undermine much of our efforts to improve the system further downstream.

1 Deming, Edwards. W. *Out of the Crisis*. Cambridge, MA: MIT Press, 1986. Pg. 32.

2 Ibid., pg. 35.

3 Kurz, Phil. "Ten Useful Tips to Help the Purchasing Agent Choose a Videotape Duplicator." *AV Video,* May 1992. Pg. 6.

4 Brody, Herb. "Good Is Never Enough," *High Technology,* August, 1986. Pg. 20.

5 Ellsworth, Ralphe E. *The School Library*. New York: Educational Facilities Laboratories, 1968. Pg. 79.

6 Port, Otis. "Quality: Small and Midsize Companies Seize The Challenge, And Not Moment Too Soon," *Business Week,* November 30, 1992. Pg. 72.

Chapter 10

ORGANIZING FOR QUALITY SERVICE

HOW WELL AN EDUCATIONAL TECHNOLOGY CENTER, COMPUTER LAB, curriculum library, repair service, print shop or media center meets and exceeds the needs of its users is partially a function of organizational structure. If the director or manager focuses on the needs and requirements of the organization's users there will be a very different organizational pattern to the center than if the focus is on policy and organization charts.

Before organizing a technology center to provide quality service to its users, we need to look inside again. The notion of customer service must also extend to customer/supplier relationships within the organization. There can be no sustainable gain in user satisfaction without an internal commitment for better service between one functional area and another. This is part of what is meant by the term "policy deployment" in quality management. The policies that determine the levels of satisfaction to be met are deployed across all areas of the organization. If you feel compelled to use the term *Total Quality Management, this,* not statistics, is what puts the "total" in quality management. The commitment to adopting better operational and management practices must extend to all the levels and phases of an agency that are beyond the eyes of the ultimate customer.

Service to Internal Customers

In any organization, no matter how small, there are certain functional areas that provide crucial internal support and service to the rest of the organization. The breakdown of any one or combination of these functions can have wide-ranging consequences on the ability of the agency to deliver services. Because the functions tend to be looked upon as "central office," "front office," or "support" activities, the people providing the internal services are seldom informed about the importance of their work. Conversely, central office staff frequently fail to see that any of their work has a direct impact on the ability of the agency to deliver timely, accurate and valuable services.

A few internal service functions are:

- Payroll
- Purchase Orders
- Accounts payable
- Insurance Coverage
- Equipment Maintenance
- Supplies
- Custodial
- Equipment Purchasing

Chapter 7 on internal and external customers described the need for all workers to recognize that the next worker depends on them to do quality work. It also explained that a flow chart is a diagram of the path taken by materials and information as they flow through the system. Management must first concentrate on helping workers within the system see the value of better cooperation between functional areas and where their work fits in the total picture. Managers who insist on putting up control charts and plotting variations in the system first do a disservice to their people and doom their quality efforts to failure.

Creating a Critical Mass

Dr. Deming, in Point 14, urges that we put everyone to work for the transformation to a quality organization. He doesn't say to do it all at once. As pointed out in Chapter 1, massive up-front training can actually create more problems than gains.

The movement toward a quality organization will require small steps and little victories. The small steps are necessary so that the organization is not overwhelmed with new methods and to minimize the risk of failure. Everyday, management must demonstrate through action its commitment to the new philosophy, even if the implementation is only begun in small ways. Otherwise the small beginning efforts could be perceived as half-hearted and lacking real commitment.

An organization boldly taken forward into the world of quality management all at once is likely to flounder and may ultimately collapse. Too much is at stake to risk such a catastrophe. Workers' jobs and families are on the line here. The aim is to change to a management method that will improve the organization, allowing it to grow and flourish, not to kill it off through well-intentioned exuberance.

The transformation must begin at the top, Dr. Deming repeats to us. Then what? Create a position of Vice-President for Quality? Associate Director of Quality, in the case of a government agency or university? Dr. Deming urges people with such titles to keep their resume up to date and begin looking for work. Quality is not the responsibility of just one person or department. The responsibility for quality belongs to top management and the work of carrying it out rests with everyone.

Although one person cannot transform a company or an educational service center, it does not take many people to begin the process of change. It requires a critical mass of people, the right number and the right kind of people. Creation of a critical mass to begin the process of transformation within an organization poses an interesting question. Just exactly what is "critical mass" and how can it be measured? Public relations practitioners and other researchers suggest that adoption of new ideas only requires action on the part of 13 to 15 percent of a given population. About 2.3 percent of a given group are known as "innovators." They probably already know about a new idea and may already be putting it to use. They are open to new ideas, innovation and change in general. Another 13.5 percent or so are referred to as "early adopters" and are willing to try new ideas based on their own evaluation of their merits. Early adopters are frequently part of the informal power structure in an organization and are generally respected by their peers. The third group, known as the "early majority," comprise about 34 percent of a population and will usually follow the first two groups if they can see a personal advantage to adopting the new idea.[1] The key then is to find the 13 to 15 percent of the work force that is required to bring along the rest.

Note that we are looking for the right "kind" of people. This is not something that can be defined by a job title. An early adopter may be driving a van or dutifully making copies of videotapes. This is the beauty of beginning a quality organization. You may never be able to predict who will get involved first or from what functional area.

The critical mass for change in any given population is not a fixed figure, but varies from around 15 to 20 percent. Motorola Corporation, a major contributor to the field of quality management, suggests that the critical mass is the square root of the number of people in the organization.[2] In an organization of 16 people, change would require four of them, or 20 percent. In an organization of 170 people, it would require 13 people or seven percent. In a unit of 32 people it might take five people, or about 15 percent. Using either 15 percent or the square root of the number of people in the organization, it is obvious that beginning change does not require a total commitment up front. It doesn't even require half of the work force to begin the transformation. One of the keys to success is to keep an open mind and eliminate the preconceived notion that all supervisors and middle level people must come up to speed first. Some of them might be your biggest roadblocks.

Many technology centers are part of a larger organization such as a university, college, school district or intermediate unit with many departments and 100 employees or more. Others are stand-alone units with a limited mission, such as a regional video/film center with ten employees. At the very least, everyone in the organization who could be called an early adopter should be involved up front with the move to a quality organization. Then we can begin finding middle-level and supervisor-level people who are likely to help the process along. This is the time to plan for success. At first, if people don't express an interest or become outright stumbling blocks, find ways to go around them. In due time, they will come around or ultimately they will have no choice but to become part of the change.

In the hunt for appropriate "middle level" managers don't confuse job titles with functions. In very small centers there may be hourly employees who "manage" a distinct function within the agency. In the very smallest units, even if they are departments within a larger organization, the critical mass may be one person, if it is the right person.

Once your critical mass has been identified, they will become key players in the reorganization effort. Make a point of providing training for these people. Invite them to participate in flow charting sessions and become team leaders. Everyone in the organization, for example, may be invited to view one of the Deming Library videotapes, but for the critical mass, attendance is a requirement. If they are the right people, you couldn't keep them away.

Reorganization?

It is not necessary to change the organization chart for the technology center. It's been done before. Half the staff has probably lived through two or three reorganizations and they know that none of them improved the level of service, made the place more productive or removed barriers to worker satisfaction. There were just as many mistakes after the reorganization as before. Unless your chain of command and organizational structure is so totally bloated it impairs communication, there is not much to gain by the effort involved with reorganization. It may even cause resentment and foster resistance if previous reorganizations were touted as methods to make the place run better.

If you follow the method of flowcharting processes without regard to departmental boundaries, natural restructuring patterns may emerge that will allow reassignment of supervisors to cross functional areas instead of departments. Just be sure to inform everyone of any staff reassignments that are made and the reasons behind the change. Nothing brings fear back into the workplace faster than letting employees find out Monday morning that they have a new supervisor or they have just been transferred to another department.

Cross functional cooperation can allow personnel to feel comfortable with exploring new organizational patterns that might allow the organization to better serve the needs of the user. The assets of one large regional center included a professional library, video/film center, print shop, software and video duplication, video production, book circulation, equipment repair, a computer center and a computer demonstration lab. Each department had its own supervisor but few had understood what the other departments had to offer. The center ran a fleet of five delivery vans to service the schools in its region which covered about 4,500 square miles. Analysis of the organization chart showed that no one had responsibility for the delivery system. It was a true cross functional activity. It delivered videotapes, books, print jobs, professional materials, and equipment to be repaired. Each department had a stake in making sure the delivery system ran. Eventually the agency formed a model to restructure the responsibilities of professional staff. The head of the professional library became a broad-based resource person, consulting with teachers on their total needs and setting up the required resources and services available from many departments.

Another became the coordinator of services that used up consumable supplies like printing paper, blank media and cassettes. Another found more time to do materials previewing and selection by turning over the logistics of material scheduling and delivery to another supervisor. It didn't happen without problems and it didn't happen overnight. It was the result of honest effort to look at the system of service and devise new structures that would break down old barriers and generate better productivity.

Avoid the Big Bang

There is little value in turning the beginning of the quality transformation into a circus. There is no need for press releases, kick-off banquets, ribbon-cuttings, project announcements or opening day conferences. There is no profit to publishing a grand design or detailed master plan. Hanging banners and declaring tomorrow quality improvement day won't do it either. These things have all been done before, for events of far less significance. The transformation takes time and goes slowly. It grows and develops as the organization matures into what Peter Senge, author of *The Fifth Discipline* calls the learning organization.

Any planned event that calls attention to the new direction of the organization will be counter-productive. Employee attention will be focused on the short-term and tangible aspects of the event. Americans are already very good at seeing the surface and the short term. At one point in the Clint Eastwood movie *Line of Fire* the villain, while posing as a businessman, makes the observation, "Americans look at the next quarter, the Japanese look at the next century." In spite of the source, the words are true and worth pondering on once in a while.

It is too easy for managers to mouth the words quality, transformation, continuous improvement, cooperation and keep the customer first. Saying it doesn't make it so. And saying it can hurt the forward momentum of the move toward quality. The words can easily become red flag words to a jaded and resistant staff. Any valuable concept can be reduced to fad status by overexposure and the failure to demonstrate a sustained commitment. Point 1 is "constancy of purpose." Always remember that quality management is not a program, a three-year project or a goal. It is a philosophy that must be continuously lived.

The best way to begin working toward a quality organization is to just do it. A participant at a Deming Four-Day Seminar referred to it as "covert quality." Eventually someone will notice the improvements. When they start to ask questions, they are ready to listen.

Cooperation

It is not enough to tell people that things will run better if everyone cooperates. Management must create opportunities and the environment in which cooperation can happen. This draws on Point 9, "break down barriers," and Point 8, "drive out fear."

Internal communication must be a high priority for early examination in any quality improvement effort. Improved communication between departments and between individual staff can yield major pay offs. Even in a small office, people separated by only a few feet may have no idea of the complexities or dimension of another person's work. Workers can begin by learning more about their own internal suppliers and internal customers. They can also learn more about the whole system by seeing what other departments do and how other functions work that may be outside of their process loop.

Informal tours, demonstrations and visits to other departments are good ways to get people to know more about the organization system as a whole. More formal methods might include swapping people between departments for a day or two, or allowing staff from one area to sit in on the planning meeting of another. Employees need to feel the importance of their own job. The culture of a quality organization does not see one job as "better" than another, only different. All are important to achieving the aim of the organization.

Why Quality Circles Failed in the United States

As pointed out elsewhere, managers new to the quality transformation frequently become enamored by the so called "tools of quality." Things like control charts and cause and effect diagrams are used far too early in the quality effort and draw energy away from the important ground work of building cooperation and teamwork. Charts and graphs can be seen, cooperation can be felt, but these are hard to point out to a visitor. Managers often fall back on charts and graphs thinking that they provide tangible evidence of the commitment to quality. In reality they are only props that give the illusion that something is going on.

Quality circles provide a similar tangible way to demonstrate that management "really means business" about this "quality thing." In the late 1970s a number of American engineers and industrialists visited Japan to study their production methods in hope of finding the secret and bringing it home. In the course of their observation they discovered little bands of hourly workers diligently studying charts and working together to come up with better ways to complete a task. These groups are called quality control circles. They work very well in Japan where it is estimated that there are over 170,000 QC circles registered with the Japanese Union of Scientists and Engineers and twice that number operating and not registered. Over three million Japanese workers are involved with QC circle activities.[3] Even waitresses in restaurants have formed quality circles to improve service.

The American visitors gleefully returned to their factories with this new idea and set about creating all manner of quality circles. The author is familiar with at least one school that experimented with QC circles as early as 1980. Americans are adept at seeing the surface but less so at seeing what is below. Only the physical aspects of quality circles were brought back to the United States. Their size, structure and organizational makeup were replicated. But the underlying philosophy, the "why," the theory upon which the QC circle concept is built was not brought back as well. The well-meaning visitors brought back a shell with nothing inside. Even Dr. Deming cast a jaundiced eye on the use of quality circles too early in the transformation. In 1984 he was quoted as saying, "This country is still ten years away from making use of quality circles."[4] The poor implementation and misapplication of the concept probably set back the quality movement in this country by ten years. His statement is still valid.

The fact is that far too much has been made of the contribution of QC circles to Japan's quality gains. It is estimated that QC circles account for ten to 30 percent of the quality control activities in Japanese companies but are not the prime of source of quality improvement.[5]

United States quality control circles in the early '80s quickly degenerated into a mechanism for management to implement its own changes. They became part of "quality of work life" and "self management" programs—programs that focused energy on making people feel good or on issues such as break time and discipline. The school mentioned above decided that the first QC circle should address the problem of assigned parking spaces. The chief problem with self-management and quality-of-work-life programs is that neither of them really deals with improvement of the process of production and service. The idea behind quality of work life was that if employees felt better about themselves and the company, they would do a better job and the company would be more profitable. By this point in the book it should be apparent to the reader that a room full of deliriously happy employees can't make up for dim lighting, defective materials, poorly designed work areas, faulty maintenance and archaic production design. Workers only have so much time and energy to invest in their work. Help them put it into improving the system of production and service. It will give them far more pride and satisfaction than new furniture in the smoking lounge.

Very few companies in the United States have sustained their QC circles over the years. Because it had such a dismal beginning in the United States and has such a bad name, the term is rarely used by quality-oriented managers. Work teams or quality teams or quality groups are the terms most often to be seen or heard today. The idea of building teams out of employees has become a booming industry in the last several years forming a sub-culture of the quality management movement. Technology directors interested in deeper study on the benefits of team building are urged to get *The Team Handbook,* published by Joiner Associates, Madison, Wisconsin.

Kaizen

The foundation for quality circles that was not brought back to America in the late '70s is a Japanese concept called *kaizen* (ky' zen). It means "ongoing improvement involving everyone."[6] Explaining the Eastern concept of *kaizen* to a Western manager is not easy. It has to do with how Western culture looks at the world. The Japanese look at things through two lenses. One shows things as a process. The other shows things holistically. The Japanese manager sees an organization as a whole process.

The Western manager also uses two lenses. One looks for results. The other looks at things analytically.[7]

Let's try to put this into the context of a multi-district regional media center that circulates video resources. The traditional media director will look at circulation (results). The director who understands *kaizen* looks at the process by which the circulation takes place. She will look at all the factors that influence utilization patterns which build circulation (a holistic view). The traditional manager focuses on teacher-demand for service to try and build circulation. The consideration of a single factor, teacher-demand, in isolation is an example of the analytical approach.

The difference between the analytical view and the holistic view affects every aspect of American management. The corporate objective of an American corporation answers several questions. What market share should we have? What shall our earnings be? How should we expand? To a technology service center the analogous outlook is: How much circulation can we get? How big can our budget be? What new technology can we install?

To a Japanese corporation the corporate objectives ask: What kind of relationship shall we have with our customers, with our suppliers, with the public? These are good questions to have answered in the vision statement of an educational technology center as well.

The inability of th American style of management to see the whole is also reflected in the difference between what is desirable and what is acceptable. Japanese companies strive for what is desirable. There is a central target value of performance that an organization always strives to meet. American management works on what is acceptable, generally through the use of specifications plus or minus $\times$ percent. Anything between the two numbers will do. The concept translates itself into the work force as well.

The difference between a desirable worker and an acceptable worker is one of holistic thinking. The desirable worker comes from knowing what the aim of the organization is, what the philosophy is and from maintaining constancy of purpose. Everyone knows their job is to work toward the aim of the system and toward continuous improvement.

The acceptable worker comes from a regimen of detailed job descriptions, performance criteria and annual reviews. The worker will meet minimum specifications. This also produces the "not my job" attitude. Under analytical management, if the worker is not functioning properly the worker is replaced. In holistic management, if the worker is not functioning properly the system is improved so that the worker can perform better.[8]

Americans love innovation. We tend to look for the big breakthrough that will revolutionize how something is done. We are a nation of inventors. Transistors, television, fax machines, telegraph, telephone, electric lights, airplanes, integrated circuits, microwave ovens, the computer, all were first pioneered in the United States. But to get any of these breakthroughs to the point they are today has required continuous revision, refinement and improvement. Japanese corporations are masters at taking technology developed elsewhere and refining it into products that are the envy of the world.

The same thing could be done in the United States. And the same can be done by an educational technology service center. But it requires looking at things through a different set of lenses and then knowing how to take action toward improvement.

Change and Improvement

Accepting the notion that continuous improvement is possible may prove to be a daunting proposition. Improvement means change. Change is a very scary thing. Many managers and corporations find that dealing with change is uncomfortable and a threat to doing business. A survey conducted by the Gallup Organization of 400 business executives showed that 53 percent thought they should be able to anticipate and take action to meet change, yet 56 percent said that they did not have a mechanism in place to deal with the changes they faced. [9]

Change is a fact of life. It is a constant. And in all likelihood the pace of change will only accelerate over time. So our challenge then as managers is to learn how to manage change. Consider the words "change" and "improvement" for a moment. Change can be either positive or negative. Improvement, by definition, can only be positive. The choice of words used when teaching workers or convincing upper management about the value of quality is important. Telling staff that we are going to "change the way things are done" raises a specter of fear and anxiety of the unknown. But explain that we are going to "improve the way things are done" and there can be only one meaning. A certain amount of anxiety may persist because staff will figure out that an improvement will require a change, but the intent, the *aim* is clear from the start.

The need for continual improvement to the system of production and service cannot be over-emphasized. As discussed in Chapter 6, systems are subject to the same laws of nature as any other form of energy. A system will being to decay as soon as it is in place. It requires constant maintenance and effort to keep operating at the same level as the day it started. But since the rest of the world is also moving forward, improvements must be made just to stay even. Many organizations look at all the money they have spent and the time they have invested in improvements and can't understand why they are no better off than five years before.

They fail to see that other systems are moving forward relative to theirs. To achieve real gains and stay ahead of emerging user expectations require continuous improvement of the component processes within the system.

Measure of Improvement

As we struggle to break free from the constraints of Western management, the desire to measure achievement and set numerical goals will die a slow, painful death. Dr. Deming's Point 11 is clear, "eliminate numerical quotas, goals and management by objective."

In quality management and under the concept of *kaizen* in particular we must learn to differentiate between two sets of measurement criteria. One is measurement of productivity and the other is measurement of improvement. Productivity is a measurement of results, referred to as R-criteria. In our educational technology center R-criteria may be circulation, printing impressions, availability rates, numbers of VCR repairs completed or number of teleconferences arranged. R-criteria management relies on performance and results as measurements of productivity. If it is the only yardstick used then the only information it produces is whether a goal has been reached or not.

Measurements of process improvement are referred to as P-criteria.[10] P-criteria measure the efforts made to improve the system of production and service. Teamwork, process analysis, skill development, time management, suggestions, communication and management support are all aspects of P-criteria. The improvement of the process is the only way to set off the Deming chain reaction and achieve lasting improvement.

Deming Chain Reaction in an Educational Technology Center

In quality management, goals are expressed as the general aims for improving the system of production and service. There are never numerical targets or percentages of improvement attached to them. Leadership in a technology center may establish goals for quality improvement to:

- Shorten order cycle time

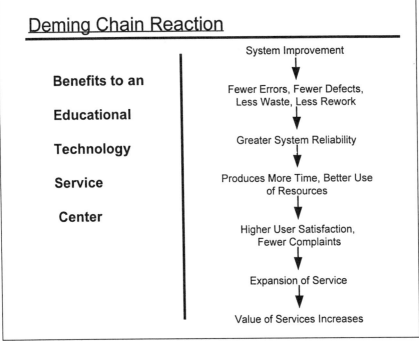

Figure 10-1.

- Raise title availability
- Reduce machine down time
- Improve title search services
- Eliminate shipment errors
- Expand access to on-line data
- Reduce computer parts inventory
- Reduce purchase order errors
- Improve response time to user requests for help
- Reduce rework in equipment repair.

Each goal requires a team effort to redesign the system and eliminate the flaws in the processes that allow the errors and missed opportunities to occur. How do we know if the improvement has created a gain in quality? Documenting results of the system both before and after the improvement was implemented makes it clear. Sections in Chapters 1 and 12 describe the use of control charts as a method of observing what the system is producing. The results recorded after an improvement is put into place become a measurement of how well management was able to improve the system.

Management is prediction, according to Dr. Deming. Management predicts that a specific change in a process will result in an improvement of the output of the system as a whole. Quality management will not state a goal in numerical terms because there is no reasonable way to predict how much measurable improvement will result from the change. It could be two percent, 38 percent, or 100 percent. Systems are matrices of complex interactions. We know this from our study of systems through profound knowledge. A single change in the process also changes the dynamics of the interactions in the system, sometimes in unknowable ways.

Although we may have run the proposed change through the Plan-Do-Study-Act-cycle (covered in detail in Chapter 12) and done everything possible to ensure that the change will actually add value to the system of production and service, it could still fail to create improvement. If a numerical goal is set, an R-criterion, it is likely that whatever numerical gain is made will not match the numerical target. If it is lower, the improvement will be perceived as somehow flawed or not worth the time it took to make it. If it is greater than the numerical target, then you can be accused of being too conservative in your estimates. In either case, attention has once again been shifted from the process to the numerical output. To expect a single improvement in the flow of a system to create measurable gains in quality is a great leap of faith. For continuous improvement to work, numerical goals, quotas and MBOs must be eliminated so everyone's energy can go into the process.

The warning of Dr. Wheeler and Dr. Chambers cited earlier merits repeating here.

> "It is futile to try and set a goal on an unstable process—one cannot know what it will do. Likewise it is futile to set a goal for a stable process—it is already doing all that it can do."[11]

Some of the value in the *kaizen* process is unknown and unknowable. The worker or team of workers who have discovered and implemented an improvement to productivity and quality, however small, can take great pride in their accomplishment. Their pride can easily be diminished if the incremental improvement does not come close to a previously stated and arbitrary goal. The multiplier effect within the organization of increased worker pride is unknowable but important to seize and develop.

Kaizen is the result of small, continuous improvements in the process of production and service. How long will it take for real improvements to become evident in the performance of the system? According to Dr. Deming and Kaoru Ishikawa, Japan's foremost quality authority and originator of the Cause and Effect Chart, it will take three to five years.[12] Breakthrough advancements in the system of production and service would be nice but they are rare. A breakthrough like the transistor is a product innovation. But for the daily routine of servicing customers, continuous improvement is required, sometimes in surprisingly small increments.

Recently the shop floor employees at Toyota's Tsutsumi Lexus plant built and installed a machine that places a print out on the windshield describing the options to be installed in the vehicle. A job previously done by hand. The machine saves four seconds of assembly time per car. But multiplied by 100,000 cars, it saves 111 hours.[13] Enough time to build 13 cars.

Closer to home, one regional media center eliminated a task in the video/film inspection process that took about 45 seconds to do. In the first year it saved 500 hours or about $2,500. Over the next seven years, adjusting for raises, it saved $20,353 by no longer doing something that added no value to the process. Moreover, it *created* 500 hours each year for staff to do something else which does add value. Admittedly this is an example of "picking the lowest fruit." That is, improvement by eliminating obvious inefficiencies and simple improvements. But improvement doesn't stop with eliminating parts of the process that have no value. Improving the process itself holds the bigger pay backs. In the last six months of 1992, Toyota's efforts to reduce complexity, improve productivity and narrow variation helped cut expenses by $500 million, without laying off any full-time employees.[14]

Four Levels of Kaizen

Kaizen gives us a four-level approach to finding system improvements. The first centers on the worker. Line workers are helped and encouraged to find methods that will make their jobs more productive, efficient and safer.

The second level centers on equipment improvements. It might include changing the layout of the work area, installing new light, or upgrading equipment.

The third level is to improve processes and procedures required to provide service or produce a product. These improvements might also include training or retraining and a review of policies that may restrict improvement.

The fourth level is a hybrid combination of the first three levels. It is only after the advances of all these levels have been maximized that Japanese management turns to innovations that will improve the system.[15]

Contrary to popular belief, Japanese management is not enamored of new technology and computers to build a competitive advantage. At the joint Chevrolet/Toyota assembly plant in Fremont, California, *kaizen* principals are so highly integrated into the plant that the term even shows up in the union contract with the United Auto Workers.[16] The Japanese managers of the plant have relied on the first three levels noted above to create a plant that produces quality at the same level as Japanese assembly lines. The jobs that require judgment and decisions to be made are not candidates for automation. Technological innovation is applied when necessary to improve performance but the human capacity for assessment and decision making is valued.[17]

Technology Access: The Ultimate Product

The overriding product of any media and technology service center is equitable access to technology. The design of the process that allows users to access various media and technology resources is the key to how well the system performs. Most educational technology centers grew gradually over the years into their present configuration. As a result the systems used to serve client needs were never really designed, but developed out of convenience or necessity. University film centers of 30 years ago became media and technology centers. Film gave way to video and video-disc. They took on computer labs, photography centers, down link operations, distance learning and video production complexes. Circulation of materials expanded into production of media for individual professors and instructional design support. The same could be said of large city film libraries and regional media centers. Satellite down links, cable access program origination, video and audio-tape duplication, VCR and computer repair all became the responsibility of the media and technology center. Some are responsible for operation of public television or radio stations as well.

But look inside the system of production and service required to offer users access to these technologies. You will generally find the same system of request forms, paperwork and scheduling that was used 20 years ago to borrow a film or a projector. Look further into the organization of the center itself and little is different. The same pyramid organization chart is there. Department supervisors deal with very narrow aspects of service, sometimes competing with other departments within the media center for resources and funding. And the hourly staff follow the routine of their department, not knowing or caring if what they do affects someone else down the line, as long as they don't get blamed if something goes wrong.

Leadership of a university center can be very proud of the new 250 station computer lab, campus-wide access to CD-ROM driven data-bases and on-line services. A regional center can promote the availability of complex videodisc packages to their schools. And a district technology repair center may have the latest in hard-drive diagnostic equipment. None of these will have any impact on the quality of education if users have to wrestle with archaic ordering methods, deal with indifferent workers and continually make backup lesson plans because the reliability of the system is poor.

Why Bother with an 800 Number?

There is a university media center in the Midwest that is a major source for rentals of non-theatrical and educational videotapes nationally. It also produces and sponsors a number of productions that are sold to the educational video market. For this reason the university media center has a toll-free 800 number. The director of a regional media center (RMC) used the 800 number to check on the price and availability of a title. After about six rings a tired voice answered.

University Media Center: Hello.

Regional Media Center: Is this the_____university media center?

UMC: Yes.

RMC: I need some information about one of your titles. I wanted to know if it was still available for purchase and the cost.

UMC: You'll have to call back when someone is here.

RMC: No one is there?

UMC: No, they're all at lunch.

RMC: Can you take a message to have someone return my call?

UMC: Well, there's no one here to take messages.

RMC: Can *you* take a message?

UMC: No, you'll have to call back later.

RMC: Why can't you leave a message that I called?

UMC: I don't take messages. Call when they're back from lunch.

RMC: Do they usually all go to lunch at the same time?

UMC: Yes.

RMC: What do you do for the media center?

UMC: Well, I don't take messages and I gotta get off. Bye.

This was someone who, having never been trained, was doing his best.

Why bother going to the expense of installing an 800 number and highlighting it in the catalog if the line won't be covered at lunch time? Furthermore, if everyone was at lunch, who was on the phone? The RMC director actually called back later and got someone who knew the title in question but not the price. She was very nice and said she would call back just as soon as possible with an answer. That was February of 1993.

User accessibility is a product. It deserves the same amount of planning and design as the production of a videotape or the creation of a computer program. The question is, How do we make it easier for people to use the resources we have for them?

The process of flow charting and tracking user inputs will show the opportunities and limitations of the system as it exists right now. Testing ideas that will improve user access will also reveal good ideas that, if they were implemented, would swamp the system and result in heavy losses for both client and center. See Chapter 12 for a discussion on broadening user access.

What Does the Technology User Want?

This is a universal question with only unique answers. Each user and each technology center will come up with a different set of answers. If we assume that access to technology is the key product, and that the system of access is appropriately designed, the next question is, Do we have what they want? Answering this requires looking at the resources provided by educational technology services from two different perspectives: filling a need and providing a tool.

The two perspectives are more philosophical than anything else. Which perspective you take will color how you will design and manage your system of service.

Technology centers that see educational technology services as providing a tool will become hardware/technology-oriented. Centers that see themselves as providing solutions are customer/systems-oriented.

The solutions-oriented center looks at what the user is trying to accomplish in the classroom. It listens to the system needs of the client and tries to provide resources that will improve the quality of communication and interaction between teacher and student.

The teacher says, "I'm trying to explain the difference between igneous and sedimentary rocks to my 4th graders."

The customer/systems center responds with a menu of possible resources to meet the need. "We have three programs on the topic at your grade level on videotape, one of which is closed captioned. We also have two packages on rock formations which include demonstrations, graphics and experiments that are interactive videodiscs with both Linkway and Hypercard software depending on what your building has. We have a 'rock box' with samples of each type of rock, and a simulation package that shows the nature of different rock formation methods over time and the erosion effects as well, on CD-ROM."

The teacher has choices and there is now a basis for sending the teacher back to class armed with the appropriate materials to solve the teaching challenge at hand.

The technology center with a hardware/technology perspective sees solutions in terms of the delivery platform. To the same teacher the answer might be, "Well, you can bring the class down to the computer lab and we'll set up some simulation programs, or we have a couple of videotapes about rocks, or we can look for something from the satellite down-link, or we can check out the multi-media PC to you. And by the way, we don't have anything that is Hypercard-based because we standardized on IBM-compatible software only."

How the center views itself is revealed in the way a simple question is answered.

"What does your center do?"

If the answer is, "We supply videotapes and computer programs to our schools," it is a hardware/technology-oriented center.

If the answer is, "We help teachers solve communications problems in the classroom," then the center is customer/systems-oriented.

Can a hardware/technology-oriented center offer quality service? Of course it can. It can be a very fine, effective operation. It also can be highly efficient and loaded with quality resources that are totally inappropriate for the user base. Such a center could go so much farther in building a satisfied client base if it began looking outward at the system of instruction it supports instead of inward at the tools in the box.

Centers that are managed by leaders who are customer/system-oriented find it easier to stay ahead of user demand. Some centers will always play catch-up. They introduced videotapes five years after everyone else in their state. They waited for the "shake out" on videodisc before buying their first package. They have no opinion on CD-ROM, have never examined titles for CD-I and don't even want to think about Asymmetrical Digital Subscriber Lines and delivering video-on-demand.

True enough, there is an old saying that, "He who does something second, can do it right." But this assumes that we can really learn from the start-up mistakes of others. Your start-up mistakes and problems may be entirely different. Your center is unique. Dr. Deming, cites the search for examples in his list of obstacles to the transformation. "It is a hazard to copy," he warns.[18] Visiting another educational technology center that has a fine reputation for being "best in class" provides nothing for the improvement of your own center. The success of integrating videodisc technology into the instructional options of one school system might be due entirely to luck and coincidence. The failure of a well-planned project could be attributed to the same cause. There is no evidence at all to assume that what worked to expand and improve quality of service in one technology center will work in another. It is not important how an educational technology agency functions. It is important to know *why* it functions the way it does. What underlying theory and philosophy guides its operations? On what assumptions does it make decisions and develop policy? On what theory will it base the efforts to improve?

The question of how to design a quality service rests squarely on the theory that will guide the management of the center. Study the theory and philosophy that guides management to understand why a successful media service operates the way it does.

Know Your User Base

If copying the example of another technology service center won't improve our center, and we are a unique agency, then what? The only recourse is to know the unique dynamics and demands of your user base. What is their predominant teaching style? What sort of students do they have? What is new on the market that might fill their needs and help them do their jobs better? And, *by what method* can our services improve the quality of education offered through our users?

Leadership must come from the educational technology service center. Few general educators are in the position of a center's management to see what is new or what is in development and likely to have applications in education within the next 36 months or so.

More than once, while acting as a consultant for district-level technology plans, the author has seen requests from teachers for a dozen computers and a network in their classrooms. Upon further investigation, including personal interviews and focus groups, the real classroom level requirements emerged. The teachers were trying to show an entire class the information presented on their 14-inch computer screen. They knew that since a network would allow many stations to see the same information, that would solve the visibility problem. But the appropriate solution was to use a liquid crystal display (LCD) panel on an overhead projector, a solution that would cost about ten percent of what had been suggested. In each case, the teachers on the planning committee had never heard of an LCD panel. And not knowing it was an option, it was never brought up. The user had to be led to the option that might prove useful.

The center that introduces new technologies and new approaches is also perceived as taking a leadership role. If the introduction is based on knowledge of user requirements, the merits of the technology relative to local need and the capacity of the system for assimilation of new approaches, then the transition is likely to be successful. But the "build it and they will come" approach no longer works. The installation of new technology for the sake of technology and for the prestige of ownership, is a tragic waste of scarce resources and human capital. With any change, or any installation of technology, the real question is, How will this improve the quality of education? If there is no hard answer to the question, then there is no reason for the investment. (See Appendix C for a discussion of the current push for an "Information Superhighway.")

Service Transcends All Products

Consumers' expectations for service are the same for any product and any organization. A company can live or die on the quality of its service. It is no different for an educational technology center. Being a government entity is no excuse for indifference to service. In fact, according to Dr. Deming, being a government agency carries a special obligation to use the resources it is given in the best, most productive manner to provide equitable access across the broadest base possible. [19]

The concept of efficiency as used in the business world has little meaning in government and educational agencies. Equity of service to the broadest base of clients possible becomes central to the design of any technology service. Any educational service support center could become highly efficient overnight. All it needs to do is focus on serving the 20 percent of the user base that accounts for 80 percent of the utilization. A regional video/film collection could become highly efficient by throwing out all the titles that do not circulate more that 15 times per year and only stocking very high demand resources. The specialized courses, the higher level science and language courses that are low incidence, but important users, will lose. [20]

In some companies customer service is a euphemism for "complaint department." The department doesn't really exist to service the customer. It is there to make excuses and minimize the cost of warranty to the company. It is too late. Service in a technology center can mean a lot of things. Everyone who has contact with a user needs to understand that they reflect the center. User attitudes toward the center will be formed by their contacts with center personnel on the phone and in person. A user inquiry, competently handled, may do more to boost confidence in the center than the content of the answer.

Some technology centers, regional, district and campus, assign staff to deliver equipment and materials to user sites. Delivery people may know many of your users by name and will be asked questions about the center or availability of some service. Drivers are important public relations people. If they don't know the answer to something, they need to be trained what to say: "I don't know, but I'll make sure someone calls you about that." Back at the van, they must then write down the question and the name of the person who asked it. At the center, they must make sure it gets into the right hands. Part of good organization is to have a structure for making things right. Even as the error rate goes down through improvement of the system, it is necessary to prevent user defections by ensuring that the opportunity to help correct an error leaves them delighted with the service. Chapter 8 has already treated the subject of warranty service in detail.

Staff Training

The ultimate delivery system of a quality/customer-oriented service is the people who work in it. One of the ways to reduce waste and rework is through uniformity within the processes of the system. People must know how to do their jobs and for what purpose their work is intended. This requires training for the job, Dr. Deming's Point 6.

Training is a management responsibility that cannot be abdicated. Large corporations have entire training departments collectively spending billions each year on job training. Keyboarding, sales techniques, equipment maintenance, new processes, business writing and math only scratch the surface of the classes handled by training departments. Most educational technology centers enjoy no such benefit of a separate training department. Yet the need for training is just as important. Unfortunately the typical pattern is to leave training of new employees to co-workers who must take time from their own work to try and show the job to the new hire.

The practice of worker teaching worker leads to heavy losses for any organization. New employees should be trained by a master of the job they are to take on.[21] The training should follow a prescribed progression and method. This ensures that employees get the same instruction and that the procedures they use are uniform from one worker to another in the same job.

For some jobs, training need not be long and involved, but it should be done by someone designated as a trainer and equipped for the unique requirements for training a new employee. The department head or supervisor may become the trainer, but only if he or she has a great deal of experience in the job to be trained for. An experienced co-worker may be an appropriate choice for a trainer. But only after being coached in the proper methods of teaching skills to a new person. The trainer should be relieved of additional duties during the actual training sessions. They should take place during a period of time specifically designated for training. If the supervisor must do the training, it should be during a prescribed time and for a prescribed duration. Not "if I get the time."

Many regional centers and university technology centers own in-house computer scheduling systems purchased from outside vendors. Most of these vendors provide training beyond the initial set up and installation. Some training may be offered for enhancements and upgrades. If new personnel are hired to operate the scheduling system it could be a good investment to arrange for formal training by the software supplier. It will probably be expensive and will appear as a cost item. But in the long term, current employees will not have to spend their time teaching a complex skill, the learning curve will be faster and the new employee will have learned proper methods from the masters of the system.

Most jobs require a skill and some sort of judgment. Training lays a foundation for beginning a skill and a base upon which to make sound judgments. Part of any employee training must include knowledge of who depends on the work that is to be done. It must also include knowledge of the mission of the agency and the requirements of the ultimate user of the technology center's services and products. Judgments on how to proceed with the job at hand can be better made with knowledge of how the work is to be used and who will use it.

Dr. Deming thinks that one can never know enough and that training should continue as long as there is something to be gained. He also points out that no amount of continued training to improve a skill, improperly learned at the outset, can improve performance.[22] A lesson all too painfully apparent to the author with regard to his typing skills.

Training resources for technology centers may appear in unexpected places. Within the resources held by a video/film center may be appropriate titles that can teach good telephone skills, how to get along with other employees, better office ergonomics or how to use specific kinds of computer applications. Videotapes on quality, like the Deming Video Library distributed by Films Incorporated, should be readily available for sessions that help explain the new emphasis of the organization.

A side benefit of building a library of videotapes for skill training and quality management is becoming a resource for the management of client schools or university department heads. Instead of serving only the needs of the curriculum and the classroom, your technology center can now respond to the growing and very real need for better training for employees in any office, including those of school and campus employees.

Some educational technology centers that are associated with larger intermediate units or universities may find seminars, workshops and courses that employees can attend to learn new skills. There are several nationally known training companies such as Padgett-Thompson and Key Productivity Centers, that conduct useful one-day skill-building seminars on a variety of topics at locations around the country. Generic business training sessions on handling multiple responsibilities, managing the office and time-management offered by these companies can boost employee skill levels, generate new interest in the job and bring back new ideas that can be shared with others.

Training is a cost. It shows up as a cost in the budget, but the long-range benefit of good, well-designed training, can never be fully known. Paradoxically, heavy losses from lack of training not only affect the performance of the center, but create losses that can be measured in low user-satisfaction, waste, errors, rework and continual fire-fighting. A technology center's investment in training will always pay off. Training improves the system by lowering costs.[23]

[1] Kindred, Leslie W., Don Bagin and Donald R. Gallagher. *The School and Community Relations,* 2nd edition. Englewood Cliffs: Prentice-Hall, 1976. Pg. 289. Fifth edition, published 1994 by Chestnut Hill Enterprises, Norwalk, CT, see page 296.

[2] Paton, Arthur E. "Creating World Class Quality: A Business And Academic Partnership." Workshop. New Orleans: AECT INFOCOMM, January 14, 1992.

[3] Imai, Masaaki. *KAIZEN: The Key To Japan's Competitive Success.* New York: McGraw Hill, 1986. Pg. 100.

[4] Walton, Mary. "Putting America Back To Work." *Philadelphia Inquirer Magazine,* March 11, 1984. Pg. 20.

[5] Imai., pg. 12.

[6] Ibid., pg. 3.

[7] Ibid., page 16. Also, Yoshida, Kosaku, *Made In Japan: 'Whole'-istically.* Videotape. And lecture, August 18, 1993, Chicago, "Deming Management Philosophy: Does It Work In the US as Well As Japan?"

[8] Yoshida, Ibid.

[9] Gilbreath, Robert D. "Needed: More Formal Structures to Manage Accelerating Rate of Change." *Total Quality,* November 1993. Pg. 7.

[10] Imai., pg. xxii & 39.

[11] Wheeler, Donald J., and David S. Chambers. *Understanding Statistical Process Control,* 2nd Ed. Knoxville, TN: SPC Press, 1992. Pg. 187.

[12] Imai, pg 106.

[13] Helm, Leslie. "Japanese Carmakers Are In Slump." *Los Angeles Times.* August 8, 1993.

[14] Ibid.

[15] Imai, pg. 168.

[16] Ibid.

[17] Reich, Robert B., *Education and The Next Economy.* Washington, DC: National Education Association, 1988. Pg. 16.

[18] Deming, W. Edwards, *Out of the Crisis.* Cambridge, MA: MIT Press, 1986. Pg. 127.

[19] Ibid., pg. 6.

[20] Ibid., pg. 199.

[21] Aguayo, Rafael. *Dr. Deming: The American Who Taught the Japanese About Quality.* New York: Simon and Schuster, 1990. Pg. 170.

[22] Walton, Mary. *The Deming Management Method.* New York: Perigee Books, 1986. Pg. 68.

[23] Aguayo, pg. 173.

Chapter 11

THE DEMING METHOD IN A GOVERNMENT AGENCY

THERE ARE NO END OF EXCUSES FOR NOT TRYING THE DEMING management method. One of the more common is, "We're a government agency, it will never work." Having said that, the prophesy will be self-fulfilling, and it probably won't work.

The fact is that many government agencies at federal, state and local levels have adopted the 14 Points and have begun the transformation into quality organizations. The United States Navy, Internal Revenue Service and Department of Health and Human Services are notable efforts at the federal level. The Defense Department has had a Deputy Under Secretary for Total Quality Management since 1990. President Clinton credits Dr. Deming's work as inspiring the movement to "reinvent" government.[1]

The United States Navy is an interesting case study. At first glance, it is difficult to think of a large, rigidly structured military organization as having customers or losing market share. With the fall of the Berlin Wall, the breakup of the Soviet Union and the emergence of numerous unstable situations around the world, the mission of the Navy is changing as it operates in a new political environment. The Navy has answered the rapid changes in the world order and fiscal realities with a major restructuring process that applies the principals of Dr. Deming to everything from material procurement to inter-service communications.[2] The Naval Aviation Depot at Cherry Point, North Carolina is an early and well-documented effort to bring quality principles to the Navy and to government service.[3]

In 1986 the base commander at Cherry Point, Marine Colonel Jerald B. Gartman, took over an aviation repair and refurbishing facility with 3,200 civil service employees, represented by seven unions and a $100 million payroll. The six Naval Aviation Depots were under the gun from the Navy Department to control run-away cost problems. Between 1981 and 1984 they had lost over $300 million. Gartman, a combat-decorated, results-driven Marine was also an ardent disciple of Dr. Deming. In 1988, two years after he took over, the facility had saved the Navy over $39 million through quality improvements. But Gartman understood the problem of only recording cost savings. "Talk about cost savings and the bean counters will cut your budget. The number of teams means nothing. It is a measure not of results but of activity. Talk about results and you were back in the money again."[4]

Results at Cherry Point came hard. Gartman attacked the problem of failure to communicate with the aviation units that had their aircraft worked on at his facility. The repaired and refurbished plane might have met specifications but it frequently didn't please the customer. Inspection at the end of the line typically revealed eight or ten things wrong, or "discrepancies." After a test flight another two or three items might be added to the discrepancy list. And after a few weeks the customer, the squadron, would return the plane with another two to six things wrong. By 1990, their refurbished aircraft averaged just one discrepancy for every two planes.

But Gartman's improvement teams went beyond the mechanical aspects of rebuilding an aircraft. They took Deming's work seriously and began to look at what would "delight" their customers. They began repainting cockpits. Repainting a cockpit is a squadron level job, so if an aircraft came in with worn cockpit paint, it would be sent back to the unit that way. Even if a million dollars worth of work had been done to the internals of the aircraft, the cockpit would still be shabby. The decision to start painting cockpits arose from two observations. One came from a study team that found the cost to rehabilitate the cockpit was very small compared to other work that was being done. The other was the Deming notion of pride in workmanship. "Our workers wanted to see a nice cockpit in there just as bad as our customers wanted to see a nice cockpit,"[5] explains Gartman.

They didn't have to paint the cockpit. It wasn't required by the contract, but they did it anyway. The standard, once removed, allowed people to move ahead and take the initiative to do more. Pride in a job well done had returned to the work force. Not through slogans and quotas. But with training, guidance, work and a sound set of guiding principals. Myron Tribus puts pride into the context of company vision. Imagine you have told your employees, " 'We're not in the business of making the best cars in the world, we're in the business of making money,' there is no way you can get their hearts and minds to work on it."[6]

There is hope for large bureaucratic, government structures to begin transformation. Another example comes from the Air Force. Ardel Nelson, a civilian personnel manager in the Air Force supply center at McClellan Air Force Base began the long journey in the early 1980s. His agency was responsible for the movement of a $5 billion dollar inventory of over 3,000 replacement and supply parts, handled by over 2,000 civil service employees. The structure of the civil service system was such that no incentive existed for managers to find ways to improve productivity. Pay scales for managers were tied into how many people they supervised. If a unit developed a way to do the same job with fewer people, the manager took a pay cut. Energy was put into finding ways to increase the number of people in a department instead of becoming more productive.

There was no way to institute cross-training of personnel either. The person who had to figure out the best way to ship an item was not allowed to calculate the rates for shipment even if they knew how—it was a different job description. There were fine distinctions between a woodworker, a wood-crafter and a carpenter. Only the enactment of the 1978 Civil Service Reform Act provided some maneuvering room in the form of allowing "demonstration projects." Nelson created a restructured personnel system and a new management system that used quality circles or process improvement teams, and the management principles of Dr. Deming. He and his managers began attending Deming's four-day seminars.

But Nelson ran into opposition from the Office of Personnel Management (OPM), the federal-level agency that had to approve the demonstration project. The implications of the project's potential success were clear. According to Nelson, OPM could lose 75 percent of its reason for being.

Permission was secured in 1987 only after a congressman got involved and the union announced its support for the plan. At the end of two years, the supply center returned $4.1 million in savings to the Air Force. And since the same Civil Service Reform Act said the cost savings could be divided between the agency and the employees, each worker received a $502 share of the savings. By 1990 the agency had 134 process improvement teams in place. Nelson is still on the long journey, but his story is evidence that even the most cumbersome bureaucracy can be transformed.[7]

What does our client really want? What will make the user of our services delighted and ready to tell others? OK, the equipment worked, it got to them on time, they got the right piece of hardware; what else could we have done?

City Government

Quality management has begun to take a slow foothold in city government as well. Entire cities have changed the way they do business and serve the public. Cities like Austin, Madison and Phoenix are now several years down the road toward quality improvement.

In Austin, Texas the city owns both the local water and electric services. In July of 1989 the municipal services office received over 38,000 phone calls. Seventy percent of them got busy signals and most calls were put on hold for an average of five and a half minutes. By 1992 the average hold time was five *seconds*. On any given day in 1989 the Austin city maintenance garage had 44 trucks on hand waiting for repair. By 1992 the average was cut to 20.[8]

The Tri-Cities area of Tennessee, including the cities of Bristol, Kingsport and Johnson City, has a regional quality education and support group that began holding seminars and quality roundtables in 1986. The community-based organization reaches into hospitals, airports, government agencies and local industries. In the first nine months, sixteen process improvement teams from a variety of businesses and agencies reported savings of $3.2 million. Success stories ranged from government bathroom cleaners solving the problem of missing toilet paper to the creation of new jobs as industries reduced scrap and increased quality.[9]

In Phoenix city departments have undergone quality audits and customer satisfaction is a critical element to future planning. Some cities have created programs for their taxi drivers, not only to school them in treating valued visitors right but also on how to find their way around the city and provide accurate information.

Mayor F. Joseph Sensenbrenner began Madison, Wisconsin's quality movement in 1983. Madison had 2,300 employees and 14 different unions within a civil service system. By starting small and being persistent, a quality culture took hold. Among other things, quality processes saved hundreds of thousands of dollars for construction of new dumping areas by changing the arrival time of trash trucks at the city trash facility. The city garage took care of 765 vehicles—everything from police cars to road graders. In 1983 the average turnaround time for repair of city vehicles was nine days. The first quality improvement team, composed of union mechanics, didn't have to do much research to explain the problem.

Most of the turnaround time was because mechanics were waiting for parts. The problem was now a management problem. The mayor took the problem to the parts manager and was informed that the city had 440 different makes, models and years of vehicles. Why was there such a variety of equipment? The parts manager explained that central purchasing would only buy vehicles with the lowest price tag. The head of the purchasing department said that he had heard the same complaint from all over the city. But his hands were tied because the comptroller's office wouldn't let him do anything except buy at the lowest price.

The mayor moved on to the comptroller who admitted that standardizing on certain makes and models of equipment would simplify the parts-ordering problem but that it would be impossible to change the policy because the city attorney wouldn't let him. Mayor Sensenbrenner paid a visit to the city attorney.

"Of course you can do that," the attorney explained. "All you need to do is write the specifications so they include warranty, ease of maintenance, availability of parts and resale value. In fact, I assumed you were doing it all along."[10]

The mayor discovered that the mechanics' problem was upstream in the system, not in the garage. The problem was a flawed system, he says, not flawed workers.

Sound familiar? Barriers between departments, lack of communication, buying on price tag alone, failure to consider total cost, lack of standardization are all symptoms of a poorly designed system. Sensenbrenner has no doubt that such problems exist in most government structures across the country. Even if the problems are known to exist, nothing can be done about them until an organizational mechanism is put into place to trace cause and improve the system. Ultimately, in Madison a 24-step purchasing process was cut to three and turnaround time was reduced from nine days to three. A preventive maintenance program, developed by the workers, created $700,000 in annual repair savings as well.[11] By the time Sensenbrenner left office in 1989, nearly every city service was involved in Deming-oriented quality improvement activities.

What Is at Stake?

Why should government bother with quality management? What is going on here? All of these cities have unions. Many are both union and civil service shops. Why is quality management being made an issue and why is it working?

"Government credibility is at stake," explains Austin City Manager, Dr. Cammile Barnett. "People have become cynical about government. We have forgotten why we are here. We have become regulators and bureaucrats."[12]

Most educational technology centers are part of some larger governmental entity. Regional media centers are connected to state government. Large district media departments are connected to a board of education. State university and community college technology centers are connected to county and state government. Even technology centers in private colleges at times take on the characteristics of a quasi-government agency.

Long gone are the days when a department or government agency can continue to exist simply because it is supported by state law or prescribed by code. With a stroke of a pen, the enactment of "sunset" legislation or the change of superintendent, whole media departments can be eliminated. Media and technology centers that fail to demonstrate their ability to satisfy user needs and provide users with instructional assets that they will brag about using are at risk. How do you make a technology center indispensable?

Indifferent and surly workers, poor materials and unpredictable service clearly will not do it. Nor will installing brand new computers, state-of-the-art video distribution systems, fiber optic interconnects, compressed video, CD-ROM drive data bases, video dial tone, public access catalog terminals, teleconference rooms, Level III videodisc systems, satellite down-links or virtual reality simulators.

Being part of a bigger government agency is no excuse for not becoming a quality organization. Educational technology managers will need to learn how to recognize the limits of their system and identify the boundaries imposed by the containing system. The limits may be civil service rules, misguided policy, unenlightened upper management, poor building maintenance or a variety of factors combined.

Even if the containing system: the university, school or district, appears to be hopelessly doomed to pursuing the old way of doing things, take heart from the stories above. The department head for media and technology must have to courage to change and the patience to live the new philosophy. Your center can become an example to the containing system. Once a quality transformation begins to take hold, the results will become noticeable outside the limits of your system. In Madison, non-quantifiable improvements included a reduction of grievances, improved staff morale, better planning, improved inter-agency cooperation and faster turnaround times.[13]

"A government agency should deliver economically the service prescribed by law or regulation. The aim should be distinction in service."

W. Edwards Deming[14]

Efficiency and Equity

There can be no finer aim for an educational technology center than to provide service with distinction. The notion of providing service with distinction is seldom heard in government agencies. Political realities hammer away at public-supported agencies to do more with less. Elections turn on "cut and slash" campaigns perpetuating the mythology that economy in government can only be achieved by cutting budgets.

Well-meaning politicians and government leaders would have us believe that creating lean, bare bones, "efficient" government is a way to improve services, reduce spending and cut waste. Unfortunately there is a basic conflict between government service and the traditional concept of efficiency as it is understood by the business world.

Consider the position of Oscar Ornati interviewed in *Public Productivity Review* magazine. "We have forgotten that the function of government is more equity-oriented than efficiency-oriented. For government, efficiency must be subsumed to equity," says Ornati.[15]

Many educational technology agencies could become highly efficient overnight. A regional media center could become more efficient by limiting its resources only to titles that circulate more than 15 times a year. It would have a smaller number of titles with a great number of copies of each to insure 100 percent availability for user requests.

Higher-level math and language courses offered via satellite to very few students for an additional cost per pupil could be eliminated. Universities could eliminate low enrollment avant garde, esoteric and special-interest course offerings to become more efficient. More courses could be offered in lecture halls through the third and fourth year. Paradoxically, there is a price to be paid for efficiency.

In a video/film center the diversity would be destroyed. Important social issue documentaries with limited appeal would not be included. Resources on complex physics topics that might be used four times a year by higher-level classes would no longer be available. The collection would evolve into a children's literature resource to the exclusion of first aid, driver education, professional development, plate tectonics, political science and 200 other topics required in K-16 education. The resources would stagnate under such a policy because it is not "efficient" to begin start-up collections of videodisc, CD-I or CD-ROM materials, initially in demand from a small segment of users.

Simplification of a system helps bring efficiency. Using a single supplier of educational video and videodisc would simplify ordering and reduce the number of potential problems with order fulfillment. It would also leave tremendous gaps in the subject and grade-level needs of the collection.

A single method for ordering, circulation and delivery would make a technology center more efficient as well. Using only machine readable, mark sense order forms and once-a-week delivery means that the system is less complex and therefore easier to manage. There are fewer variations to provide for and fewer combinations of inputs to deal with. The more rigid and inflexible the system, the more efficient it can become.

It is axiomatic that increased flexibility lowers efficiency. The expectations of our users are shaped by the level of service they experience on a daily basis. A modern consumer can call a bank and expect to receive an instant report on an account balance, or find out if a check cleared. A complete computer system can be purchased on the phone, paid for by credit card, delivered overnight and made operational by noon the following day as a matter of routine. Groceries can be paid for with cash, check or credit card. The advent of automatic teller machines no longer limits the hours when we can obtain cash. Yet buying a dog license can still take a week and issuing a library card three days.

The frustration level of the public with government services is raised by its experience with service in the private sector. To provide service with distinction, we must be willing to create flexible systems that will serve our clients' needs. Resource orders might be taken by phone, on paper forms, via fax or through on-line access systems. Operational hours can be extended through 24-hour user access dial-in scheduling systems. Circulation for non-standard circulation periods might fill the needs of many users. Instead of purchasing new titles once a year, continuous purchasing throughout the year might make a technology center more responsive to unexpected and changing user needs.

But all of these flexible arrangements, designed to meet the rising expectations of our users, can destroy the integrity and reliability of any technology service center. What is required is planning for quality service as discussed in Chapter 12. Management must know the requirements and expectations of the user, but also must have an intimate knowledge of the capacity of the system to provide service.

Long-range planning and forward vision can provide a rational method for identifying services that will meet and exceed client needs without at the same time destroying the system of service.

1 Hillkirk, John. "World Famous Quality Expert Dead At 93." *USA Today,* December 21, 1993. Page B1.

2 Kelso, Admiral Frank B. "Total Quality Leadership: The Way Of The Future." *United States Naval Institute Proceedings,* May, 1991. Pg. 107.

3 Naval Aviation Depots were at one time called Naval Air Rework Facilities. The Admiral in charge of the six facilities had their name changed. He felt that the word "rework" implied that the work had not been done right in the first place, a serious breech of quality principals.

4 Walton, Mary. *Deming Management at Work.* New York: Perigee Books, 1990. Pg. 165.

5 Ibid., pg. 170.

6 Dobyns, Lloyd and Clare Crawford-Mason. *Quality . . .Or Else.* New York: Houghton-Miffilin, 1991. Pg. 265.

7 Walton, *Deming Management At Work,* pg. 223–224.

8 *Hidden Assets: Empowering Government Workers.* Videotape. Deerfield, IL: Coronet/MIT Video, 1991.

9 Walton, *Deming Management At Work,* pg. 127.

10 Sesenbrenner, Joseph. "Quality Comes To City Hall." *Harvard Business Review,* March-April, 1991.

11 Kline, James J. "Total Quality Management in Local Government." *Government Finance Review.* August, 1992. Pg. 7–11.

12 *Empowering Government Workers,* op. cit.

13 Kline.

14 Deming, W. Edwards. *Out of the Crisis.* Cambridge, MA: MIT Press, 1986. Pg. 6.

15 Quoted in *Out of the Crisis,* pg. 198.

Chapter 12

PLANNING FOR QUALITY SERVICE

IN THE LATE 1980S AND INTO THE 1990S IT BECAME POPULAR FOR editorial and commentary writers, politicians and some business leaders to make impassioned pleas for education to be run more like business. There have also been articles denouncing quality management as the misapplication of business methods to education.

Take a moment to look behind the implication that schools should be run like a business. First of all, American businesses on the whole are not particularly well-run. The decline of American productivity, world competitive position and $150 billion annual trade deficits are ample evidence of this. Three out of four small businesses fail in the first three years and roughly 60,000 businesses file for bankruptcy each year.

There are many examples of fine American businesses. Some have transformed themselves into the mold of a Deming company. But these are few are far between. "Pockets of excellence," as Dr. Deming calls them will not pull the rest of the companies up out of the depths of poor performance.

In a book published by the National School Boards Association, Lewis J. Perelman points out that successful business practice is "rarely transferable from one business to another." Research by the Hay Group found that the more a company tries to diversify away from its original business, the less successful it is. Nationally known examples of failure he cites are: Exxon's attempt to run a typewriter company, Mobil Oil's failed venture in running the Montgomery Ward department stores, AT&T's computer sales and Sears' expansion into financial marketing.[1]

217

His book, *Technology And Transformation of Schools,* should be required reading for every library, media and technology manager.

Yet high-level educational administrators turn to local and national business leaders for advice on how to run school districts and universities. Blue ribbon panels of business leaders are convened to construct key recommendations that if followed, so the logic goes, would reshape schools and help cure the ills of American industry. If nothing else this gives business leaders a forum for blaming the education system for their own failures to produce quality and remain competitive in the global economy. Typically, American business points to the "excessive" amount of money spent on training workers in skills they say the schools should provide. Training in America is viewed as a cost. In Japan it is viewed as an investment in the most valuable asset a corporation can have, its people. Japanese companies and Demingized companies in the United States invest far more time and money on training than an average U.S. company. In Japan all employees are extensively trained, while in the United States more than two-thirds of corporate training is only for college-educated employees: managers, sales people and skilled technicians. Hourly workers who do the basic work of an enterprise receive very little training. Even more depressing is the fact that 90 percent of the training dollars come from only one percent of American companies.[2]

One of the magic bullets of business, recommended to, and taken up by schools, universities, government agencies and non-profit associations, is "strategic planning."

As already noted in Chapter 5, strategic planning generally results in three outcomes. It delays action that might be taken to improve things. It tends to focus attention on solutions to problems instead of developing a vision of what is required for the future. And, since it is a result of consensus, it represents things that people are least likely to argue over, therefore ensuring that the status quo is preserved. Or as Perelman puts it, "helps assure mediocrity."

Perelman observes that, "No strategic plan has ever been implemented. Anyone who has ever tried to adhere rigidly to a prefabricated 'strategic plan' in war, politics, poker, business or any other competitive field suffered disaster."[3] It has been argued that much of the starvation in the Soviet Union under Joseph Stalin in the late 1940s was the result of rigidly following five year collective farm plans.

Efficiency by its very nature prevents flexibility. Any regional media center or campus technology center could operate with fewer staff members, smaller budgets and fewer problems if it only allowed one way to order things, one way to circulate materials, only supported one computer operating system and offered fewer choices of titles with greater depth. The trouble is that it would no longer serve the needs and expectations of its users. The inflexible nature of the service would greatly limit the type of client it could serve and compromise the greater mission of the organization. The same applies to planning and explains Perelman's assertion that no strategic plan has ever been implemented. Management is ill-prepared to recognize or adapt to a changing operating environment.

The concept of flexibility in planning is not new. Nor is it unique to quality management.

> "The purpose of planning is not to prescribe a ridged course of action, but to provide a point of departure when changing situations demand it."
>
> *19th century military philosopher*
> *Carl Von Clausewitz*

> "A rationalistic approach [to planning] is characterized by pretension to the universality of its solutions . . . and lack of flexibility. Its very efficiency prevents flexibility, [ensuring] that alternate means are not available if the objective is changed."
>
> *British defense analyst*
> *Gregory Palmer*

The preceding two quotes, although drawn from a military perspective, are highly instructive in the real value of planning. Planning should create a common aim. It should prescribe a general method for proceeding toward the aim and provide flexibility to accommodate changing circumstances.

If stock market value is taken as an indicator of corporate performance, the evidence further piles up against strategic planning as a tool for success or excellence. A study of U.S. corporations compared those that did extensive corporate planning with companies that had little or no formal planning structure. The study found that the companies with highly developed plans were more likely to perform close to the average performance of the market. Companies with little planning tended to perform either far above or far below the average.[4] The planning corporations insured that their performance would be average. The last thing an educational technology center needs is to be average.

"It would be a mistake to export American management to a friendly country," Dr. Deming tells us.[5] Why would we want to impose it on our education system?

So what about planning? Is it a totally useless exercise? The lesson to be learned about planning is to understand the aim of planning. The aim in quality planning is not to solve problems or set numerical goals. The aim is to plan for how to *change the system*.

Perelman points out that the lessons we can take from business are not on how to *run* the business of education, but on the methods of how to *change* the way we do business. He points out that, "As troubled as it is, American industry is far ahead of public education in learning how to adapt to the transformations of the postindustrial age." He urges that education policy makers and administrators study the *processes* by which corporations are transforming themselves to meet the challenges of the new global economy.[6] Companies that are most successful in the transformation, like Ford, Saturn, Federal Express, Motorola and Xerox, have adopted the Deming management method.

At some point, after making a personal commitment to becoming a quality manager, after much study and struggle to accept the discomfort of casting aside old, comfortable ways, the question will come up, How do I make this happen?

In Chapter 10 we learned that starting with a "big bang" isn't necessary and may be counter-productive. After the mental commitment has been made by management, Deming's Point 14, "take action to accomplish the transformation," must be put into place. The old saw that actions speak louder than words has never been more true than in the application of the Deming Method.

Planning Means Having an Aim

Stephen Covey, author of *The 7 Habits of Highly Effective People,* describes the ability to, "begin with the end in mind" as an essential attribute of a good leader.[7] Leadership for quality improvement requires someone who is able to visualize what your system will look like five, ten or twenty years from now and construct the methods that will take it there. Although the quality journey never ends, there are always short-term activities that serve as milestones and measurements of progress. Visualizing the aim of the organization creates a picture of the most desirable route to take along the way.

Sometimes having a vision of what "could be" is a liberating experience. It allows us to let our imaginations run free and construct a vision of the best possible world for our organization. Russell Ackoff refers to this as "idealized redesign." It is a detailed statement of how you would design your system right now, if you could have whatever you wanted. The exercise is limited by only two factors. The elements of the system must be technologically feasible and it must be robust enough to survive normal operational demands.[8] Idealized redesign is another form of planning with the end in mind first.

Next time you talk to someone who puts together picture puzzles, a child or adult, try this experiment. Ask them, "What do you do first when you work on a puzzle?'

Typically they will explain that they arrange all the similarly colored pieces together or they build the outer edges first. Rarely will they say, "I look at the box to see what the picture is supposed to look like." But that is exactly what is required; otherwise they would never know how to assemble the pieces. Constructing a vision for a technology center and developing the method to get there require the same approach. You have to have a box top to look at and show other people, otherwise no one will know what your vision of the organization looks like.[9]

A Vision

An essential first step for taking action that will have meaning is to establish an aim for the organization. The aim may take the form of a "vision statement" or a "mission statement" for the organization. It need not be complex or lengthy. The difference between a mission statement and a vision statement may appear to be arcane and too subtle to define but the distinction is important. A vision statement tells what we want to be and a mission statement tells what we plan to do.[10]

Florida Power and Light, a public utility and the first United States company to win the Japanese Deming prize has a 27-word vision:

> During the next decade, we want to become the best managed electric utility in the United States and an excellent company overall and be recognized as such.[11]

In 1961 John F. Kennedy established a mission statement for the space program in a speech to congress:

> By the end of the decade we will put a man on the moon and return him safely to Earth.

Both statements are simple and clear. Both establish a direction and a focus for the organization. The value of every activity from that point on will hinge on the contribution it makes toward the aim of the organization.

Vision and mission statements are not arrived at during an overnight writing session, and they should not be written alone. The development of a workable vision statement comes from the ideas and input of many people in the organization. It took Ford Motor Company three years to develop a written mission, set of values and a set of guiding principles. Their mission statement is:

> Ford Motor company is a worldwide leader in automotive and automotive-related products and services as well in newer industries such as aerospace, communications and financial services. Our mission is to improve continually our products and services to meet our customers' needs, allowing us to prosper as a business and to provide a reasonable return for our stockholders, the owners of our business.[12]

Consider the following as a mission statement:

> It is important not merely to produce and sell products, but to produce and sell quality products, without fail. Not only from the

production side, but also from the distribution side, we must constantly review whether customers are satisfied with our products and whether customers are satisfied with our service. We must be perfect in satisfying.

The statement was written in 1940 for the Matsushita corporation in Japan. The importance of doing quality work and satisfying customer needs existed in Japan long before Homer Sarasohn (who preceded Deming to Japan), Dr. Deming and Dr. Juran visited there in the 1950s. What they gave the Japanese was the *method* through which they could achieve their quality aims.[13]

Visions and quality aims do not tell us what we should be doing differently to accomplish the aim. Our vision must be translated into a set of quality goals with the aid of an appropriate method by which the goals can be accomplished. The planning process provides the means by which vision can be turned into action to accomplish the aim of the organization.[14]

Quality Goals

Quality goals relate to major issues within an organization. They deal with issues such as product performance, service reliability, quality improvement, development of new products and services and performance of such functional areas as the billing department or the delivery system. It is here that the work of Dr. Deming differs from the view of Dr. Joseph Juran. Juran teaches that quality goals convert the larger aim of a vision or mission statement into specific, quantifiable measurements and should be tied to a specific time frame. Agencies just beginning with serious quality improvement may find this useful. Some examples of quality goals include:

- Improve product and service quality ten times by 1989. (Motorola, 1987)

- Reduce the cost of (poor) quality by 50 percent in five years. (3M, 1982)

- Reduce billing errors by 90 percent. (Florida Power and Light)[15]

Dr. Deming, as discussed in Chapters 6 and 10, teaches that if quality goals are tied to numerical goals, then the focus of the organization will remain on making the target number and not on improving the process. Grades in school do the same thing. Effort is expended to make the grade, not learn the content or skill.

Quality goals are aimed at improving the system and working upstream to multiply the gains that each improvement brings. If an organization is sufficiently mature as a quality organization, the implied requirement that quality goals require continuous improvement is apparent. Imposing a deadline for improvement may actually be limiting and delay real improvement while the work force stretches out the activity to fill the allotted time. Likewise, establishing a target number places an artificial cap on efforts to improve the system.

Examples of quality goals for educational technology centers can be found in Chapter 10. Quality goals address functional areas that have a direct impact on client satisfaction, the cost of operations, development of services and future performance of the organization. To reach these goals and implement the activities and improvements that will achieve them require planning. If we are responsible for the installation of a new computer lab or a fiber-optic network planning is essential. Bid specifications must be developed and written. Educational and technical needs must be defined. Space needs to be built or acquired. Local electrical service needs to be installed. The list goes on and on. Implementation planning defines who will be responsible for what. It organizes what must be done and in what sequence to make the most effective use of the time and resources available.

This kind of planning is not the management by objective that Dr. Deming rails against. MBO, when used to rate and rank individual performance is destructive. The damage done by MBO at the individual level is detailed in Chapter 1. Implementation planning flows from the need to organize and direct the activities that will be required to start a new service, install new equipment or improve a process within a system. The plan will not be centered on meeting a numerical goal. It will be focused on activities that help meet the larger, quality goals of the organization.

A Philosophy of Service

At some point the management of an educational technology center or library should write its management philosophy. This can be a difficult task without further study of the Deming method and a deeper understanding of what quality means to a service agency. Like it or not, most organizations have a management philosophy already but would never think of putting it into written form. The philosophy would be guided by current practice mostly founded in the work of Frederick Taylor's scientific management theory developed at the turn of the century.

Current management philosophy that governs the actions of a government or educational organization might include such positions as:

- Do more with less
- Cut costs whenever possible
- Buy from the lowest bidder
- Avoid costly innovations and new equipment
- Meet no more than minimum customer expectations
- Finish the year with a surplus
- Spend every dime in the budget
- Set monthly performance goals and reach them
- Make the boss look good
- Avoid doing anything more than absolutely necessary

A transformed organization will begin to develop a set of values or an operational philosophy that will provide general guidance and direction upon which all other policy actions and improvements will be based.

Dr. Juran calls these "policies" and gives examples:

- We will promote from within
- We will not be undersold
- Our products should equal or exceed competitive quality[16]

The philosophy describes the position of the organization in terms of how it shall interact with other organizations and the people who have contact with it. Examples include:

- Provide long term benefit to our clients

- Develop sources of supply that enhance our mission
- Develop services that exceed user requirements
- Establish a work environment that is safe
- Make management decisions and requests for operational changes based on fact and data, not guesswork and gut feelings
- Create a working relationship with clients that makes them part of the improvement process

Committing a philosophy to writing with the endorsement of the organization's governing body provides management with a sanction for its actions and establishes real guidance for development of future improvement plans.

The Seven-Step Action Plan

In *Out of the Crisis* Dr. Deming details a seven-step action plan that he credits to Dr. Phyllis Sobo. The seven steps, already detailed in Chapter 3, are only outlined here.

- Step 1. Struggle. [Management will struggle with all 14 Points, the deadly diseases and the obstacles.]
- Step 2. Take pride in the new philosophy.
- Step 3. Create critical mass.
- Step 4. Understand the customer/supplier relationship in every system.
- Step 5. Construct an organization to guide the continual improvement of quality.
- Step 6. Create teams to improve the input and output of every stage in the process.
- Step 7. Implement statistical process controls as part of the organizational structure. [17]

Following the sequence of these steps is important. Many school-based efforts toward quality management have jumped from Step 2 to Step 7 with disastrous results. The recently transformed school administrator attempts to regulate absence rates, tardy counts, repair requests and bus arrival times through the elaborate plotting of points on run charts, cause and effect diagrams and histograms. Lacking a supportive base of employees trained in quality principals and an internal communication system that is trusted, the efforts are tolerated and then dismissed as another in a long parade of management gimmicks.

It may take years to repair the psychic damage such misapplication has done to the supervisors and workers in the system. They will remain suspicious and fearful for years and the credibility of any further quality improvement effort will remain suspect.

A looser interpretation of Step 7 might apply to the use of data as a decision-making tool without going the full step into the mathematics of statistical process control. Much of the data required to learn how to improve a process can be collected and analyzed by observing patterns formed by a plot of points on a visual display.[18] The important concept behind Step 7 is that decisions affecting quality improvement are to be made based on hard data, not on guess work, hunches or gut feelings. Decisions made based on "experience" are also suspect since the experience may be based on historic precedents that have no relevancy to the current state of the system or the needs of the customer.

Statistical process control (SPC) becomes necessary to determine the upper and lower limits of the process. SPC also tells us if the system is stable or unstable, a concept already covered in Chapter 6. Imposing specifications or upper and lower limits of performance (quotas), is not a legitimate source of data. It simply diverts energy into watching the numbers instead of improving the processes that create the performance.

Action to improve the quality of a system in the absence of profound knowledge can do more damage than good. Managers must recognize that their own study of quality improvement must never end. Although an organization may see itself as approaching Step 6, management must continue with Step 1 as well. Continuous learning is part of the struggle process. Unless you are willing to constantly challenge yourself with new learning, new insights and deeper understanding of the Deming method, then your agency will stagnate. Quality may rise to a higher level. But it will remain there and eventually backslide to old levels unless continuous improvement applies to the function of management as well. Management can only provide continuous leadership if it is also providing itself with continuous learning. In education this continues to be a do-it-yourself endeavor. American business spends millions on management training and continual upgrading of skills. Teachers who ultimately rise to levels of supervision and management in education rarely receive additional management training through their school district. The personal transformation required by adoption of the Deming philosophy is a source of professional strength and continuous learning that may not be available through the institution.

Another Guide to Action

John Jay Bonstingl, in his book, *Schools Of Quality: An Introduction to Total Quality Management In Education* describes 13 principles that should guide the development of an individual approach to quality improvement.[19]

- Learn as much about total quality management and its application to education as you can.
- Make a personal commitment to total quality and *kaizen*.
- Provide leadership by building networks of support for the transformation.
- Celebrate successes, even small ones.
- Tie compatible existing philosophies and practices together under the total quality umbrella. Site-based management, team teaching, interdisciplinary courses, whole language, authentic assessment, mastery learning and effective schools research are examples.
- Make your journey a slow and steady process.
- Approach your transformation with patience, forgiveness and a helping hand.
- Don't be afraid to fail. Quality organizations are places where it's safe to take risks, okay to fail on the way to successes.

Compared to What? Benchmarking

A minor controversy exists in the quality management literature and between various quality leaders. It centers on the practice known as "benchmarking." Dr. Deming and quality consultant Philip B. Crosby are adamant that benchmarking is a form of copying. Dr. Deming cites the "search for examples" as a serious obstacle to attaining real and lasting quality improvement. Dr. Deming objects to the benchmarking process because it encourages corporations to borrow apparently successful practices from one company and put them into place back home. Deming views this as exceedingly dangerous because one can never know with certainty that the practice being copied is actually responsible for the superior performance of the company being observed. It also implies that the practice and technique used by one company is transportable into another system and operating environment. Dr. Deming cautions against copying and is fond of quoting, "Never mistake coincidence for cause and effect."[20]

On the other side of the issue is Dr. Juran, who believes that benchmarking is one of the most important tools for successful quality management.[21] Juran looks at benchmarking as a tool for setting world-class quality goals. He teaches in his books and seminars that the search for best practices may include any source, including competitors and corporations in other industries. For example when Xerox wanted to improve the shipping operations for photocopier parts, it benchmarked the clothing mail order company, L.L. Bean of Freeport, Maine. L.L. Bean has a reputation for fast delivery and a high degree of accuracy. During 1991 their order error rate was under one-tenth of one percent. The Xerox study of Bean's order fulfillment and shipping facility found that Bean could fill an order three times faster than Xerox could fill a part order. That and other ideas helped Xerox reduce warehousing costs by 10 percent in the first year.[22]

There are many impressive stories of successful benchmarking activities. But Juran also stresses that the search must include an examination of the "means used to attain the results."[23]

The controversy over the use of benchmarking is fueled by the Malcolm Baldrige National Quality Award. The award invites companies to have their quality performance judged against a set of seven criteria categories with 28 sub-criteria. Each criteria area is worth a specific number of points with a total possible score of 1,000. In 1992 there were 6 winners. In 1993 there were two. Nine of the sub-criteria for the 1994 award, totaling 315 points, specifically mention benchmarking as an area to be addressed in the performance documentation. [24]

Deming calls the award criteria "misguided." Unlike the Japanese Deming Prize, the Baldrige Award contains no system for showing companies how to improve. Philip Crosby sees the criteria as a collection of "techniques." He explains, "Quality is a culture, a way of life deliberately selected . . . not a set of procedures." [25]

The idea behind benchmarking is that one company should be able to benefit from the experience of another, as Xerox did with L.L. Bean. One university video and technology center, the logic goes, should be able to study the practices of another and take back the best practices for implementation.

"Experience teaches nothing without theory," Deming repeats in his seminars. Because there is no theory embodied in the criteria to show the way to improvement, Deming sees the criteria as devoid of knowledge to guide the practice. Brian Joiner, a quality consultant in the Deming method shares his concern. "There is a danger that companies will just go around and copy one another without understanding," he says, "but seeing what other people are doing and understanding it with the aid of theory is a very powerful force to help move the country forward." [26] Joiner takes a little more pragmatic view of the value of benchmarking against the need for theory. "The Baldrige Award is more like a yardstick. It helps you see where your deficiencies are." [27]

It would be nice if every manager who embarked on a benchmarking expedition was already grounded in the theory of process improvement and systems thinking. Or at the very least understood Dr. Juran's teaching that the search for the "means" of the superior performance is an important component of benchmarking. Unfortunately this is not always the case with many quality improvement efforts. Having read one or two journal articles, the ill-equipped manager, director, dean, principal or school superintendent will only further the problems of an organization by prematurely forging ahead. To make a quality plan work, management must have allowed itself to go through a substantial period of reading, study, questioning and struggle before attempting the real work of transforming the organization.

Without knowing the underlying theory that guides the successful practice, the organization will only be going through the motions that it has copied and will have no basis upon which to judge performance or create additional improvement.

A mounting body of evidence is beginning to bear out Dr. Deming's concerns. The International Quality Study (IQS), sponsored by Ernst & Young and the American Quality Foundation have found that the practice of benchmarking will not improve performance unless the company already has a comprehensive quality program in place. The report further discovered that corporations with poor performance records that attempt benchmarking actually do themselves more harm than good.[28]

For the most part, low-achieving companies are not organized for quality. They have no internal structure or coordinated plan for improving processes, there is no management commitment and no training for workers in quality. The study reports that an attempt to improve one part of the company by copying the practices of the best in class can bring such heavy losses to the rest of the company that it can end up worse off than when it started. The phenomenon is referred to as "suboptimization."

It is possible for one department in a technology center to enact practices observed during a benchmarking visit and inadvertently undermine the performance of another activity. The failure to have a structure in place, coordinated by management, to guide the quality transformation creates an environment where the best efforts of one unit will do nothing but disrupt, or suboptimize, the operations of another and set back employee confidence in future attempts to build quality. The whole organization is suboptimized and cannot possibly move ahead until each component knows its real job.

Unfortunately the critics of benchmarking and quality management in general seize upon the news that "benchmarking doesn't work" instead of developing an understanding for the place of benchmarking (if there is one) as a quality tool. Joshua Hammond, president of the American Quality Foundation, explains that there is a pronounced learning curve when an organization becomes quality-oriented. Corporations and others new to quality management mistakenly assume that one approach or another, like benchmarking, or forming quality teams, will produce visible results. They try to tie quality efforts to the bottom line as well. The result, he says. is that "you get a measure of how many people are being trained, not what difference it's making in performance."[29] The continual shift from one management practice to another is caused by frustrated managers searching for a formula or model to help solve system problems. The search is a phenomenon known as "Program of the Month" syndrome.[30] It is typical of analytical, Western thinking that only sees problems to solve instead of processes to improve. It sees pieces of the solution but not the whole. The search for examples and the hope for instant pudding are both prime obstacles to quality performance as described by Dr. Deming.

Organizations that have matured in quality management might actually find a great deal to gain from the practice of benchmarking, but only after much internal work and years of improvement. Managers from organizations that are just starting out on the quality journey are simply not prepared enough for the benchmarking activity to have any meaning. They have no idea what to look for according to Darel Hull, reengineering and benchmarking manager for AT&T. "Most benchmarkers aren't prepared to discover anything when they go out on a site visit. They may stumble over a lot of great things and not be in a position to recognize the potential," he says.[31] Ronald D. Schmidt, chairman of Zytec Corporation, a 1991 Baldrige winner, shares this view. Unless a quality culture has already been built within the organization, "it won't know how to exploit insights gleaned from benchmarking."[32]

Do not confuse benchmarking with the common professional practice of swapping good ideas. Attending professional conferences and listening to presentations made by other technology professionals is not benchmarking. It is a source of new ideas and applications that may have relevance back home. Sometimes it is a source of validation for operational assumptions or ideas. Seeing that someone else, or some other technology center is proceeding with a new service or application of a new technology takes the idea out of the realm of science fiction. It proves that it can be done.

A wealth of good ideas can be obtained by attending roundtable sessions of media and technology directors where everyone is asked to bring a printed list of "Ten Things That Work" and explain one or two of them to the group. It is an easy way to see how shared problems are approached by different centers. Some of the ideas work and some don't. The ideas are generally simple things like:

- Place a material condition form in every video box. In addition to places to indicate any defects found in the tape, also ask: "Did this program meet the objectives of your lesson?"

- Celebrate the 20th, 25th, etc., anniversary of your agency with embossed foil seals that carry the agency name and dates. Stick them on video boxes, videodisc cases, letters, annual reports, et al.

- Place resource lists of related titles inside video boxes.

- Have an introduction sheet made up for each driver and include it in the first delivery each year.

- List the staff by name in the catalog. In newsletters mention specific people to contact for help with various services. It helps get your staff known and gives callers a specific name to ask for.

- Have a separate newsletter aimed at administrators, school boards, trustees and others in management or policy-making positions. Keep it short and deal with technology in the context of policy and planning. Articles about fiber optic deployment, quality management and technology planning are appropriate.

These are useful practices but do not describe *processes* that are components of a system. Benchmarking involves a detailed examination of an entire process, including the methods and theory upon which the design of the process is based.

Success Comes with Time

Time and constancy of purpose are key factors in the success of any quality effort. Survey results that were widely reported in the business press in 1992 painted a dismal picture of the benefits of quality management. Unfortunately there was no indication of how long the companies surveyed had been using quality management or engaged in quality improvement activities.

A survey conducted by Development Dimensions International of 7,000 people involved in quality management in both North America and Europe turned up hard evidence that persistence over at least a three-year-period is required before measurable quality improvement can be seen. The study found that of organizations working on quality improvement for more than three years, 65 percent improved operational results, and 69 percent improved customer satisfaction. At the opposite end of the scale are organizations that have been dealing with quality improvement for two years or less. Fewer than 40 percent of them achieved high levels of success in the various quality indicators that the study examined.[33]

The same study asked executives to rank 15 quality strategies according to how likely they are to have a long-term benefit. Quality management topped the list. Benchmarking ranked ninth with only three percent of the respondents seeing it as having the most long-term benefit. It is unlikely that benchmarking will go away or the debate subside. Readers of "Total Quality Management Newsletter" who responded to a 1992 survey reported that 54 percent of them had engaged in benchmarking in the previous year. Further, 79 percent expected to conduct benchmarking the following year.

By now the lesson must be clear that there is no magic bullet for quality. Teamwork training, benchmarking, control charts, technology, workplace quality and the Baldrige criteria will not alone help an organization create quality performance. For each technology service center some mix of strategies will be appropriate. And the mix will change to some extent as the years go by and the center matures as a quality organization.

The study and understanding of profound knowledge will equip technology directors with the knowledge that the *interactions* between the strategies, the dynamics of how one approach feeds and nurtures another, is what makes quality management really work. Any approach or quality tool taken alone, without benefit of profound knowledge, can only be, in the words of Dr. Deming, "An attempt to substitute wishful thinking for knowledge."[34]

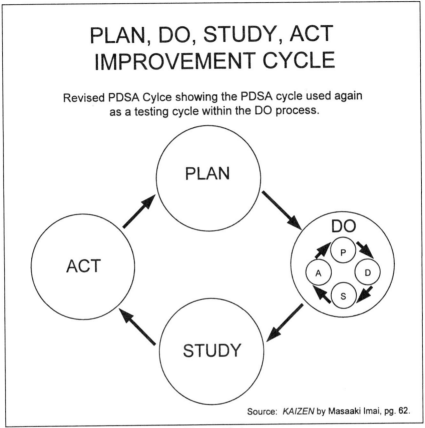

PLAN, DO, STUDY, ACT IMPROVEMENT CYCLE

Revised PDSA Cylce showing the PDSA cycle used again as a testing cycle within the DO process.

Source: *KAIZEN* by Masaaki Imai, pg. 62.

Figure 12-1

Plan-Do-Study-Act: The Structure for Improvement

To students of the Deming method, the cycle of Plan-Do-Study-Act (PDSA), shown in Figure 12-1 eventually becomes second nature. The PDSA cycle, also known as the Shewhart Cycle,[35] is a fundamental tool for implementing process improvements. The Shewhart Cycle was originally referred to as Plan-Do-Check-Act (PDCA). Dr. Deming changed Check to Study in 1990. What follows is an introduction to the cycle and some examples of its application in a technology center.

The beauty of using the PDSA cycle is that it allows innovations, process improvements and new service ideas to be tested and observed prior to full-scale implementation. Because of this broad application to quality improvement, PDSA is a fundamental guide for any improvement activity. Its advantages are that it provides a common structure understood by everyone involved. It creates an environment where fact and accurate data are valued over hunches and gut feelings. It allows for failure and provides a mechanism for modifying the original assumptions to create process changes that will improve performance. It provides a method for continuous improvement by the spiraling nature of the cycle. It provides an indicator of when further action on the system will no longer create further improvement. And, it creates a motivation for the improvements to become standardized procedures.

First-time users of the PDSA Cycle may want to focus on some problem of customer service or an internal process that has created a great deal of rework and wasted time. PDSA can also be used to launch a new service and provides a way to test systems in a controlled way prior to full deployment to your users.

Step One—Plan

Find a process that has a lot of problems or complaints, the place where your staff has to say "I'm sorry" the most. This could be an area highly visible to your user like delivery errors. Or it could be an entirely internal process like mislabeled video boxes. Flowcharting activities may reveal a sub-system or process that could be a prime candidate for improvement through PDSA. Pick a process that is easily measured: time, volume or length. Or select a process that is quantifiable: errors, missing information or short counts. Typing errors on purchase orders, wrong items shipped, order entry errors, misdirected phone calls, billing errors, repair returns and equipment scheduling conflicts are examples.

A team might be an appropriate group to plan the approach to creating the desired improvement. In a small technology unit or department the team may be two people. The result of the cycle will always be better when the talents of more than one person are brought to bear on the problem.

Establish a clear aim for the team. Management may have to set the aim. Making the aim simple and clear: reduce packing errors, eliminate equipment damage in shipping, reduce VCR repair turnaround time, gives focus and purpose to all the activities of the team from there on. The team should begin to ask questions about the process and about what kind of data would be useful to gather. It may decide how to construct a test of the proposed improvements and how it will evaluate the results of the test. It will also need to design a method for gathering and recording the data.

Step Two—Do

Now the improvement team can gather the required data and make observations on the nature of the process. A flowchart can show the process graphically. A run chart will show the performance of the system over a period of time and will provide a visual reference on how many errors there are in relationship to the number of opportunities. For example if a technology repair service worked on 35 VCRs over a two-month period and six of them were returned for rework, there is a 17 percent rework rate.

Once the team decides that it has asked the right questions and has the necessary data, it can construct a series of suggested changes that might bring about the desired improvement. A number of quality management charts and tools are available to assist in this effort and are outlined in Appendix A. Among them are the Pareto Chart and the Cause and Effect Diagram.

The Pareto Chart provides a graphic distribution of the sources of defects in a process. It allows the improvement team to sort out what Dr. Juran describes as the "vital few from the trivial many." Figure 12-2 shows the distribution of material pulling errors and the characteristic of each type of error. The chart clearly shows that fully 50 percent of the errors were attributable to one type of error. It points out the single largest source of problems to be eliminated and allows all improvement efforts to be focused on a single element. In a subsequent cycle, the Pareto Chart shows a 90 percent reduction in the prime cause shown on the first chart and reveals the next error cause to be worked on.

A Cause and Effect Diagram, also known as a Fish Bone Diagram, like the one in Figure 12-3 is useful in sorting out the sources of errors

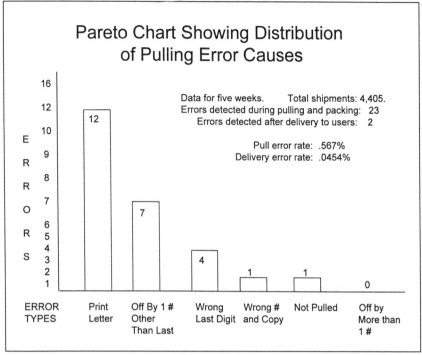

Figure 12-2

and suggesting areas for improvement. Most charts are organized into four categories: Methods (including policy), people, equipment and material. For solving a problem, the "effect" contained in the box at the end of the diagram describes an existing condition that is the subject of the improvement process. For creating a desired result, the effect box describes the desired outcome of the process. In either case the "effect" is not numerical but descriptive in nature. "No returns of VCR repairs," "reduction of late deliveries," "reduction of caller hold time," are examples.

Along the four branches or ribs extending from the backbone are listings of cause factors attributable to one of the four categories listed above. The diagram helps sort out all the cause factors that come into play to fulfill a specific process. It also focuses improvement on the causes directly related to the effect. In this case, two cause factors are cited as having the most influence on pulling the wrong copy of a title for ship-

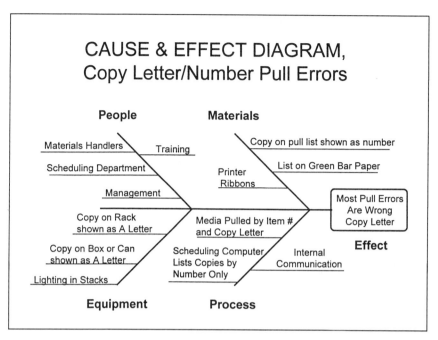

Figure 12-3

ment: How the copy is listed on the pull list; and how it is actually labeled
on the video box and the storage rack. The pull list, used by staff to pull
media for shipment, shows the title number followed by a *number* to indicate which copy should be sent. But the video boxes and film cans, along
with the rack location label, show the added copies as a *letter*. Although
this sounds simple, it requires the material handling staff to make a mental
translation from a number to its corresponding letter in the alphabet about
200 times a day.

A secondary cause factor that emerges is poor lighting in the media
stacks. The lighting had been the same for years, and although known to
be shadowy in some places, was accepted as a "fact of life." Once identified as a possible cause factor to a problem that directly affected customer
satisfaction and created a source of rework, efforts can be made to find
creative solutions that will increase lighting levels.

Both problems are system problems and beyond the ability of hourly
workers to improve. Only management can control the technology

center's relationship with the software supplier to change the pull list print out to show letters instead of numbers. And only management is in a position to make lighting improvements a possibility.

In some cases the team may decide that a small scale test is in order. One delivery route may be handled under a different set of procedures for several weeks. The intake procedures for printer repairs may use a new approach for a time, or the request forms for producing an in-house video tape might be modified and tested with the next few productions.

The intent of the test period is to experiment without doing any damage to the system as a whole. It is called working "above the waterline" so that if the new ideas don't work, they won't sink the system and do irreparable harm.

Step Three—Study

What happened during the test? Did the changes improve anything? Are the changes compatible with other component of the system? Will they benefit the system and the organization as a whole? Did we move toward our original aim stated in Step 1?

What if nothing happened or things got worse? Then you have learned what *not* to do in the future. You have gained valuable knowledge about what won't work in the system without the risk of bringing heavy losses to the organization.

Step Four—Act

Put the new ideas and the lessons learned from study to work. Make the new procedures or the improvement to the process the new standard. Deploy the change across the system so that from that point on the old way will no longer be used. This requires that staff be trained in the new procedure. The training must also include how the change was arrived at and why it is important for the procedure to be uniform across the organization. The improved process will remain in place until the next improvement cycle recommends another change.

The importance of standardizing procedures cannot be over-emphasized. It is essential that improvements, proven through the PDSA cycle, be followed by everyone in the process. Standard operating procedures

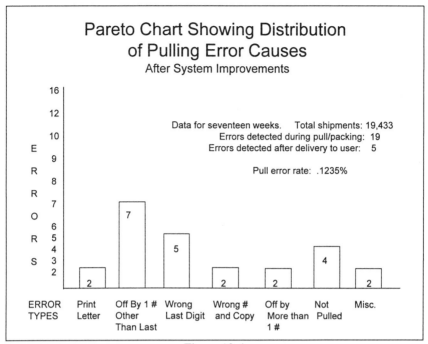

Figure 12-4

(SOP) for each process are so important that they must take the form of regulations for the system to be optimized.[36] Management is responsible for making the new standard operating procedure a matter of policy and seeing that everyone follows it. The system will continue to run under the improved process until the next improvement upgrades the standard again. Unfortunately, in the American practice of quality management the single improvement cycle becomes symbolic of a finish line. The new standard of performance becomes an upper limit. In Japan, each quality improvement standard becomes a "starting line." It is the point of departure for the next improvement cycle in the unending cycle of improvement.[37]

Figure 12-4 is a Pareto Chart showing a drastic reduction in print letter pull errors after system improvements were made. It also clearly indicates the next error source to be studied. Regular tracking of the system will confirm if the improvements remain consistent and stable.

The issue of standardizing functional procedures is a two-edged sword. Kaoru Ishikawa, the developer of the Cause and Effect Diagram and one of the foremost quality leaders in Japan warns that there are some people who are "born regulators." They like nothing better than to set policy and procedure as a means to controlling the workforce and the output of the organization. He also warns against allowing engineers and headquarters staff to prescribe operating procedures and process methods. Generally, they are too far removed from the process they are trying to regulate to provide effective guidance. The result is only to "hinder efficiency and ignore humanity."[38]

Ishikawa cites the value of common aims and a common understanding of the system by all employees. This common bond of understanding the aim of the system makes the implementation of necessary standards easier. It speaks well of the need for teams to investigate alternate methods of production and service with the intent of improving the existing practices. Team involvement gives wider ownership to the new procedures, allows improvement initiatives to come from the shop floor and acts as a catalyst to overcome resistance to new methods.

PDSA and New Services

The social shift from an "either/or society" to a "multiple option society" observed by John Naisbitt more than ten years ago in his book *Megatrends* has long since come to pass. Regional, district and university media and technology centers have responded to the new expectation of choices on the part of users in a variety of ways. Few, however, take the initiative to provide choices without first experiencing user demands for something different, the possibility of defections or loss of funding. In other words, they wait until a crisis forces a reassessment of how services are offered. Sometimes alternate choices for users come to the center by default, as when a computer scheduling system is upgraded and a new feature allows greater subject searching or the preparation of more specialized resource lists.

Technology centers that are managed by a quality method do not wait for crisis or for things to fall in their lap. They are constantly looking at new products, upgrades, new techniques and new media that might be useful to their client base. Do they sieze on every innovation, idea and product that comes along? No, but quality managers are aware of their existence and know how to assess their potential value to their center and their users. Each service improvement is a candidate for implementation with a PDSA Cycle.

It used to be that ordering resources for delivery either on campus, across a district or among many districts took only one or two forms. For years, after the advent of mainframe computers, mark sense cards were used. Users filled in tiny blocks on IBM cards that would be read by a card reading attachment to the scheduling computer.

In some cases phone-in scheduling was possible, but a cumbersome task. By the early 1990s large media centers could routinely accept requests for material by phone, mark sense card, order form, fax and through computer modem connections. An innovation called PhoneBook, made available through TekData, a major supplier of media management systems, turns a common TouchTone phone into a remote terminal, allowing users to place orders for materials directly into the scheduling computer 24 hours a day. Some centers have combined this with a toll free 800 number to insure equitable access and avoid an unfair burden of phone bills for teachers calling in from home.

How do we implement these changes? Do we plug in the PhoneBook system one day and expect it to work? Can we introduce a new order form to 5,000 teachers and expect them to start using it? And if they do, how will it affect the media scheduling process?

To find out, the PDSA approach is applied. We can see how this works by following the introduction of paper order forms to a regional service that had previously allowed ordering only with mark sense cards.

Step One: Planning for Paper Forms

The existing order system handled an average of 45,000 orders each year. Each order arrived as an IBM card marked with the user's number, title number, request date and alternate request dates. The cards were processed through a card reader to enter the request data into the computer scheduling system. Although the process sounds highly automated and very efficient, it was the source of a tremendous amount of rework. In any given week, almost 20 percent of the cards had to be rejected because they were either improperly marked, missing information or couldn't be read by the card reader. The card reading process was not able to keep up with the volume of orders that arrived in the center in late summer and early September when almost 50 percent of the total yearly orders arrived. Because of a policy that requests would be taken in the order received, the cycle time for receiving an order and returning a confirmation was as long as six weeks.

The result was that many of the rejected orders had to be entered by keyboard while the operator tried to visually decipher information from the mark sense cards. Limitations of the computer system dictated that the single available terminal could not be used while the card reader was in use.

Users, expecting their order confirmations to return a week later, called constantly to ask about the status of their order. Staff time that could have been spent scheduling material was being used to trace down order back log and make apologies.

Order cards that could not be processed had to be returned to users with a form explaining why their order could not be filled and asking them to redo the cards—more waste and rework; more negative communication with users that translated into frustration and lack of confidence in the service.

The planning process began by asking, "What does the user want?"

- Rapid turnaround of orders
- Something easier to use than a mark sense card
- Accurate order fulfillment
- Less paperwork
- More than one title ordered on each form
- No return of order cards for lack of information

Then the process asked, "What does the scheduling system require?"

- "Plain English" order forms
- Flexibility of entry options
- A way to avoid returning orders for lack of information

- More than one or two items ordered per form

- An arrangement that is compatible with computer entry fields

- "No harm,"—the new order system could not damage the system or put new strains on the personnel

- System must remain compatible with the existing card order system

Plans then proceeded with the design of a new order form. Personnel directly involved with order entry were part of the team that designed the new form. They checked the arrangement of information on the form and spent a great deal of time discussing the positive and negative impact a new entry might have.

Step Two: Do—Testing the New Form

Once the proposed form, now known as a bulk order form, to play off the popularity of buying certain foods and candy in bulk, was designed and the instructions distilled into a readable form, it was time to test the form with real users. Six schools, out of 150 in the service area, were selected for the test during the last three months of the school year. A cover letter explaining why the new form was developed and a set of instructions were sent to the contact person in each of the six schools along with a supply of blank forms. Within a week orders began arriving and were processed according to procedures established to handle the new forms. Verbal feedback and written notes on the forms from users provided useful ideas for modifying the form and clarifying instructions. Overall, the users in the test schools reported that they much preferred using the bulk form over the IBM cards.

Step Three: Study—What Did We Learn?

Internally, scheduling personnel worked out a system for sorting incoming orders by month. That way orders for the next few weeks would not get lost in orders set for several months ahead. Standard procedures were also developed to indicate if an item had been booked, turned down, shared or become a snag in need of further processing.

The new form asked users for their eight-digit user number, their name and school building. This was designed to eliminate the need to send back cards that lacked a user number and therefore could never be traced back to their source. It also eliminated returning cards with incorrect user numbers. Since the name and building were on the form in "plain English" it could always be searched by an alternate method. The form also established a minimum number of titles that could be ordered per form as six. There are twelve lines per form. This was done to encourage continued use of the card system for users who ordered things one at a time. Computer operators found that once the user number had been entered then key stroking was limited to entering each requested title and date, saving a tremendous amount of time.

If the bulk order form became as widely accepted as the testing appeared to indicate, it would mean altering the computer system to allow for more terminals and training additional staff in the scheduling process.

Step Four: Act—How Do We Make This a Regular Service?

The use of the bulk order form became an institutionalized part of the ordering system the following September. The agency newsletter contained a feature story on the benefits of the new ordering method and a blank form was printed in the new resource catalog that was sent to all 5,000 teachers in the service region.

An upgrade for the media scheduling system was purchased along with two additional terminals to accommodate the expected volume of orders that would be handled through the bulk order forms.

The response was overwhelming, and the improvement of cycle time evident immediately. Previously it was common for the surge of September orders to be backed up until Columbus Day. In the first year of the bulk form, backlog was cleaned up by the end of September. Over 30 percent of the orders received came in on bulk forms. In the second year, order backlog was gone by the second week in September and 60 percent of the orders for the year were on bulk forms. By the third year, all backlog was gone by the end of the first delivery week of September. Although no new staff was hired, some personnel were cross-trained to handle order processing during heavy load periods.

Ironically, the move away from mark sense cards as a technological solution to the problem of efficiently handling 45,000 orders was responsible for a quantum increase in service reliability. The bulk forms and the entry by hand actually created higher productivity, lower turndowns, fewer order returns, less rework, fewer misunderstandings, higher user-satisfaction and greater user-confidence in the system.

The situation is not unlike the experience of Japanese management at the Geo/Corolla assembly plant in Fremont, California mentioned earlier in this book. After the plant reopened under Japanese management and matched the productivity of Toyota plants in Japan, General Motors officials were distressed to see millions of dollars of recently installed hi-tech equipment standing idle while the same work was again being done by hand or with simpler machines.[39]

The paradox of doing orders by hand that were once done by machine was not lost on the customer. Several teachers, after raving about how easy the new ordering system was to use, asked if the new system didn't create more work internally. The answer is complex, but the short answer is, "No, just different work." The use of the mark sense technology, in the absence of any alternate ordering method, conspired to suboptimize the scheduling system. But the development of a new ordering method created an environment that optimized the ordering process for the customer, even though the actual order entry procedure might be viewed as suboptimized internally.

Although on the surface the system appears to be slow and labor-intensive, there is almost no rework, so all time devoted to scheduling is for making the entry just once. There is very little interruption of the process for reentering information or correcting errors.

The bulk order form proved to be the most popular way to order materials and eventually the mark sense card will be phased out of service. To give users maximum flexibility in transmitting orders to the center a fax line number was widely advertised along with the on-line PhoneBook scheduling system which runs 24 hours a day.

Users now have multiple choices in how they can order and how they can return the orders to the center.

And It Starts Again

In the PDSA cycle the improvement process begins again. Constant feedback from order-entry staff and clients might reveal bottlenecks on the flow of orders or changes in the form that might speed entry. These become opportunities for improvement that will trigger another testing cycle.

In smaller organizations where many staff members are cross-trained and doing many kinds of work, it is not possible to maintain true continuous improvement of every process all the time. The order entry system may have to function with the new improvements for a year, 18 months, or more before it is ready for another PDSA cycle. Some other process in the technology center creating losses might have to be addressed next, like purchase order cycles, catalog preparation or new equipment acquisition. To continue focusing all of an agency's improvement efforts on a limited scope of processes will eventually cause another process down the line to be suboptimized. A new barcode material check-in system, for example, could create a back up of items to be returned to shelves, taking up cart space and frustrating workers.

There is something to be said for allowing the new standard to remain in place for sometime as well. At some point there can be too many "improvements" too quickly arrived at. If staff is having to relearn procedures every few days or weeks, it creates an unstable work environment, can affect productivity and counteract the intention of the improvement to the process.

Overcoming Resistance to the New Philosophy

The first resistance that must be overcome is within. If you have made it this far through the book then your personal resistance to adopting the Deming philosophy is probably already gone. Either that or you have been searching the text for reasons why the Deming method will not work in educational technology.

Consider the history of change and innovation in American education. Gerald Bracey, well known educational writer and psychologist, describes education's "pathological failure to adopt good practice."

Bracey draws an analogy with the kitchen staff of a good restaurant. He notes that restaurants are constantly searching for good ideas in the menus of other restaurants. Some well-known restaurants regularly take the entire kitchen staff to visit a highly regarded establishment and then take time to discuss and learn more about what they found. He points to this as a contributing factor in the growing diversity of menu offerings typically found in restaurants over the last thirty years.

When an educational institution finds a new and effective teaching practice, other institutions frequently resist adoption because of the "pathology of envy" described by Bracey. He explains that it can be best stated as, "If you have a new idea, I'd better get one too, but it can't be yours."[40] This leads to increased competition between schools. Instead of looking for the best practice, administrators look for "something new to do. Or appear to do."

At the risk of making this sound like benchmarking, there must be a willingness to examine the quality management practices of other organizations during the struggle to begin the transformation. The investigation is not with an eye to copying the practice of one center in another, but to observing the road that has already been taken by one organization. The observation allows for preparation and planning to anticipate both the roadblocks to be removed and the successes to be expected. Sometimes the greatest resistance is within ourselves. We have changed our mind and accepted a new idea, but failed to overcome the internal resistance to take action. We run on fear and comfort. The old ways are known and comfortable, even if we do spend a lot of time fighting fires.

Taking action to put the new ideas to work is scary. It means moving into the unknown. It means risking failure and setbacks. Risk is an unnatural act. But fear is removed by making the unknown into a known through information and knowledge. Sometimes you just have to do it.

Quality Is Too Much Extra Work

The "extra work syndrome" is the most commonly cited reason for resistance to adopting a quality improvement philosophy. The key to overcoming resistance is unrelenting commitment and communication of quality principles by management. As a media and technology center begins to shift away from management by numbers and quotas to customer satisfaction, workers can begin to see a direct relationship between their daily work and the aim of the agency. The quality of service and the quality of internal processes become the same instead of two separate processes.[41]

This requires clear communication of quality goals to the staff and continual communication of how well the organization is moving toward those goals. Quick "stand up" progress reports from process improvement teams are also part of the communication process. Keeping quality efforts visible and reporting on progress and improvements regularly helps make quality an instinctive part of the work day instead of something extra to be done.[42]

The documentation that is sometimes a necessary part of quality improvement is also cited as a serious cause of resistance. Frequently it is caused by poor planning, improper selection of measurement tools or introduction of process charting too early. It is important to remember that not all of the quality tools outlined in Appendix A have to be used all the time or with every process. In many cases great improvement can come from a minimal number of charts and documentation.

Deming Prize winner Florida Power and Light made extensive use of a storyboard system developed by the president of Komatsu tractor as a quality planning tool.[43] The storyboards, known as the Quality Improvement Story, are a visual component to a seven-step analysis, justification and improvement planning method. After FP&L won the Deming Prize it began to back away from the storyboard approach because of worker complaints about the red tape it created.[44]

Proper training in the use of appropriate charts by employees is essential. Without it, employees will view the activity of documenting errors and rework as "added" work with no meaning. Workers and management alike must be able to see where the data gathered will create a benefit and improvement in quality for the organization.[45]

"Drive out fear" is Point 8. Consistent commitment to quality, open communication and proper training in process improvement all help to drive out fear in the workforce. Fear can be a powerful source of resistance to quality improvement and therefore must be driven out long before the introduction of control charts or any other process tracking tool. If the use of any kind of tracking tool is introduced too early, any information will be suspect. Without a feeling of security that the data will not be used against them, workers will only fill in what they think management wants to see. Nothing will improve.

Taking the path of least resistance can also work as a strategy for introducing process improvement to your center. It may be that the computer repair service is the system with the most user complaints and the highest rework costs, but the department supervisor is uncooperative and resistant to new approaches. It may do harm to forge ahead in a department where your insistence on quality is not welcome. Find another area to work in first. Building small but visible successes can provide evidence that the new philosophy works and help break down the arguments that justify continued resistance.

AT&T Universal Card Services, a 1992 Baldrige Award winner, began its quality effort by what Greg Swindell, vice-president for customer-focused quality improvement, calls "gentle persuasion." If any of the organization's ten department executives showed any resistance to the notion of implementing a quality improvement effort, Swindel followed the line of least resistance and went somewhere else. Eventually all of the executives adopted the corporate quality strategy. The president had assigned each of them to work with some cross-functional improvement team and observe the team's progress.[46] The first-person exposure to the improvement process at work, no doubt lead to a greater trust of the new approach and eventual adoption.

It Doesn t Always Work the First Time

After studying Dr. Deming and learning about Japan's post-war economic growth based on an unrelenting pursuit of quality, it is easy to assume that all Japanese efforts at producing quality work and delivering quality service are highly successful. A case in point is the Japanese National Railway (JNR). Today JNR is known for high speed "bullet" trains that run on precise time schedules. But in 1970 JNR was a battleground for an attempt to bring quality improvement activities to a government-run organization.

Management of the railway proposed a major campaign to improve productivity as a solution to frequent budget deficits and poor employee moral. The program gained acceptance by some segments of railway employees, but quickly ran into resistance from the union. The union accused management of using the program to break the union and exploit the workforce. It filed suit with the Japanese equivalent of the United States Labor Relations Board claiming that productivity was an "unfair labor practice." The union agreed to drop the action if management would stop encouraging productivity. Ultimately the railway withdrew the productivity improvement program, but only after the suicides of several executives.

The railway learned several things from the experience. The program was introduced too fast. Not enough time was spent explaining the need to improve productivity to the employees and there was no cohesive management position on how and why quality should be improved.[47]

Effective internal communication is essential if the organization is to be successful in putting the principles of Dr. Deming to work. Communication and agreement of purpose between all levels of management and supervision come first. Next comes accurate and consistent communication with all staff to explain the intent of the new direction, the benefits it will bring and the quality goals that have been established. Communication is an obligation of management.

Rebuild Intrinsic Motivation

Quality improvement is a humanistic approach to management. It requires an understanding of people and what motivates them. Dr. Deming describes understanding psychology as one of the four parts of profound knowledge, without which the other three parts are suboptimized. The job of a quality leader is to build and rebuild intrinsic motivation that may have been beaten out of the worker by the system. The system of rewards for performance, competition between workers, annual reviews, and merit raises all destroy the intrinsic motivation to simply do a good job and take pride in one's work.

To adopt the Deming Method requires a belief that most people want to do a good job. Very few people take a job with the intent of being careless, inefficient and unproductive. Quality management means treating employees as your greatest asset instead of as a cost factor. No one in your organization took the job they have because they lost a lottery. At some point, even the most despondent worker actually wanted to work there.

Systems of performance review and merit raises contribute to the notion that one job is better than another. Never tell an employee that you want to find a better job for them. What have you just said about the position they are in? People may be moved into different jobs, or to positions that make better use of their talents and temperament, but no job is better than another. If there is anything to be learned from management in Japan, it is that all work has honor. The work of a custodian, truck driver and computer operator are to be honored. We would do well to remember that in America from time to time.

Keep Persistence of Vision

As the manager of a technology service center and the leader of a quality journey, it is important that you remain persistent in your quest for knowledge. The long-range vision of leadership sets the agenda for any organization. Where your center will be twelve years from now and how it will be delivering services will be determined largely by actions taken right now.

Keeping the faith in the principles of quality can be exhausting even when things are going well. It can be intolerable when there is no one else around who shares your vision or understands your aims. Take the time to recharge your batteries, read everything you can on quality, even if it doesn't make much sense right now. If you read a good article, contact the author with questions. Go to seminars and watch videotapes, even if they are aimed at business and industry or military practitioners. Learn how to translate the language of industrial quality into service and quality in education. Make yourself available to other educational administrators interested in quality management. If your agency has a video/film library create a section on quality management videotapes and make them available to the schools and colleges in your service area. There are even self paced CD-I resources that provide training in quality management, quality tools and decision analysis.

Continue to take a holistic view of how quality is achieved in an organization. There is a tendency among some organizations to bounce around from one quality practice to another. Efforts are shifted from self-management to quality circles to just in time to statistical process control to quality of work life to team building in a frustrating search for a quick payoff and visible results. It creates a "program of the month" mentality and diverts energy that should be focused on the quality aims of the organization.[48] Part of management's job is to see the whole picture of the system of production and service. Quality management requires harmonious coordination of the interactions that are created by many people and appropriate quality tools working together toward the quality goals of the organization.

The movement toward becoming a quality organization can sometimes appear to be very slow. Keep sight of the aims established for improvement of service and product. Consider sharing your experience, even early experiences, successes, failures and insights. Write for a professional journal or newsletter or submit a proposal for a workshop at a state or national conference. It is a way of reaching out to like-minded administrators and letting your colleagues see that their concerns are not unique; that they no longer need to be "exiles among their peers."

Aim for Service with Distinction

Why are we here? What is the aim of our technology center? What business are we *really* in? What products and services do users need? What does our user really expect? What else can we offer that will serve our users better? What would be useful to our users three, seven or twelve years from now? What do our center's employees expect? By now you must realize that these are not just metaphysical questions but sources of guidance for management action.

With a clear aim, understood by everyone in the center, we are prepared to ask Dr. Deming's universal question, "By what method?" The aims of improving service, improving access to information, reducing downtime, reducing turnaround time or eliminating scheduling errors all have noble intentions. And, like the America 2000 goals for education, they are devoid of method. The "how" is missing. The teachings of Dr. Deming, elaborated by others, provide a clear answer to "how?" The answer is quality.

Four elements, quality in process, quality in people, quality in materials and quality in policy, combined through application of a systematic quality approach, yield the performance required to provide service with distinction.

Don't let problems and complaints drag quality efforts down to the level of exercises in fire-fighting. Russell Ackoff provides three areas to always concentrate management efforts. First, focus efforts on meeting and exceeding what the customer *wants,* not on what they don't want. This includes internal customers of work processes as well as clients of technology services. Second, learn what it means to do the right things, not just do things right. And last, focus attention on managing the interactions of the system, not the actions. Management must create an environment where the interaction between people and the interaction between processes allows for continuous improvement. Continuous improvement allows both systems and people "to do better tomorrow than the best they can do today."[49]

An educational technology center may be part of a government bureaucracy, but that is no longer an excuse for indifferent service, sullen employees and lack of organizational focus. The focus should be creating a distinctive level of service that clients will brag about using.

Quality Tools

There are many tools and many approaches that may be employed to make quality management work, some of which have been touched upon in this book. Sorting out which tools are appropriate and which approaches are right for a specific improvement project for your media and technology center can take some time. The process of quality improvement is dynamic. Tools used for one project may not be appropriate or necessary for another. Control charts that were used daily last year may only need to be checked every few months as the system improves and the performance becomes predictable. Approaches that appeared too sophisticated at the start of the quality journey may have a great appeal two or three years later. Appendix A provides a brief examination of the primary charts used for quality improvement.

Continued Study

Continued study is an inseparable part of continual improvement. This is not the last book, or the only resource you will use to learn how to provide high quality service in your agency. A few years from now, after the culture of the organization changes, the content of this work may appear to be pedestrian. That will be a good indicator that progress has been made.

Quality management seeks to improve the system as a whole, not the individual parts. Therefore the approach to managing quality must employ the methods and tools as a whole, working together. The 14 Points and profound knowledge work together and multiply the benefits of any one point taken alone.

Each approach and tool of quality management interacts with another and creates interactions that produce the chain reaction of quality that we seek. Learning how to use two or three approaches well might take several years. In the spirit of continuous improvement, recognize that learning to master the nature of true quality management may take a lifetime.

[1] Perelman, Lewis J. *Technology and Transformation of Schools*. Alexandria, VA: National School Boards Association, 1987. Pg.101.

[2] Dobyns, Lloyd & Clare Crawford-Mason. *Quality . . .Or Else*. Boston: Houghton Mifflin, 1992. Pg. 108.

[3] Ibid. Pg. 98.

[4] Ibid. Pg. 103.

[5] Deming, W. Edwards. *Out of the Crisis*. Cambridge, MA: MIT Press, 1986. Pg. 6.

[6] Perelman. Pg. 101.

[7] Covey, Stephen R. *The Seven Habits of Highly Effective People*. New York: Simon and Schuster, 1989. Pg. 99.

[8] Ackoff, Russell L. *The Art of Problem Solving*. New York: Wiley & Sons, 1978. Pg. 27.

[9] The "Puzzle Picture Question" comes from Robert Baggs, currently a consultant on corporate quality with Harold S. Haller and Company, Cleveland, Ohio.

[10] Walton, Mary. *Deming Management At Work*. New York: Perigee Books, 1990. Pg. 235.

[11] Ibid. Pg. 30.

[12] Walton, Mary. *The Deming Management Method*. New York: Perigee Books, 1986. Pg. 135.

[13] George, Steven. *The Baldrige Quality System*. New York: Wiley and Sons, 1992. Pg. 22.

[14] Juran, Joseph. *Juran on Quality by Design*. New York: Macmillan, 1992. Pg. 31.

[15] Ibid. Pg. 32.

[16] Ibid. Pg. 31.

[17] Deming, *Out of the Crisis,* pg. 86.

[18] Walton, *The Deming Management Method,* pg. 97.

[19] Bonstingl, John Jay. *Schools Of Quality: An Introduction to Total Quality Management In Education*. Alexandria, VA: ASCD, 1992. Pg. 44.

[20] Deming, W. Edwards. Quoted in Four-Day Seminar, Philadelphia, February 18, 1993.

[21] Godfrey, A. Blanton. *At the Cutting Edge of Quality: Ten Clear Trends for Quality Over the Next Decade*. Wilton, CT: Juran Institute, 1993. Pg. 9.

[22] Port, Otis. et al. "Quality." *Business Week: Special Report*. Nov. 30, 1992, pg. 72 & "Beg, Borrow and Benchmark," pg. 75.

[23] Juran, Joseph M. *The Last Word: Lessons Of A Lifetime in Managing For Quality*. Juran Institute, Wilton, MA: Juran Institute, 1993. Pg. 18.

[24] See the Malcolm Baldrige National Quality Award Criteria. Available from the National Institute of Standards and Technology, Gaithersburg, MD at no charge.

[25] Dobins. Pg. 182.

[26] Ibid.

[27] *The Prophet of Quality, Part II*. Videotape. Chicago: Films Inc., 1993.

[28] Port. Pg. 68.

[29] Ibid.

[30] *Deming's Point One*. Piqua, OH: Ohio Quality & Productivity Forum, 1991. Pg. 9.

[31] "Studying Best of Class Requires More Than Hit or Miss Strategy," *Total Quality Newsletter,* September 1993. Pg. 2.

[32] Port. Pg. 69.

[33] "Study: Perseverance Necessary to See Quality's Payoff," *Total Quality Newsletter,* June 1993. Pg. 4.

[34] Dobyns. Pg. 182.

[35] Dr. Deming credits the development of the PDSA cycle to his mentor and father of modern statistical analysis Dr. Walter A. Shewhart.

[36] Ishiakawa, Kaoru. *What Is Total Quality Control?: The Japanese Way.* Englewod Cliffs: Prentice Hall, 1985. Pg. 62.

[37] Imai, Masaaki. *KAIZEN: The Key To Japan's Competitive Success.* New York: McGraw Hill, 1986. Pg. 63.

[38] Ishikawa. Pg. 62.

[39] Aguayo, Rafael. *Dr. Deming: The American Who Taught the Japanese About Quality.* New York: Simon & Schuster, 1990. Pg. 48.

[40] Bracey, Gerald W. "Filet of School Reform, Sauce Diable." *Education Week,* June 16, 1993. Pg. 28.

[41] "How To Overcome the 'Quality Is Too Much Extra Work' Syndrome." *Total Quality Newsletter,* December 1992. Pg. 1.

[42] Ibid.

[43] Walton, *Deming Management At Work,* pg. 49. And, Gabor, Andrea. *The Man Who Discovered Quality.* New York: Random House, 1990. Pg. 170–177.

[44] Mathews, Jay. "The TQM of The '80s Needs Help Today," *Philadelphia Inquirer,* June 13, 1993, section D, page 1.

[45] Op cit., "How To Overcome the 'Quality Is Too Much Extra Work' Syndrome."

[46] Geber, Beverly. "TQM vs. PQM." *Quality Perspective,* Special Issue, Training Magazine, September 1993, Pg. 14.

[47] Imai. Pg. 185.

[48] *Deming's Point One: Create Constancy Of Purpose.* Piqua, OH: Ohio Quality And Productivity Forum, 1991. Pg. 9.

[49] Ackoff, Russell. "Avoiding Implementation Errors." *Quality Network News.* American Association of School Administrators, May/June 1993.

Appendix A

Charts for Quality Management

Included here is a brief explanation of the primary types of charts used to track data and graphically represent components of a system.[1]

CAUSE AND EFFECT DIAGRAM—also known as a Fish Bone Diagram for its shape and an Ishikawa Diagram after its developer. The head of the fish represents an "effect" that is to be examined, generally during a brainstorming session. The effect is usually negative and the focus of an improvement team's activities. A desirable effect may be used instead when the diagram is used as part of the planning process for developing a new service. The four ribs of the fish are generally headed *methods* (or *policy*), *material, people* and *equipment.* Sometimes additional ribs are added. The most common addition is labeled *measurement.*

The improvement team uses each rib to classify the various "causes" of the effect under study. The resulting chart gives a graphic representation of the system of causes that created the undesirable effect.

CHECK SHEET—A simple chart used on a daily basis, generally to count the number of "things gone wrong." The chart may have a number of categories to assist employees in keeping track of errors over a period of time. The counts of errors under each category can provide a way to decide what kind of problem

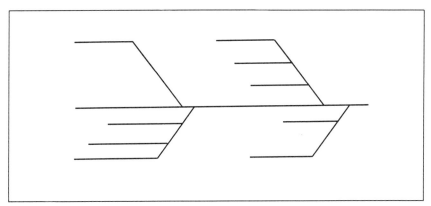

Cause & Effect Chart

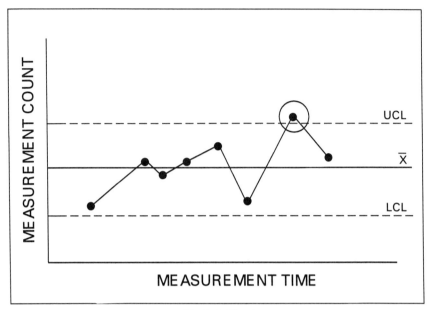

Control Chart

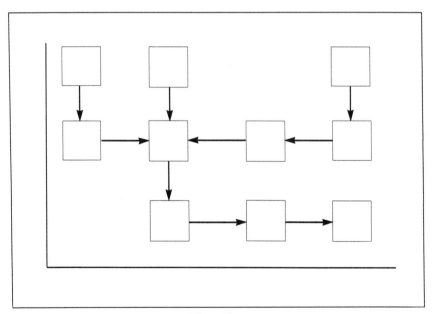

Flow Chart

is in need of most attention and clearly identify the source of problems. The numerical counts are a source of data when statistical process control formulas are applied to the process.

Counting number of delivery errors, complaints about product quality or broken videotapes is relatively easy. A little tougher, but just as important, is tracking opportunities missed. A run chart can show the number of phone calls requesting technical assistance (opportunities) and then show how many requests were not adequately met, according to the customer.

CONTROL CHART—Originated by Dr. Walter Shewhart while working for Bell Labs in 1924. A control chart shows a series of points along a horizontal axis that represents a period of time. The vertical axis contains a scale representing the number of factors counted at each point in time along the horizontal scale. Points could be the number of items delivered, requests processed, delivery errors, reshelving errors or late deliveries. The difference between a Run Chart and a Control Chart is the Control Chart will also show two parallel horizontal lines representing the upper and lower control limits of the system. These control limits are only drawn after they have been derived form statistical process control formulas based on the data provided in the chart. They are not specifications, rather they are the statistical upper and lower limits within which we can say the process is stable. The control limits show us how well the system functions on a day to day basis.

After statistical limits have been established, workers and management can easily determine if action is necessary when errors occur. Points (errors) within the two lines are said to be the result of "common causes" found with the design of the system. Investigation of every common cause error is a waste of time since the cause is actually built-in to the system. Only improvement of the system, management's responsibility, will reduce or eliminate common cause errors.

Points outside the lines, outliers above and below the line, are said to be due to "special causes." A single point outside the control limits does not necessarily signal a need for action unless it is known that it is likely to occur again. A series of special cause points is a clear signal that action must be taken to bring the system back into a stable operating condition.

Information from a control chart provides us with a starting point to measure the performance of the system after improvements have been made. The intent of quality improvement with control charts is to narrow the variation between control limits and decrease the frequency of errors. Both are accomplished only by improvement of the system, not by simply redrawing the lines.

Beginning control chart users mistakenly draw in their own limits based on how they think the system should perform. This practice is not process control and will undermine any quality improvement effort.

FLOW CHART—A flow chart is a graphic representation showing the path that information and/or materials must take as it moves through a process. Flow

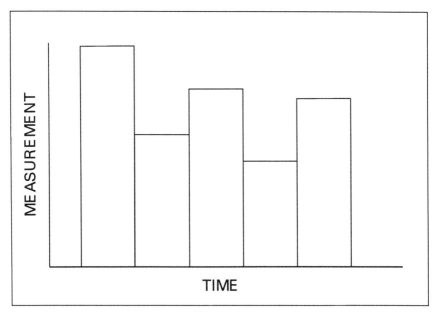

Histogram

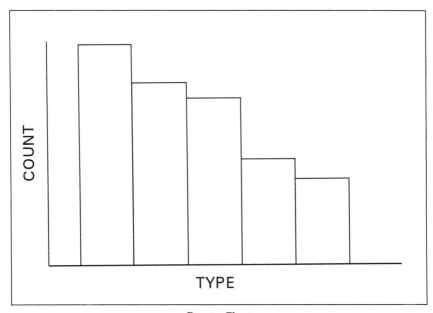

Pareto Chart

charting is a valuable activity for allowing workers to see their place in the larger process and identifying points in the process that could be improved.

HISTOGRAM—Graphically shows the distribution of variation for a specific value being measured. The typical Histogram is a bar chart with each bar representing the number of times a particular variation occurred. The classic Histogram will show the highest bars in the center and progressively shorter bars extending off to either side. Tracking the arrival time of a delivery van might show most of the arrival times falling within a specific five minute period. Then progressively fewer arrival times in the five minute periods earlier or later. Interpretation of Histograms that are skewed one way or the other can indicate flaws in system design or tampering with the system by workers or management.

PARETO CHART (Juran Chart)—Pronounced *pah-ray-toe,* and named for the early 20th century Italian economist Vilfredo Pareto who discovered the principal of maldistribution of wealth or what is commonly called the 80/20 rule. Dr. Joseph Juran assigned Pareto's name to the principal in 1950 when he documented the unequal distribution of quality loss. His work described a process in which the sources of quality loss can be sorted by frequency of their cause to determine the source that creates the greatest number of flaws. Juran's method identified a way to separate the "vital few from the trivial many," a phrase he coined as well.[2]

The Pareto Chart is a bar chart that documents the number of times each error cause occurs. The cause with the greatest count, represented by the highest bar, signals the primary cause for most errors and thus the cause to be addressed first. It also shows the "trivial many" which are causes that, while annoying, need not be addressed until the "vital few" are corrected. Pareto Charts show an organization where to direct limited resources to achieve the most system improvement.

QUALITY IMPROVEMENT STORY—Used extensively by Florida Power and Light. Originated by the president of Komatsu tractor corporation in Japan as a visual method for designing and justifying process improvements. For more information on the use of the Quality Improvement Story, see *The Man Who Discovered Quality,* by Andrea Gabor.[3]

RUN CHART—Run charts are used by employees to plot the day to day operations of a process. The chart has a time scale on the horizontal axis and a vertical scale for plotting the factor to be quantified such as errors or opportunities for service. Lines between points on a Run Chart give a picture of general trends within the system. Data points provide information that is applied to statistical formulas that will determine if the system is stable or out of control. See also Control Charts.

SCATTER DIAGRAM—A Scatter Diagram shows the relationship between two variables over time. The effect of various lighting levels on typing errors for example.

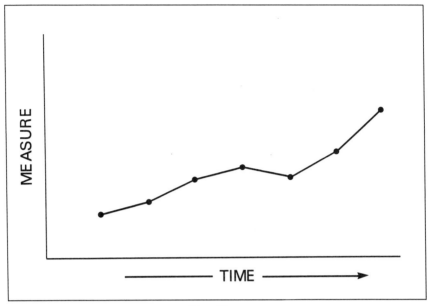

Run Chart

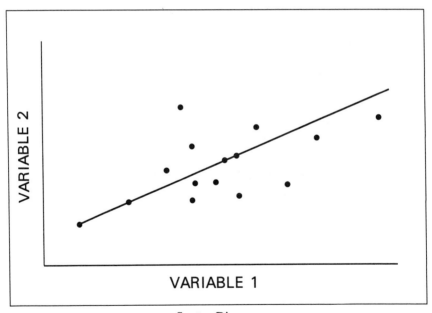

Scatter Diagram

The diagram is frequently used as a diagnostic tool to see how one variable is affected by changes in another.

[1]Descriptions of the basic quality tools have been derived from the following sources:

Fellers, Gary. *The Deming Vision: SPC/TQM For Administrators*. Milwaukee, WI: ASQC Quality Press, 1992.

GOAL/QPC. *The Memory Jogger For Education*. Methuen, MA, 1992.

Imai, Masaaki. *KAIZEN: The Key To Japan's Competitive Success*. New York: McGraw Hill, 1986.

Ishikawa, Kaoru. *What Is Total Quality Management? The Japanese Way*. Englewood Cliffs: Prentice Hall, 1986.

Walton, Mary. *The Deming Management Method*. New York: Perigee Books, 1986.

[2]Juran, Joseph M. *Juran On Quality By Design*. New York: Free Press, 1992. Pg. 70.

[3]Gabor, Andrea. *The Man Who Discovered Quality*. New York: Penguin Books, 1990. Pg. 177.

Appendix B

Quality Management and the Video/Film Industry

The following was originally published by the National Association of Regional Media Centers in the Spring 1993 issue of their membership publication: *'etin*. The events are true, names have been omitted to avoid embarrassing the parties involved.

I got a phone call a couple of weeks ago from one of our sales representatives. We had a pleasant conversation and I asked what was on his mind. He said nothing really, but his sales manager required him to make 40 calls a month and this was being logged as a call. Such waste. My time and his. He knows my agency doesn't buy until July, but, out of fear, he is diligently making 40 phone calls to meet the quota set by his boss. He will turn in his monthly activity report showing 40 phone calls, no more, no less. His boss will report to the company president that the sales force is "really out there beating the bushes for sales." The amount of damage this kind of "management" does to the corporation is unknowable. The productivity loss from fear driven, demoralized workers is incalculable.

Dr. W. Edwards Deming, the prophet of quality, who showed Japan the way to capture markets, expand business and create jobs, would not approve. Three of Dr. Deming's 14 points are found in this one instance: Point 8, "drive out fear"; Point 11, "eliminate numerical goals, quotas and management by objective"; and Point 12, "eliminate barriers to people taking pride in their work."

Another Example of Loss

In 1991 our agency purchased 75 videotapes from a well known educational video producer. A particular tape in this order was circulated twice in the first year, a slow mover, but not uncommon for a first year secondary title. The next year, on the second circulation, one of our users, our customer, complained that the title was missing several minutes at the beginning of program.

266

We investigated, and sure enough; rewind the tape to the beginning, press play and it starts in mid-sentence 5 or 6 minutes into the program. A defective tape from the distributor's lab.

Now defects like this a rare, 1 in 100,000 perhaps, maybe more. But they are random events caused by variation in the system of production and expected from time to time. What to do? Contact the producer for a replacement. Simple.

Our first call by our office manager yielded a courteous but firm response that since the purchase order was more than a year old, the replacement policy did not apply and it would cost us $250 to replace the item. "Even though the tape was sent defective from the company?" Answer: "Yes."

Our second call was made by the director of the regional media center (RMC). After several frustrating transfers within the voice mail system, a message was left for the head of customer service to contact us about the problem. A customer service representative called back the next day. The same one our office manager had spoken with. Same response, the replacement would be $250. The rest of the conversation went something like this:

RMC: Did Mr. [Jones] (head of customer service) get my message?

Customer Service Representative: Yes, he gave it to me to return.

RMC: But I wanted to talk to Mr. [Jones].

Service Rep.: He gave the message to me to handle.

After repeating our problem the representative replied, "You may not be aware of it, but we have a replacement policy for damaged tapes, 50 percent off the first year only, full price after that."

RMC: But the tape isn't damaged. It came from your company missing some of the beginning of the program.

Service Rep.: My boss would say there was no telling what happened out there, I'm not saying you're lying, just he would have a hard time because it is more than a year.

RMC: How about I mail the tape to you and then you can explain how we could remove five or six minutes of the program between the leader and the start of the tape stock? Besides, explain why I would *want* to do that. Having the tape out of circulation means that future bookings cannot be filled, which will result in disappointed users, and that makes us look bad.

Service Rep.: Because it is more than a year old, it can't be replaced, but since it is part of a large order, we'll take care of it.

RMC: Let me ask you, are you saying that we should check every tape when it comes in to make sure there is a program on it?

Service Rep.: Yes, you should check every tape soon after it comes in. At least within a year.

RMC: OK, I just wanted to be clear where the responsibility for product quality lies, with us or with the producer.

Service Rep.: Look, we have good tapes, but because it is more than a year, I'll have a hard time getting my boss to approve it.

RMC: Even if it arrived defective?

Service Rep.: That's right.

RMC: That's why I called Mr. [Jones], then you wouldn't be in such a tough spot. Will you let Mr. [Jones] know I would still like him to return my call?

In the course of the conversation we got a return authorization number and spent our own money to UPS their defective product back to them. We still haven't heard from Mr. [Jones]. The company does not know what its aim is.

We spent perhaps 30 minutes on their 800 line; more waste: the office manager's time, the director's time, the representative's time, plus discussions off the phone with others about the lunacy of the situation. To view 75 tapes at an average of 20 minutes each would take at least 25 hours. At $7.50 an hour that is $187.50 plus benefits.

The dissatisfied customer, studies have shown, tells 16 to 22 people. The satisfied customer will tell two to four. How many has the author told this story to, and named the company? At *best* you must create four satisfied customers for every one dissatisfied customer just to stay even. To grow, you must create customers who will *brag* about using your product or service. This applies with equal force to media producers and to regional media centers.

Best Efforts

How long will this company last? The customer service worker is running on fear and adherence to inflexible and arbitrary policies. He quotes policy and can do nothing to help the customer. He is doing what he is trained to do. He is doing the best he can. How could he do otherwise? He is trapped in a system that he is powerless to change. His boss is, no doubt, trying to cut the cost of warranty by enforcing a strict one year policy, no matter what the source of the defect.

In an effort to optimize his own cost center, he has brought losses to another department. He has no clue what this has done to sales potential. Why would we want to buy from this company again? The content of their product line will not save them if customer service fails. Why should we get special treatment and have the defective item replaced because it was part of a large order? Pity the customer who bought two tapes and discovered one to be defective a year later.

Imagine discovering a defect in the transmission of your car and being told, "Nope, we won't fix the problem. You should have bought 25 or 30 cars for a rental fleet. You're just a little customer."

Heavy Losses

The video/film industry will continue to incur heavy losses by adhering to the failed methods of American management. Management by numbers, management by objective, management by results, quotas, focus on visible numbers, focus on short term results, merit reviews, commission sales—all destructive to productivity. The company that becomes transformed, that begins to focus on improving the process of production and service will gain the market. The company that recognizes itself as a *system* of production and service, and arms itself with knowledge may learn how to continually improve, grow and prosper. The same applies to a regional technology center.

Ever wonder why a country of 230 million people has three auto companies and a country of 130 million has nine? Because the country with nine of them uses the management principles developed by an American 45 years ago. W. Edwards Deming.

Aftermath: Subsequent to the publication of this article, the author received seven letters and nine phone calls from various educational video/film companies. The specific company involved with both of these incidents was not among them. Some of the calls were meant to reassure the author that their company was committed to quality service. A few sent their customer satisfaction policies. At least three indicated that they had sent copies of the article to all of their sales and customer service personnel.

Appendix C

Technological Overkill and the Failure to Understand Profound Knowledge

The current national push for an information "superhighway" and numerous state and regional fiber optic/cable initiatives are examples of action taken without profound knowledge. What will play in the general press and on Capitol Hill are miles apart from the reality of instructional need. The notion of students sitting at their computers accessing an on-line database to learn about the parts of a flower is quaint but technological overkill. And although politicians and well meaning educators are quoted in the general press, saying that this highway will improve learning, it will not. No amount of "greater access to information" will improve learning without improvement of the systems that apply the information, in this case, the education system in America. Assuming that education will be able to afford the installation of "off ramps" from the information highway, the practice of teaching will look much the same after the connections are made.

The more serious problem of overcoming shortages of teachers in certain fields is a more cost effective use for fiber optic systems. The capacity for several high schools to share a teacher electronically and open up sections of fourth year German, or offer physics to a high school that has no physics teacher, would greatly enhance the opportunities for equitable access to education in America. But course-sharing between buildings and districts is difficult to explain because it addresses such a basic need. And basics are not what gets reported on or funded.

The advent of lower cost, high quality CD-ROM drives and the concurrent advances in computing power may have diminished the need for access to powerful on-line data bases at the K–12 level. Most any research oriented information source required in K–12 education is available in CD-ROM format for local installation and access.

The notion that an elementary student needs to make a first hand visit to a rain forest or talk to a deep sea diver in real time via satellite is specious. Typically the experience only reaches students in gifted programs or other enrichment courses. The logistic arrangements for satellite time, phone links, class scheduling changes and the disruption it creates in the school day is simply not worth the alleged benefit that is derived from real time experience. The ability to have students speak live with a diver exploring a ship wreck is unique, but does nothing to further understanding that could not be done by other, less costly means. But that doesn't sell. The perversity is mind boggling.

The methods of providing authentic but cost-effective experiences to students are never mentioned in the general press or on Capitol Hill. But the highly expensive, more complex and visible activities like interactive teleconferences with someone underwater around the world not only get reported on, but get cheers for their "innovative value."

Does advanced technology really improve instruction? Does the ability to use technology in ever more complex combinations mean that the system of education is being improved? Not at all.

It is a delusion that the general media willingly reports on and technologists use to justify new projects and added technology that only make the system of education more complex but not improved.

The pattern will continue until the planning process is opened up to educators who do not own a technology agenda. When will school districts begin to establish cross-functional planning groups that are able to focus on what is truly required to improve instruction and meet the needs of teachers? Technology can improve the interactions between teacher and student that help create learning. But allowing the local technology czar to make implementation decisions in the absence of a cross-functional process improvement team is only tacking on new equipment to an existing structure. The system of instruction isn't improved, it just gets bigger.

Bibliography and Resource List

PUBLICATIONS

Ackoff, Russell L. *The Art Of Problem Solving*. New York: Wiley & Sons, 1978

———. "Avoiding Implementation Errors." *Quality Network News*. American Association of School Administrators, May/June 1993.

American Association of School Administrators. *Introduction to Total Quality Schools: Compilation of Articles on the Concepts of TQM and W. Edwards Deming*. Arlington, VA, 1991.

Aguayo, Rafael. *Dr. Deming: The American Who Taught The Japanese About Quality*. New York: Simon and Schuster, 1986.

Association for Supervision and Curriculum Development. *Educational Leadership*. Magazine. Vol 50, Number 3. November 1992.

Backaitis, Nida. *Managing for Organizational Quality—Theory And Implementation: An Annotated Bibliography*. San Diego, CA: Navy Personnel Research and Development Center, 1990.

Baker, Joel. *Discovering the Future: The Business Of Paradigms*. St. Paul, MN: ILI Press, 1985.

Bonstingl, John Jay. *Schools of Quality: An Introduction to TQM in Education*. Alexandria, VA: Association for Supervision and Curriculum Development, 1992.

Bracey, Gerald W. "Filet of School Reform, Sauce Diable." *Education Week*, June 16, 1993.

———. "The Second Bracey Report on The Condition Of Public Education." *Kappan*, October 1992.

Brandt, Ronald S. ed. *Readings From "Educational Leadership": Effective Schools and School Improvement.* Arlington, VA: Association for Supervision and Curriculum Development, 1989.

Brody, Herb. "Good Is Never Enough," *High Technology,* August, 1986.

Byrne, John A. et. al. "Reinventing America." *Business Week: Special Report.* January 19, 1992.

Clements, Michael. "Ford Sees Record Mid 90s Car Sales." *USA Today,* December 2, 1993.

Covey, Stephen R. *The Seven Habits of Highly Effective People.* New York: Simon and Schuster, 1989.

Darling-Hammond, Linda., and Arthur Wise. *Effective Teacher Selection.* Santa Monica, CA: RAND Corporation, 1987.

Deming, W. Edwards. *Out of the Crisis.* Cambridge, MA: Massachusetts Institute of Technology, 1986.

———. *New Economics For Business, Industry and Education.* Cambridge, MA: MIT Press, 1993.

Dickson, Paul. *The Official Rules.* New York: Delacorte Press, 1978.

Dobyns, Lloyd, and Clare Crawford-Mason. *Quality or Else: The Revolution in World Business.* Boston, MA: Houghton Mifflin, 1991.

Ellsworth, Ralphe E. *The School Library.* New York: Educational Facilities Laboratories, 1968.

Feigenbaum, Armond V. "Quality and Productivity," *Quality Progress.* November 1977.

Fellows, Gary. *The Deming Vision: SPC/TQM For Administrators.* Milwaukee, WI: ASQC Quality Press, 1992.

Gabor, Andrea. *The Man Who Discovered Quality.* New York: Random House, 1990.

Geber, Beverly. "TQM vs. PQM," *Quality Perspective, Training Magazine* Special Issue, September 1993.

George, Stephen. *The Baldrige Quality System: The Do It Yourself Way to Transform Your Business.* New York: Wiley & Sons, 1992.

Gilbreath, Robert D. "Needed: More Formal Structures to Manage Accelerating Rate of Change." *Total Quality,* November 1993.

Glasser, William. *The Quality School,* 2nd Edition. New York: Harper & Row, 1990.

Gleick, James. *Chaos: Making a New Science.* New York: Viking, 1987.

GOAL/QPC. *The Memory Jogger for Education: A Pocket Guide of The Tools For Continuous Improvement In Schools.* Methuen, MA: GOAL/QPC, 1992.

Godfrey, A. Blanton. *At the Cutting Edge of Quality: Ten Clear Trends for Quality over the Next Decade.* Wilton, CT: Juran Institute, 1993.

Greenwald, John. "What Went Wrong?" *Time,* November 8, 1993.

Hamel, G. and Prahalad, C. K. "Strategic Intent." *Harvard Business Review,* May-June, 1989.

Harvard Business School. *Unconditional Quality.* Boston, MA, 1991.

Hovelson, Jack. "GM Drops 10 Day Reports; Sales Totals 'Meaningless.'" *USA Today,* December 2, 1993.

Imai, Masaaki. *KAIZEN: The Key To Japan's Competitive Success.* New York: McGraw Hill, 1986.

Ishikawa, Kaoru. *What Is Total Quality Control? The Japanese Way.* Englewood Cliffs, NJ: Prentice-Hall, 1985.

Juran, Joseph M. *Juran on Quality by Design.* New York: Macmillan, 1992.

————. *The Last Word: Lessons of a Lifetime in Managing for Quality.* Wilton, CT: Juran Institute, 1993.

Kelso, Frank B. "The Way Of The Future: Total Quality Leadership." *Proceedings of the United States Naval Institute,* May, 1991.

Kilian, Cecelia S. *The World of W. Edwards Deming.* Knoxville, TN: SPC Press, 1992.

Kindred, Leslie W., and Don Bagin and Donald R. Gallagher. *The School and Community Relations,* 2nd edition. Englewood Cliffs: Prentice-Hall, 1976.

Kline, James J. "Total Quality Management in Local Government." *Government Finance Review.* August 1992.

Kurz, Phil. "Ten Useful Tips to Help the Purchasing Agent Choose a Videotape Duplicator." *AV Video,* May 1992, pg. 6.

Levy, Steven. "The Case of the Purloined Productivity." *Macworld,* March, 1993.

Macher, Ken. "On Becoming a Visionary," *Association Management,* Feb 1987.

Malcolm Baldrige National Quality Award: 1994 criteria. Gaithersburg, MD: United States Department of Commerce, 1993.

Mathews, Jay. "The TQM of The '80s Needs Help Today," *Philadelphia Inquirer,* June 13, 1993.

McGonagill, Grady. *Removing Barriers to Educational Restructuring: A Call For Systems Literacy.* Washington, DC: American Association of School Administrators & The National Education Association, 1992.

McWhirter, William. "Back On The Fast Track." *Time,* December 13, 1993.

Naisbitt, John. *Megatrends: Ten New Directions Transforming Our Lives.* New York: Warner Books, 1982.

National Center For Effective Schools Research and Development. *Focus in Change,* Fall 1992, No. 8.

Ohio Quality & Productivity Forum. *Deming's Point One.* Piqua, OH, 1991.

———. *Deming's Point Four.* Piqua, OH, 1988.

———. *Deming's Point Seven.* Piqua, OH, 1989.

Olson, Lynn. "Florida District Vows to Infuse Quality Principles into Schools." *Education Week.* March 11, 1992.

———. "Quality-Management Movement Spurs Interest in New Awards for Education." *Education Week.* March 18, 1992.

———. "Schools Getting Swept Up in Business's Quality Movement." *Education Week.* March 11, 1992.

Perelman, Lewis, J. *Technology and Transformation of Schools.* Alexandria, VA: National School Boards Association, 1987.

Port, Otis. et. al. "Quality." *Business Week: Special Report.* Nov. 30, 1992.

PQ Systems. *Improvement Tools For Education* (K-12). Miamisburg, Ohio, 1993.

Reich, Robert B. *Education and the Next Economy*. Washington, DC: National Education Association, 1988.

Rummler, Geary A. and Alan P. Brache. "Managing The White Space." *Training,* January 1991.

Sagor, Richard. "The False Premises of Strategic Planning." *Education Week,* April 1, 1992.

Savary, Louis M. *Creating Quality Schools*. Arlington, VA: American Association of School Administrators, 1992.

Schenkat, Randy. *Quality Connections: Transforming Schools*. Alexandria, VA: Association for Supervision Curriculum and Development (ASCD), 1993

Scherkenbach, William W. *The Deming Route to Quality and Productivity*. Rockville, MD: Mercury Press, 1986.

Scholtes, Peter. *The Team Handbook*. Madison, WI: Joiner Associates, 1992.

Senge, Peter M. *The Fifth Discipline*. New York: Doubleday, 1990.

Sensenbrenner, Joseph. "Quality Comes to City Hall." *Harvard Business Review*. March-April, 1991.

Shewhart, Walter A. *Statistical Method From the Viewpoint of Quality Control*. Mineola, NY: Dover Publications, 1986. Reprint of the original work published in 1939.

Tidman, Keith R. *The Operations Evaluation Group*. Annapolis, MD: Naval Institute Press, 1984.

Total Quality Newsletter, "How To Overcome the 'Quality Is Too Much Extra Work' Syndrome." December 1992.

————. "Study: Perseverance Necessary to See Quality's Payoff," June 1993.

————. "Studying Best of Class Requires More Than Hit Or Miss Strategy," September 1993.

Tribus, Myron. *Deployment Flow Charting*. Los Angles: Quality and Productivity, Inc., 1989.

Walton, Mary. *The Deming Management Method*. New York: Perigee Books, 1986.

————. *Deming Management At Work*. New York: Perigee: Books, 1991.

———. "Putting America Back To Work." *Philadelphia Inquirer Magazine,* March 11, 1984.

Weisman, Jonathan. "Skills In The Schools: Now It's Business' Turn." *Kappan,* January 1993.

———. "Some Economists Challenge View That Schools Hurt Competitiveness," *Education Week,* November 13, 1991.

Wheeler, Donald J. and David S. Chambers. *Understanding Statistical Process Control.* Second edition. Knoxville, TN: SPC Press, 1992.

Zemke, Ron and Chip R. Bell. *Service Wisdom: Creating and Maintaining The Customer Service Edge.* Minneapolis, MN: Lakewood Books, 1989.

VIDEOTAPES

Creating the Total Quality Effective School. Effective Schools Research, 1992. 800 343 4312.

The Deming Library Starter Set for Educators. Eight parts app. 30 minutes each. Chicago: Films, Inc., 1988-1993.

Dr. W. Edwards Deming: The Prophet of Quality. Two parts app. 60 minutes. Chicago: Films, Inc., 1992. 800 343 4312.

Fundamentals of Total Quality Management. Compact Disc-Interactive. Self-Paced Interactive Continuing Education Program. Atlanta, GA: AMPED, 1993.

Heartbeat of America. Frontline Series. Videotape. App. 58 min. Washington: PBS, 1993.

Hidden Assets: Empowering Government Workers. Videotape. App. 30 minutes. Deerfield, IL: Coronet/MIT Video, 1991.

If Japan Can, Why Can't We? Videotape. Chicago: Films Inc., 1980.

In Search of Quality: Quality Through Systems. Videotape. Two Parts. Deerfield, IL: Coronet/MTI Film & Video, 1991.

Made in Japan: 'Whole'-istically. Videotape. Los Angeles: Quality Enhancement Seminars, 1989.

Quality . . . or Else: A Course of Study. Three parts app. 60 min. each. Chicago: Films, Inc., 1991.

Theory of a System for Educators and Managers. App. 30 min. Chicago: Films, Inc., 1993.

ASSOCIATIONS AND ORGANIZATIONS

American Association of School Administrators: Total Quality Network.
1801 North Moore Street, Arlington, VA 22209
(703) 528-0700

American Society for Quality Control
PO Box 3005, Milwaukee, WI 53201
(800) 952-6587

Films Incorporated, TQM Marketing
5547 North Ravenswood Avenue, Chicago, IL 60640-1199
(800) 343-4312

GOAL/QPC
13 Branch Street, Mrthuen, MA 01844
(508) 685-3900

Malcolm Baldrige National Quality Award
National Institute of Standards and Technology
Route 270 and Quince Orchard Road
Administration Building, Room A537
Gaithersburg, MD 20899-0001
(301) 975-2036

Philadelphia Area Council for Excellence/PACE
1234 Market Street, Suite 1800
Philadelphia, PA 19107
(215) 972-3977

Productivity-Quality Systems, Inc. (PQ-Systems)
10468 Miamisburg-Springboro Road
Miamisburg, Ohio 45342
(800) 777-3020

TQM-Education Network of the American
Association for Supervision and Curriculum
c/o Center for Quality Schools
John Jay Bonstingl, Director
PO Box 810
Columbia, MD 21044

Index

About the Author

 Mark L. Richie is director of a regional media center serving 63,000 students in New Jersey. He is a past president of both the American Film and Video Association and The National Association of Regional Media Centers, an AECT affiliate.

His study of quality management includes two four-day seminars conducted by Dr. W. Edwards Deming and a seminar with Dr. Joseph Juran. He is a certified school media specialist, holds a master's degree in public relations and has conducted over 45 workshops on a variety of topics at state, regional and national conferences.